"I put back *Dusty Booze* in one sitting. Aaron Goldfarb is a drinker's drinker, and a writer's writer. He's as well-versed in spirits as nearly anyone writing today, yet manages to uncover entirely new worlds in the pages of this book. By turns suspenseful, humorous, and philosophical, *Dusty Booze* is a propulsive read as deeply concerned with the obsessive, treasure-seeking mindset of collectors as with the vintage bottles themselves."

—CAREY JONES, author of *Every Cocktail Has a Twist* and *Be Your Own Bartender*

"An investigation into the secretive and competitive collectors and their methods, unsolved mysteries, and mythological caches. The once worthless dusties inspire Goldfarb to debate the monetary value of quality versus rarity and the proximity to fame. And unlike, say, stamp collectors, the author and every other dusty hunter must grapple with the decision whether to taste a moment in time or to keep time locked away in a bottle."

—CAMPER ENGLISH, author of *Doctors and Distillers: The Remarkable Medicinal History of Beer, Wine, Spirits, and Cocktails*

DUSTY BOOZE

IN SEARCH OF VINTAGE SPIRITS

Aaron Goldfarb

ABRAMS PRESS, NEW YORK

Library of Congress Control Number: 2023946468

ISBN: 978-1-4197-6679-4
eISBN: 978-1-64700-939-7

Printed and bound in the United States
10 9 8 7 6 5 4 3 2 1

Abrams books are available at special discounts when purchased in quantity
for premiums and promotions as well as fundraising or educational use.
Special editions can also be created to specification. For details, contact
specialsales@abramsbooks.com or the address below.

Abrams Press® is a registered trademark of Harry N. Abrams, Inc.

ABRAMS The Art of Books
195 Broadway, New York, NY 10007
abramsbooks.com

TO ELLIE AND WILDER

"BROWN-EYED WOMEN
AND RED GRENADINE, THE
BOTTLE WAS DUSTY BUT
THE LIQUOR WAS CLEAN."

CONTENTS

xi   PROLOGUE

PART I: THE SPIRIT OF TODAY

3   1: THE GLUT ERA

On Decanters: Chessmen, King Tut, and "the King"

Key Japanese Export Dusties

25   2: VINTAGE BOOZE'S BIG BANG

Pre-Phylloxera 'Gnac

51   3: MR. DEMILLE, I'M READY FOR YOUR BOOZE STASH

67   4: THE RISE OF THE SECONDARY MARKET

How to Decipher and Date Old Bottles

Did It Really Used to Be Better?

Key Bourbon Dusties

87   5: CHANGING LAWS SPAWN A NEW INDUSTRY

The Jack Daniel's Collector Loophole

PART II: SPIRITS FROM THE PAST

107 6: DUSTY HUNTING MOVES BEYOND BOURBON

The One and Only Don Henny

115   **7: THE SEARCH FOR OLD MONK JUICE AND TRAGIC WISDOM**

Key Liqueur Dusties

127   **8: THE MONA (LISA) OF RUM**

Key Old Rums

141   **9: WHY IS THERE SO LITTLE VINTAGE TEQUILA?**

Key Tequila Dusties

159   **10: THE DUSTY MIXOLOGIST**

Key (and Necessary) Vintage Cocktail Ingredients

PART III: A SPIRITED FUTURE

177   **11: THE MERCENARIES**

Minis and Maxis

197   **12: YOU SHOULD DRINK A SPIRIT OLDER THAN YOU**

Private Labels and Personal Bottles

211   **13: YEARNING FOR YESTERYEAR**

223   **14: DUSTIES ON THE AUCTION BLOCK**

Fakes, Refills, Counterfeiting, and Teenage Funny Business

A Few Key Scotch and Single Malt Dusties

255   **15: THE WHOLE STORE SCORE**

What's Next?

269   **16: ASK THE DUST**

277   **ACKNOWLEDGMENTS**

279   **VINTAGE RESOURCES**

281   **INDEX**

286   **ABOUT THE AUTHOR**

PROLOGUE

THE MOST COVETED liquor collection in Los Angeles was not located at a trendy bar or a Michelin-starred restaurant or some exclusive, private club frequented by movie producers or record label execs or even social media influencers who were getting their tabs comped in exchange for a post.

Instead, I had been told, it was in an indistinguishable storage unit, somewhere in or near Hollywood—depending on who you ask—with the sole key to its padlock residing in the hands of a powerful local law firm. It had been there for decades, this world-class booze cache, ever since one of the most famous celebrities in all of California state history had died, and his—or her?—many descendants had begun fighting over the estate.

"Alfred Hitchcock?" I asked.

No.

"Humphrey Bogart?"

No.

"Frank Sinatra."

I'm not telling you. But no.

I was on the phone talking to Kevin Langdon Ackerman. A filmmaker based in Los Angeles himself, Ackerman is one of the country's top dusty hunters, a seeker and finder of vintage spirits.* Even though it's not his job, it's what he's best known for online, where I first came across him as @the_debonair_bourbonair on Instagram.

"Steve McQueen?"

No.

"Marilyn Monroe!"

No.

"Ronald Reagan?!"

Please *stop.*

The problem for Ackerman—aside from not being a descendant of the deceased A-lister—was his concern that several other dusty hunters were also aware of this collection, and all were surely vying to find it and to eventually possess it and then maybe even drink it.

This had happened to Ackerman before, and I could still hear how crestfallen he was as he told me about the three pristine cases of 1940s Old Overholt rye whiskey that had been pulled out from underneath him, some years back. In fact, he didn't even really want to talk to me because he was worried I might end up telling some of his competition about the stash and adding them to the hunt. He was so worried that he wouldn't even tell me what A-lister once owned this supposed booze collection that was supposedly somewhere in Los Angeles. It was the one piece of leverage Ackerman had over me and the other potential pursuers.

These other guys—and, in this hobby, it's almost always guys, for better or worse—were people like Eric Witz, a mild-mannered Boston-area man who had become a self-taught historian of strange and obscure spirits due to his incredible knack for locating bottles from the past.

---

* While pedants love to explain that the etymology of "vintage" comes from the wine world—deriving from the Latin *vindemia,* or "grape-gathering"—the term is now used for old spirits as well.

Or Pablo Moix, a former actor a and fast-talking restaurateur who dusty-hunted the Pacific coast so thoroughly in the early 2000s that he eventually used his stash to open the premier vintage spirits bar in Los Angeles.

Perhaps Owen Powell and Brad Bonds might be interested in finding this stash, to stock at the vintage retail stores they would open in Kentucky during the pandemic.

There was also Jonah Goodman, a curly-haired Kentucky boy in his early twenties, who somehow started dusty-hunting before he could legally drink—his ambitions, savvy with the internet, and willingness to hop around the globe at a moment's notice had allowed him to quickly become one of the best at this crazy game.

They wouldn't just need to scoop Ackerman, though; they'd all need to outwit the courts, buddy up to the lawyers, smooth-talk some possibly avaricious heirs, and eventually make them an offer they couldn't refuse.

"Marlon Brando???"

You don't have to be much of a spirits connoisseur, or even a drinker, to have noticed that whiskey is red-hot these days, with brands like Pappy Van Winkle, The Macallan, and Yamazaki becoming legitimate commodities, sold for thousands upon thousands of dollars a bottle, both legally and less than so. Unfortunately, by the mid-2010s, finding these bottles in your average American liquor store had become an impossibility unless you knew "a guy," and tasting even a few ounces began to cost more than a fancy dinner for two. Thus, many spirits enthusiasts began moving on to something more accessible, which, oddly, necessitated stepping back in time.

A weird quirk of spirits history, but especially bourbon history, is that for most of its existence, it existed merely to be drunk. Shocking, I know. No one collected it and certainly no one sat on massive bunkers of it, speculating that it would be valuable one day. These days, though,

I know of a personal wealth manager down in Tampa who spends half a million dollars per year on rare bourbon . . . and he's a teetotaler.

In fact, for most of the latter half of the twentieth century, no one was really buying bourbon at all, seeing it as an old man's drink at best, good ol' boy Southern rotgut at worst. That meant many bottles lingered on store shelves, and many more bottles sat in home bars, in cellars and basements, and in attics, never opened, gathering dust.

Thus, in the late 2000s, just as modern bourbon was having a renaissance, the concept of "dusty hunting" arose. That is, trekking to out-of-the-way liquor stores in small towns and sketchy neighborhoods (if the clerk sits behind bulletproof glass, that's good!) in search of old bottles that never got sold for whatever reason. Or going to estate sales and flea markets and even scouring places like eBay, Craigslist, and eventually Facebook for someone's grandpa's bottle of 1980s Wild Turkey or 1970s Old Grand-Dad or maybe even 1950s Weller that had sat in a basement or attic or locked liquor cabinet for decades.

Not all dusty bottles were desirable, of course—when my grandpa died, the best thing I found in his liquor cabinet was some neon-green Midori from the mid-1980s—and many were hard for neophytes to date and assess. But if you taught yourself how to read barcodes and Julian dating, learned how to identify tax stamps and DSP (distilled spirits plant) numbers, and knew where good "juice" was being distilled (and when), you could end up scoring some major rarities—ones most folks weren't well schooled enough to know were tastier than just about anything being released to market these days.

Dusty hunters are interesting characters, no question, Indiana Jones mixed with Comic Book Guy from *The Simpsons* with a dose of John Laroche from Susan Orlean's *The Orchid Thief*—spending years of their lives going to seedy liquor stores, filling their houses with dusty bottles, and talking about arcana from the past all day are not necessarily activities that lead to the most socially adept individuals. But they're also avid drinkers, which gives them a certain edge that, say, stamp collectors surely lack. Indeed, many of these dusty hunters have beautiful wives and lucrative day jobs—the latter a bit of a necessity in order to have such purchasing power and disposable income.

Though I'm a big spirits collector myself, I've never exactly been a dusty hunter; however, I've always been fascinated by them. And I certainly understand the mentality—the sickness, some might say—that drives someone who already has twelve hundred bottles of whiskey to buy more of it.

To paraphrase Rob, the obsessive record collector at the center of Nick Hornby's *High Fidelity*: I'd feel guilty writing about them if I wasn't, well, kinda one of them.

Though this is a fairly new hobby, it is one seemingly facing its end days, as there are simply fewer and fewer undiscovered bottles still out there to find. Dusty booze is a nonrenewable resource. They're not making more bottles of 1950s bourbon. Vintage spirits are likewise one of the only collectibles that its collectors also consume. You could thumb through *Action Comics* no. 1 or look at the stats on the back of Mickey Mantle's 1952 Topps card or even drive a 1965 Shelby Cobra, and that doesn't make it disappear from the face of the earth, doesn't make it no longer able to be traded, sold, or enjoyed by another collector. But vintage spirits innately have to disappear as they are enjoyed. At least in America, this has caused dusty hunting to become more professionalized online as well as at bars and retail.

Though the collecting of vintage spirits is mostly seen as yet another silly, late-stage capitalist, uniquely American pursuit, the fever has spread to other countries; there are dusty hunters across the entire globe, and many have their own specialties and foibles, like Rotem Ben Shitrit, an Israeli man who has amassed around ten thousand bottles of vintage "minis," and a Belgian man who dresses and talks a bit like Ali G and simply goes by the name "Don Henny"—yes, he only collects bottles of Hennessy Cognac. U.K. collectors tend to lean toward single malt Scotch, Germans love old bourbon, Italians pursue obscure rum, most tequila collectors seem to reside on the West Coast.

There are many reasons vintage spirits are trendy these days. There's an incredible return on investment—all it takes is time and some effort, and you might just find a $15 bottle of Old Fitzgerald that's actually worth $1,500 on the open market.*

This isn't just a book about the collectors, however, but about the producers too. For most vintage spirits lovers, there's a belief that they just don't make liquor like they used to—maybe distilleries have become too automated, ingredients too much of a bulk commodity—and to taste "handmade" whiskey, rum, tequila, or Chartreuse from decades past is a delight we simply don't get with today's conglomerate-owned, GMO-sourced, factory-produced, celebrity-endorsed crap.

However, the top reason, the unspoken reason, the true reason I believe vintage spirits are so hot these days is that they allow us to revisit the past. Vintage spirits are drinkable time capsules in the sense that once bottled, the liquid doesn't really change. Find a bottle, and you can truly taste what some bygone bourbon would have tasted like in 1934, soon after Prohibition ended. Or try what Don Draper and Roger Sterling would have been sipping on Madison Avenue in the 1960s. Or something from 1979, when your humble author was born. Your buzzed mind can escape the harsh present day and drift off to yesteryear.

But for many dusty hunters, it is indeed the thrill of the hunt that drives them above all else.

That inspires them to never pass a liquor store on some lonely highway because maybe—maybe!—there could be something interesting in

---

* I will mostly abstain from discussing the values of bottles in this book, as the market is currently moving too fast to keep up—imagine if I wrote a book on Beanie Babies in 1998 and here you are reading it now, thinking your Twigs the Giraffe is worth $1,800.

there for the taking. That has them going to just one more estate sale, hoping the dead geezer had great taste in bourbon—but not enough taste that he didn't leave a few sealed bottles around to survive him.

That had Ackerman intrigued with finding this A-list celebrity's A-list collection.

And now me as well.

PART I

THE SPIRIT OF TODAY

I

THE GLUT ERA

TO UNDERSTAND WHY there are desirable vintage spirits even available today, one needs to understand why so many seemingly great things became undesirable in the past.

The first place to start is with Prohibition.

Prior to 1920 there were nearly two hundred operating bourbon distilleries in Kentucky. In the Northeast, mainly centered around Maryland and Pennsylvania, there were hundreds, if not thousands, of rye distilleries, many of them small-time farm operations making something called Monongahela rye.

Prohibition would kill American whiskey distilling in so many ways. Though not completely.

There's an old joke in Kentucky about drinkers in the state during Prohibition. Back during those nearly fourteen dry years, from 1920 to 1933, the only way you could legally obtain whiskey was by a doctor's prescription. Suffice to say, there were a lot of sick Kentuckians during those years.

Yes, as improbable as it sounds, the Volstead Act of 1919 didn't completely shutter every liquor brand. Amazingly, six companies were granted the ability to sell "pure whiskey for medicinal use," all of it bottled-in-bond at 100 proof, government stamped, and boxed up with your doctor's prescription attached to the back of the bottle, all authorized by the U.S. Treasury Department. Some of these bottles even came with a dosage cup on the cap, no different than you'd find with a bottle of Pepto Bismol today.

Sick—or, rather, "sick"—patients were allowed to purchase a pint from their pharmacy every ten days, for about $3 apiece (roughly $50 in today's money).

What qualified for a prescription? Any of a number of things: high blood pressure, pneumonia, digestive issues, tuberculosis. While referred to as "medicinal" whiskey, these releases were aged distillates no different than those sold before or after this ignoble era.

The most significant changes were in the packaging. All medicinal whiskey came in pint-size hip flasks—thin, flat, and able to be stowed in your back trouser pocket—often ornate in design too, whether the embossed glass cursive lettering for "A Overholt," the diagonal ribbing on bottles of Special Old Reserve, or the waffled glass of Old McBrayer, meant to resemble something that would literally come from the apothecary shop.

"These were not necessarily connoisseurs' bourbons," says Joshua Feldman, a whiskey historian who has long collected and tasted examples from the era. Though many of them were well aged and quite tasty.

A few of these medicinal whiskey brands, like Old Overholt, and distilleries, such as A. Ph. Stitzel, when Julian "Pappy" Van Winkle himself was at the helm, you might recognize; others you almost certainly wouldn't, like American Medicinal Spirits Company (AMS), the biggest whiskey packager during Prohibition.

By 1933, when Prohibition finally ended, there were only six bourbon distilleries left in Kentucky and one in Tennessee, while the Maryland and Pennsylvania styles of rye had gone almost completely extinct.

New things would be needed to fill the void.

WITH PROHIBITION DECIMATING America's bourbon and rye industries, with very little aged whiskey even left in the country, other, non-American spirits categories finally had a chance to take hold. Early on, that meant imports of Canadian whisky* and Scotch, as well as mature rum from the Caribbean.

Most notably, however, was vodka, which would completely change the way Americans drank in the latter half of the twentieth century.

We should go back to the Russian Revolution for a second, though. As it was heating up in 1917, Russians began escaping their own country, and some of those were indeed local vodka makers, often traveling to America with nothing more than the clothes on their backs and a vodka recipe sloshing around in their heads.

One such refugee was Rudolph Kunett, who arrived penniless in New York in 1920, just as Prohibition was beginning. The son of a Ukrainian distillery owner, who was reportedly the world's largest rectifier and blender of liquor, Kunett began his new American life as a salesman for the Standard Oil Company, before eventually becoming a general manager at Helena Rubinstein, the eponymous cosmetics company started by a Polish refugee.

In the early 1930s, Kunett met up in Paris with an old friend, Vladimir Smirnov; his late father, Pyotr Arsenjevitch Smirnov, had founded the family's vodka distillery in Moscow in 1864, and the Kunetts had once supplied him with grain. The distillery had fallen on hard times since the Russian Revolution, and Kunett was able to secure its vodka recipe and North American rights.

---

* When referring to Scotch, Canadian whisky, or Japanese whisky, whisky is typically spelled without an e. (This is a sentence that has been printed in every single booze book ever written, and I pray that one day I no longer have to write it.)

Prohibition was just ending, and Kunett opened America's first vodka distillery, now known as Smirnoff, in 1934 in a building that still stands at 77 South Street in Bethel, Connecticut, near the New Haven Line's train tracks. Unfortunately, no one wanted Kunett's foreign hooch, and he maxed out at selling five thousand cases in one year—most Americans had yet to even hear of this weird Russian spirit and still greatly favored classic Western liquors like whiskey and gin.

Eventually Kunett had no real choice but to sell his Smirnoff to John Gilbert Martin of Heublein (which also distributed the British product A.1. Steak Sauce), who in 1939 offered $14,000 and a royalty of 5 percent on each bottle sold for the next ten years. As the *New York Times* wrote about the man in 1995, "Martin set out to see if he could sell Smirnoff, the vodka of the czars, in an age when there were no czars."

A chance break occurred in the early 1940s when Martin noticed that a South Carolina liquor distributor was having success by capitalizing on vodka's neutral flavor with a questionably accurate slogan: "Smirnoff White Whiskey—No Smell, No Taste."

Martin was an offbeat salesman during these more staid times, and he was more than willing to lean into this strategy.

"It was strictly illegal, of course, but it was going great," Martin told the *Hartford Times* in 1964. That same year Congress declared bourbon a "distinctive product of the United States." But it was already too late—neutral and approachable vodka was well on its way to becoming king. "People were mixing it with milk and orange juice and whatnot," boasted Martin.

Noticing a new breed of post-Prohibition drinkers who had never been in bars and were, thus, more eager for buzz than flavor, Martin began marketing it for use in cocktails, namely the Moscow Mule, which he cocreated in 1941.

A. J. Liebling cracked in his 1959 memoir, *Between Meals*: "The standard of perfection for vodka (no color, no taste, no smell) . . . accounts perfectly for the drink's rising popularity with those who like their alcohol in conjunction with the reassuring tastes of infancy—tomato juice, orange juice, chicken broth."

Further bolstering the spirit's popularity was an aggressive, celebrity-fueled advertising campaign—not to mention somewhat softened feelings toward Russia, despite the ongoing Cold War—featuring stars like Woody Allen, Johnny Carson, Eartha Kitt, Langston Hughes, Zsa Zsa Gabor, and Groucho Marx.

Often, when I'm writing about the history of booze, I find myself recalling scenes from *Mad Men*. For vodka, it's in the opening episode of the third season when the great Roger Sterling bursts into Don Draper's office with some contraband he'd just procured while on his honeymoon in Greece—Cuban cigars and Stolichnaya vodka.

A jet-setter always on top of trends, Sterling had visited Greece in the summer of 1963; "Stoli" wouldn't officially start being exported to the United States until 1965. It was immediately seen as exotic and highbrow compared to the stuffy spirits dominating the U.S. market. If the then-thirtysomething Draper and fortysomething Sterling had previously been J&B Scotch and Canadian Club whiskey fans, so had many Americans.

But whiskey was starting to be seen as your "old man's" drink to the hippie youth. It was not fit for the progressive ways of the 1960s; it would later also be seen as too antiquated for the disco drinks of the 1970s, and that's why it hardly appears in any of them.

Vodka would eventually win over the baby boomers now coming of drinking age, becoming an exotic and "lighter" alternative to whiskey; it would also supplant gin as the preferred base spirit for the martini.

By 1976 vodka had finally overtaken whiskey as America's top-selling spirit, and in 1978 Smirnoff was the number one spirits brand in all of America. It was ideal in, say, a Harvey Wallbanger or a Sex on the Beach.

After hitting an all-time peak sales number in 1970 with eighty million cases moved, bourbon would go on a steep decline for the bulk of the 1970s, '80s, and early '90s. Vodka would, in fact, dominate so much for the next several decades that the American whiskey industry was nearly destroyed. Everyone was drinking vodka; no one was drinking America's "distinctive" national spirit, and a bourbon glut occurred.

Yet I'd always wondered: Why did Kentucky continue to make so much damn bourbon if no one was drinking it? Eddie Russell, the current master distiller for Wild Turkey, filled me in.

"Because people like Jimmy"—his father, the legendary master distiller Jimmy Russell—"had a belief it would be back one day," Eddie told me.

And that's why so many mature barrels were never dumped, and why so many great bottles of American bourbon and rye just sat on shelves, never purchased, never opened, never even dusted, for the latter half of the twentieth century.

It's why some of these bottles were inexplicably still sitting in stores in the first decade of the twenty-first century.

Few people passing by, on their way to grab some Grey Goose or Patrón or even Jägermeister, realized that those dusty bottles contained some of the best bourbon and rye whiskey ever produced in America.

While today vodka is pretty much the only spirit that doesn't have any sort of vintage market to speak of.

NOW, BOURBON COMPANIES weren't completely sitting on their hands during the glut years. Many of them were throwing any ideas they could think of at the wall, hoping something would stick.

There was flavored whiskey, kicked off by Wild Turkey Honey Liqueur, which debuted in 1976.

There was also something dubbed light whiskey, distilled to such a high proof that all the flavor was stripped so it ended up tasting like vodka.

"'Light' is right," claimed Schenley's Light Red Label. "You've tried some whiskeys that growl. Now try a new kind of whiskey," read the copy for Crow Light, adding, "It whispers." "Underwhelm me . . . again," said the ads for Four Roses Premium American Light Whiskey. "It's whiskey without the whelm."

Not surprisingly, these were all abject disasters, and virtually no one collects them today outside of brand completists.

Then there was one gimmick that actually sorta worked: putting this glut of whiskey into gimmicky decanters.

"It was a way for us to get rid of old bourbon," Fred Noe, master distiller of Jim Beam and the great-grandson of the actual man, once told me. His company first released decanters in 1953, but it really ramped up production during the glut era, dumping its standard Kentucky straight bourbon into decorative vessels made by the Regal China Company out of Chicago. "We just had so much inventory—one hundred fifty months old, sometimes."

Jim Beam would release several dozen different decanters every year for decades. They became such a critical part of its business that it even acquired Regal China in 1968.

And that's why the dusty world, and the antique world, remains absolutely flooded with Jim Beam decanters, both open and sealed and shaped like everything from Corvettes to Poulan chainsaws to former vice president Spiro Agnew. Simply go on eBay, type in "Jim Beam decanters," and you'll be gobsmacked by the pure breadth of what is still out there. (Of course, if it's available on eBay these days, it legally must be an empty decanter, something I'll discuss further in a bit.)

"In the sixties and seventies, people collected the shit out of them. It was nuts," Noe told me. Many of these decanters were gifted to people who might not even like bourbon and thus would never open them.

In fact, in an era when no one was really buying bourbon or drinking bourbon, there was an International Association of Jim Beam Bottle

Collectors, with chapters in various cities across the globe and yearly conventions like 1975's in Sacramento, California.

"The thing was, all these collectors got old and died off, and no young people took up the hobby," says Noe.

But dusty hunters eventually did, though not necessarily in pursuit of just Jim Beam.

Thankfully, other distilleries of the glut era had followed suit, producing and filling their own decanters that are very much desired today. From 1971 to 1989, Wild Turkey released decanters annually, including the occasional mini-decanter. The glazed ceramic artwork, always shaped like the namesake bird, is of a surprisingly high quality and so is the whiskey, which was usually 8-year-old bourbon bottled at the brand's iconic 101 proof.

Julian Van Winkle III, scion of the soon-to-come Pappy Van Winkle dynasty, put his Stitzel-Weller Distillery stock in decanters modeled on Rip Van Winkle, and Ezra Brooks made ones in the shape of dueling pistols, potbellied stoves, and the Iowa State Capitol building.

The crème de la crème of glut-era decanters, however, is surely the Old Crow Chessmen set, a 1969 release that offered 10-year-old National Distillers–produced bourbon in all thirty-two different chess pieces.

Many modern bourbon collectors have labeled the bourbon from the Old Crow Chessmen the best thing they ever drank.

ON DECANTERS: CHESSMEN, KING TUT, AND "THE KING"

As recently as 2018 or so, wheeling and dealing on glut-era decanters was a great way to score incredible vintage liquid for a thriftier price, but collectors have since caught on. Unlike regular dusty bottles, decanters were also more easily found at flea markets and garage sales, whose proprietors might just think they had a goofy little statuette on their hands, not some world-class whiskey. Unlike typical vintage bottles, there were also two fears keeping even some of the most avid dusty hunters away from decanters.

First, since the bottles are opaque with poor closures and thick walls, it's always difficult to tell how much liquid remains in a vessel and virtually impossible to tell if the liquid is clear and of a high quality. For that reason, collectors have created crowd-sourced spreadsheets and even a Facebook group ("Bourbon Decanter ounces to ounces") in an effort to list the expected weight of a full decanter of various releases. Many collectors also will demand that a decanter be, uh, decanted into a glass bottle (preferably while being filmed) before shipping, to make leakage or breakage less likely.

Second, there are health concerns with drinking from old decanters, which were often made of a leaden ceramic and, according to the U.S. Food and Drug Administration (FDA) in a 1991 warning, have been found to leach lead into the liquid. How much of that lead can get into your body if you drink from vintage decanters? Well, that's up for debate.

Joshua Richholt, a longtime vintage collector who at one time owned an example of literally every single Wild Turkey decanter ever produced, has his doctor test him once a year for lead poisoning. (He remains lead-free.) Mike Jasinski, an expert on testing drinking water (who will be more formally introduced in a bit), once used the graphite furnace auto analyzer in the laboratory at his job to analyze bourbon pulled from ceramic decanters to see if they were safe to drink, posting his results to the Straightbourbon.com message boards in 2013.

Ultimately, he found that yes, the decanters had higher lead levels than the acceptable limit for drinking water (15 parts per billion [ppb]), but they weren't much higher, ranging from a 1968 Jim Beam decanter as low as 18 ppb to a 1971 Old Fitzgerald figural at 103 ppb.

Of course, no one drinks as much vintage decanter bourbon as they do tap water, so Jasinski figured he was safe, and so are you (though please consult your own health care professionals). If you can still find any. Here are some key dusty decanters to look out for the next time you go antiquing.

OLD CROW CHESSMEN

Not just the top decanter series that vintage geeks actively pursue, but one of the top overall dusties. This one-time release, in 1969, offered 10-year-old, 86-proof National Distillers–produced bourbon inside all thirty-two different chess pieces, sized from 12 to 15.5 inches and glazed in golden bronze for the white pieces and an almost-black "Viridian Green" for the opposing side. A full set also came with a 45" x 45" chessboard made of deep-pile carpet. Many vintage collectors who have tried a Chessman, myself included, consider this extremely dark bourbon some of the most exceptional liquid they have ever tasted. Unfortunately, poor closures mean that most of the decanters have evaporated (a full decanter should weigh about four pounds). Prices have skyrocketed in recent years to several thousand dollars per piece. A bucket list pour for any vintage enthusiast.

ANY STITZEL-WELLER AND WILD TURKEY

Just as all Stitzel-Weller and Wild Turkey dusties are greedily pursued, their decanters are as well. While Stitzel-Weller bourbon was thrown in a variety of decanters, some attractive (Cabin Still Sportsman's and several Old Fitzgerald glass decanters), many ugly (the Old Fitzgerald rounded porcelain decanters with artwork more befitting a McDonald's giveaway cup), some downright strange (the Cabin Still Kentucky Hillbilly series), all Wild Turkey decanters—released between 1971 and 1989—came in fairly handsome ceramic turkeys, though collectors should be cautious of the high likelihood of breaking their wattled necks while handling.

MICHTER'S KING TUT

Released in 1978 to commemorate the *Treasures of Tutankhamun*, a blockbuster traveling tour of the Egyptian boy pharaoh across America, this Michter's decanter is not particularly great-tasting liquid—"pot still sour mash whiskey" at 86 proof without an age statement. However, the stunning packaging, a gold-colored bust of King Tut, as well as the industry darling that is Michter's today, means that many collectors aspire to own a Tut decanter, or at least order a pour at a vintage bar in order to flex their photogenic purchase on Instagram.

MCCORMICK ELVIS

Similarly, forty different Elvis Presley decanters produced by McCormick Distilling Company, a lightly regarded Missouri outfit, from the late 1970s into the '80s have been gaining a lot of traction from collectors of late—not necessarily for their contents, but for the cool visual of a drinkable Elvis in various poses and attires, including "Aloha" Elvis, depicting his 1961 benefit performance at the Pearl Harbor National Memorial, and "Elvis Karate," featuring the King in a red-belted karate gi. Maybe the 2022 Baz Luhrmann movie helped drive this recent interest, though I thought it suffered from third-act problems.

NOT PARTICULARLY COLLECTED

JIM BEAM DECANTERS

Not all goofy decanters from the past are sought-after, however. Even before the glut, starting in 1953, Jim Beam began packaging some of its vast stock of inventory in decorative decanters made by the Regal China Company and shaped like classic cars, garden tools, and famous politicians. Unfortunately, most of what remains is lightly aged, 80-proof swill. It's nearly impossible to go to a flea market and not find a few empty Jim Beam decanters selling for a few bucks each.

Bourbon was being shoved into goofy decanters and languishing on shelves in America in the 1970s and '80s, but there was one place on the planet where it had become red-hot, a fact that would lead to unexpected reverberations in the market that are still being felt today.

In the early 1970s, William G. Yuracko was head of Schenley International's export division, working out of the Empire State Building, and tasked with trying to sell to foreign markets his company's bourbons that weren't selling at home. He quickly found success turning Germans on to his portfolio's cheaper, lower-shelf bourbons like J.W. Dant. In 1972 he began taking reconnaissance trips to the Far East to see if there was any sort of market there as well. The country had lifted all restrictions on imported spirits in 1969, and back then Japanese people mostly drank Scotch or their own homegrown whiskey, which was likewise based on a Scotch flavor profile and was moving some thirty million cases per year.

"Bourbon was unknown and a total departure from the taste pattern," Yuracko claims.

Yuracko soon realized that getting Scotch-swilling Japanese old-timers to switch to American-made whiskey would be nearly impossible. He decided to write off middle-aged customers and instead focus his efforts solely on Japan's youth, the "post-college consumer . . . whose tastes were not yet formed and who was attuned to Western products and ideas," like Coca-Cola and Levi's.

"They were having their own youth revolution, [like] what we had gone through in the '60s, they were going through in the '80s," explains Chuck Cowdery, author and bourbon historian. But if America's youth was rejecting "brown goods," as Yuracko called them, in order to drink lightly colored vodka and tequila, he thought he could get young drinkers of Japan to reject Scotch in favor of bourbon, and take some of the growing glut off his hands.

Unfortunately, then, as now, it was very hard for foreigners to make headway in Japanese business. Yuracko knew he'd need a local liaison, so he offered a distribution partnership with Suntory, the Japanese whiskey giant that already controlled 70 percent of the local market. Brown-Forman, another American whiskey powerhouse and Schenley's top competitor, would eventually offer Suntory the same deal.

"I cannot overestimate the importance of the decision taken by Schenley management to place their most important brands in the same house with their major competitor," Yuracko explained in a paper he authored for the *Journal of Business Strategy* in 1992. (I spoke to Yuracko, now eighty-nine years old, by phone after he had just finished his weekly Tuesday tennis match. Why this man has not been inducted into the Kentucky Bourbon Hall of Fame is beyond me.) "This would be tantamount to Ford and General Motors giving all their top models to Toyota to market in Japan."

It was a major gamble for everyone involved. Suntory could, of course, intentionally torpedo all bourbon sales to ensure that Japanese whiskey would face no serious competition, or it could favor one bourbon brand over the other. The fact was, however, neither Schenley nor Brown-Forman had much to lose. Bourbon was flailing so badly at this point, so many other distilleries had already gone out of business, that if they didn't take the gamble, they might be extinct soon enough as well.

Suntory didn't want to simply do a trial either. According to Yuracko, Suntory wanted a "critical mass" of bourbon, "a product for every taste and price level . . . and each brand was given its own identity and market niche." Schenley offered Ancient Age, J.W. Dant, and I.W. Harper. Brown-Forman handed over Early Times, Old Forester, and Jack Daniel's.

Since most drinking in Japan was done outside the home, Schenley and Brown-Forman together began setting up bourbon bars all over the country. The bars had "an unsophisticated atmosphere that would appeal to young people already attracted to American clothes, cars, and customs," Yuracko explained, playing country music, serving stereotypical American food like hamburgers, chili, and fried chicken, and pouring only Suntory's six bourbon brands. Yuracko would go to each bar's opening, presenting employees with a certificate that each was now a certified Schenley bartender.

Instead of buying single glasses of bourbon, or cocktails, young customers of that era purchased entire bottles, stored in cabinets along the bar, each adorned with a neck tag denoting whose was whose. In an era before social media flexing, it became a youthful challenge to see who could drink the most personal bottles. Thanks to heavy advertising from Suntory, one brand quickly began to rise above the others.

"I.W. Harper was the eye-opener," explains Cowdery. A bottom-shelf product in America, it was able to be sold at an elevated price in Japan, before Schenley eventually fully repositioned it as a premiu 12-year-old product. I.W. Harper was selling only two thousand cases internationally in 1969, but by 1991 it was the largest-selling bourbon brand in Japan at more than five hundred thousand cases per year. So much so that,

Cowdery explains, "It was profitable to buy cases of I.W. Harper on [the American] wholesale market and privately ship them to Japan."

Eventually Schenley had to take I.W. Harper off the market stateside in order to satisfy demand in Japan. (Perhaps this is why so little vintage I.W. Harper is seen in the States today.) Soon enough, other brands took notice and decided to see if they, too, could become "big in Japan." By 1990, two million cases of bourbon were headed to the country every year.

Japan gave these old bourbon brands a new lifeline. For example, Four Roses had long fallen out of favor with American drinkers by the 1970s. In 1967, Seagram's turned the once-venerable brand into a dreaded blended whiskey, cut with grain neutral spirit and added flavoring.

"By the time the nineties rolled around, it was just your average blended whiskey," Al Young, Four Roses' legendary senior brand ambassador who worked at the company for fifty years, told me before he died in 2019. But in Japan, Four Roses was still a legitimate straight bourbon whiskey, high-quality liquid packaged in sleek, Cognac-style bottles with embossed silver roses. In Japan, it was a big hit. Just as Schenley and Brown-Forman had partnered with Suntory, in 1971 Four Roses struck up a partnership with Kirin, Japan's top beer brand.

If brands like I.W. Harper, Four Roses, and Early Times were saved by Japan, others were specifically created for it, particularly luxury brands.

"The Japanese people were always willing to pay for high-end products," recalls Yuracko.

There was, notably, Blanton's, which was spawned in 1984 by two former Fleischmann's Distilling execs, Ferdie Falk and Bob Baranaskas. The two had acquired the Buffalo Trace Distillery (then known as the George T. Stagg Distillery) as well as Schenley's key bourbon, Ancient Age. Believing, like Yuracko, that the future of bourbon was overseas, they called their new company Age International.

Blanton's, the world's first commercial single-barrel bourbon, packaged in a now-iconic grenade-shaped, horse-stoppered bottle, was such a hit in

Japan that by 1992 the Japanese company Takara Shuzo had purchased Age International for $20 million. It immediately flipped the actual distillery to Sazerac, while retaining the brand trademarks for Blanton's.

Accustomed to Scotch with big age statements, Japanese consumers began to demand bourbons of a similar maturity. Bourbon in America had typically been released after about four years—common wisdom among distillers like Jimmy Russell was that it got too oaky if it was aged much longer. But if Japan wanted well-aged bourbon, American distilleries and bottlers were more than happy to fob off their mature glut stock to them.

Russell, who started visiting Japan in the 1980s, released a 13-year-old Wild Turkey to the market. Heaven Hill specifically bottled an Evan Williams 23 Year Old for Japan and created new brands like Martin Mills 24 Years.

Marci Palatella, an exporter with her firm International Beverage, created Very Olde St. Nick in 1984, with some releases as old as 25 years. There was Old Grommes Very Very Rare Kentucky Straight Bourbon Whiskey, which in the late 1980s started sending Japan bottles as old as two decades. A.H. Hirsch, aged 15, 16, and eventually 20 years, landed in Japan as early as 1989, and it is still some of the most coveted bourbon of all time (so much so that Cowdery wrote an entire book, *The Best Bourbon You'll Never Taste*, about it).

Private labels were big business too. Kentucky Bourbon Distillers (today more commonly known as Willett) provided a 20-year-old Rogin's Choice to a top American whiskey bar in Osaka that counted some five thousand "self-imported" bourbons. Julian Van Winkle III kept his nascent company afloat in the mid-1980s and onward by providing special bottlings to local bars, many under names like Society of Bourbon Connoisseurs.

America's bourbon malaise would last nearly three decades, reaching its nadir in 2000 when a mere thirty-two million cases were moved stateside, less than half of the 1970 peak. Of course, it's always darkest before the dawn, and, thanks to Japan's example, things were already being put into place for bourbon's homeland revival.

By the time bourbon had crawled its way out of the glut in the late 1990s and early 2000s, people like Van Winkle III were more than willing to start offering Americans bottles of 23-year-old "brown goods" too. If Japan liked it, perhaps we would as well.

A new generation of Americans didn't just like this bourbon, we loved it.

And this modern breed of drinkers was more than willing to buy it, trade it, sell it, stockpile it, fetishize it, and look back into the past to find vintage examples of it that their forebears had skipped over.

Even today Japan remains one of the final frontiers for American dusty hunters, with loads of great bottles dotting the country. But, just like America, it's not as great as it used to be.

Back in 2020, I spoke to John Rudd, an American who ran a blog called the *Tokyo Bourbon Bible*. Living in Japan in the early 2010s, he recalled finding bottles of gold wax A.H. Hirsch, Van Winkle 1974 Family Reserve 17 Year, and early editions of the vaunted Buffalo Trace Antique Collection (BTAC). He always let it sit there, never worried it would run out.

Then, one day, there was literally nothing left.

"I asked a liquor store owner what happened, and he told me, 'Some American guy named Alex came by and purchased all of it.'"

KEY JAPANESE EXPORT DUSTIES

Throughout this book, there will be several sections detailing the key bottles that collectors pursue in various spirits categories. If you're enjoying the narrative, feel free to skip these sections to return to later for reference.

As far as vintage spirits collecting goes, whiskey has long been king, specifically American bourbon or rye; perhaps that's because there's simply so much of it still out there due to the aforementioned glut. Or maybe it's because whiskey collectors are a lot more avaricious than drinkers in other categories.

Many of the key bourbon dusties (see page 81) have been found in Japan over the years, though the days of stumbling upon them just hanging out on shelves, priced to move as they were in 1988, are sadly over, and many are now stickered at modern secondary market values. But there are also some key, Japanese-only exports one should seek out that the vast majority of modern American bourbon drinkers might not even know ever existed.

GLUT ERA

JULIAN VAN WINKLE III BOTTLINGS

Starting in 1983, in the two decades before the Pappy scion moved his operations to Buffalo Trace Distillery in 2002, Van Winkle III sourced liquid and bottled many brands for himself (and others) at Old Commonwealth Distillery, which had formerly been known as the Hoffman Distillery. Not just the Old Rip Van Winkles you're probably aware of, but also many brands that ended up in Japan. Those would include early batches of the revered A.H. Hirsch, Old Grommes (Old Grommes 16 Year Old is the same juice as A.H. Hirsch, while other bottlings are Stitzel-Weller and Jim Beam), and Very Olde St. Nick (look for Lawrenceburg, KY, on the label; later bottlings, courtesy of Even Kulsveen of Kentucky Bourbon Distillers and using Heaven Hill stock, will list Bardstown, KY).

OBSCURE HEAVEN HILL LABELS

Apparently, so the lore goes, in the 1990s, many Japanese businessmen would go to Max Shapira of the Heaven Hill Distillery and ask if he could make them their own private label bourbon to sell back home. Shapira was in no mood to put in such effort, but he was more than happy to hand them a binder of obscure labels that Heaven Hill already owned, ones with names like Virgin Bourbon, most of which were acquired from small distilleries that went under during the early years of the bourbon glut, and allow them to pick one for themselves. His only requirement was that they place a minimum order that was big enough to fill an entire shipping container to Asia. Look for any Japanese export distilled at Heaven Hill (DSP-KY-32 will be printed on the back label), preferably bottled at 100 proof or greater and 15 years or older, with a dark red tint to the bourbon—a telltale sign it is going to be exceptional. (Of note, Heaven Hill continues to bottle and sell all these obscure labels today on an extremely small scale—say, *twelve* total bottles' worth, available only at the distillery gift shop—in order to keep the trademark active "in commerce.")

AMERICA, F@#K YEAH!

As mentioned, Japan had a hard-on for American cosplay during the tail end of the glut era, and, thus, many export brands were developed to be as stereotypically American (to Japanese eyes) as possible. Van Winkle III, under the Commonwealth name, bottled something called Loredo Pass that came in a cowboy boot–shaped decanter. National Distillers released a Kentucky Colonel gift set that included an ice bucket wrapped in a denim blue jean. Heaven Hill presented The Yellow Rose of Texas. If you hear Lee Greenwood in your ear while looking at some red, white, and jingoist bottling, it will almost certainly be good.

TAKARA BLANTON'S

The earliest Blanton's bottlings were specifically made for the Japanese marketplace, and those releases are still highly desirable. (From 1993 on, look for "Blanton's Single Barrel Bourbon ウイスキー" on the neck label.) For many years, expressions not available in the United States included Single Barrel Bourbon (with either a black or cream label), Silver Edition (a discontinued duty-free offering), Takara Black (packaged in a box), Takara Red (packaged in a box), Takara Gold (aged 2 years longer and packaged in a gaudier box than standard Gold), and Blanton's Straight from the Barrel.

WILD TURKEY EXPORTS

Over the years, there have been a few Wild Turkey exports that are good, but really only sought-after by Turkey fan boys. For the Japanese market, those would include Wild Turkey 1855 Reserve as well as various 8-, 12-, and 13-Year-Olds.

THE POST-GLUT DUSTIES

FRED NOE SELECTS

Starting in 2010, Fred Noe—the master distiller of Jim Beam—selected three different small-batch, barrel-proof bourbons for the high-end Japanese supermarket chain Seijo Ishii. Packaged in the same style of bottles as the brand's high-end, barrel-proof Booker's—named after Fred's dad, the even more venerated master distiller Booker Noe—these are differentiated by having Fred's visage on the label. (Typically considered tastier than Booker's, the bottle count is much lower than standard Booker's as well.) Seijo Ishii gilded the lily even further by putting the bottles in bamboo tubes—not exactly sanctioned by Jim Beam, which had yet to be bought by Suntory, something that would happen in 2014. Each of the three releases can be differentiated by the picture and proof on the label.

JAPANESE FOUR ROSES

While Four Roses was fobbing off swill to its homegrown market starting in 1967, it gave Japan all its good stuff. Today there is still a Four Roses Super Premium that is export-only for Japanese retail. It is not exceptional juice by any means, but the handsome bottle, with a silver rose inset, makes it a desirable souvenir for American visitors.

KEN'S CHOICE

Private labels remain fairly strong in Japan, and this is perhaps the most coveted of recent times. Ken Matsuyama owns two top bourbon bars in Tokyo, known simply as Ken's Bar. They have very few seats and play American jazz, another passion of Matsuyama, who is an accomplished musician himself. Starting in 2015, he began private bottling select casks from America under the Ken's Choice and Ken's Choice Jazz Instrumental series, featuring jazz artists or instruments on the label. The always well-aged liquid has variously come from Wild Turkey, Heaven Hill, George Dickel, and other American distilleries—some are finished in sherry casks or barrels from the cult Chichibu Distillery, which also handles all the bottling. New releases continue to come out, which can be scored for a fairly reasonable price if you're willing to visit Ken.

2

VINTAGE BOOZE'S BIG BANG

MODERN VINTAGE SPIRITS collecting doesn't begin in Japan, however, or in America, or even with glut-era bourbon. It actually starts with Cognac and a debonair London bartender by way of Italy. Born in 1955 in the small town of Maiori along the Amalfi Coast, Salvatore Calabrese had entered the bar industry by age eleven. During his school's summer break, his father got him a gig at the Hotel Reginna Palace bar, where he ran errands for the head barman, Signor Raffaello. Even at such a green age, Calabrese was awed by the Rick Blainesque Italian who spoke several languages and sported a cream jacket to work, never even a red speck appearing on it as he mixed Americanos for tourists.

Calabrese would rise through the ranks in Maiori, by age twenty-one becoming the youngest maître d' on the Amalfi Coast when he was hired at Hotel Panorama, before he headed to the larger pastures of London. In 1982 he answered a classified ad in the *Evening Standard* and was soon working at the then little-known bar at Dukes Hotel. By the mid-1980s Calabrese had garnered notice in the city for inadvertently creating the "Direct Martini" or "Naked Martini," a bottle of gin pulled straight from the freezer and combined with a single dash of vermouth—he invented it after a customer complained his martinis weren't cold enough or dry enough.

He was soon receiving hosannas across the globe, from journalists like Stanton Delaplane and Herb Caen as well as the novelist Kingsley Amis. It was also at Dukes where Calabrese would pioneer the whole idea of vintage spirits. Much like his Direct Martini, it happened a bit inadvertently.

Dukes Bar was tiny, with just six small tables, and Calabrese needed to figure out a way to up the average spend of each customer, especially as the barman made most of his income off a percentage of sales. He realized he couldn't get customers to drink more, so maybe he could get them to drink better, by getting them to drink older.

Unfortunately, there wasn't really a market for that sort of thing. At the time, in London, there was a market for vintage wine and port, which make sense—those liquids clearly age in the bottle, often into something spectacular. But when it came to spirits, drinkers were all about the contemporary.

"I wanted to go as far back as the Napoleonic era, as far back as when George Washington was around," says Calabrese, still spry and fashionable in his late sixties with gray hair softly slicked back and a manicured white beard, and sporting hip, rectangular eyeglasses, as we spoke over Zoom one Monday morning.

Calabrese thought Cognac, which he continually calls "the noblest spirit," was the answer. In a way, it was preternaturally designed for vintage enthusiasm; much like wine vintages are determined by the year the grapes were picked, Cognac—distilled wine—labels its vintages along with the harvest. Unfortunately, both Dukes' general manager and beverage manager at the time thought Calabrese was crazy.

"I was out of my mind because where would I find something that old, and would I even be able to sell it?" Calabrese recalls.

Luckily for Calabrese, hotelier Arthur Rapp was a regular at the bar. One day the charismatic Calabrese painted a picture for the big boss of building a special collection of vintage spirits. Rapp gave Calabrese the go-ahead—but finding his first piece of liquid history would be harder than he expected.

Calabrese first tried the major auction houses, Christie's and Sotheby's. No luck. He crossed the street to the oldest wine merchant in town, Berry Bros. & Rudd, but it didn't have anything either. So Calabrese began asking around. It would take nearly two years for him to get a good lead. Eventually he was introduced to a private collector, though the man was reluctant to sell anything to Calabrese. Finally, the barman talked him into parting with just one bottle, a 1914 Croizet Bonaparte Cognac Fine Champagne, which he purchased for a modest £70.

Calabrese offered it at Dukes for £15 a glass. The previous collector had warned him that it probably wouldn't even taste good, but Calabrese presumed otherwise. He knew that, unlike wine, spirits don't age in the bottle and, if stored well, will taste just like they had when first bottled all those decades ago. A spirit is alive only for those years it is in a barrel; once it is bottled, it becomes like a mammoth locked in permafrost.

To intrigue customers, Calabrese told them that when this very Cognac was made, World War I had just begun.

"You can see history, you can touch history—but you can't taste it. I wanted to sell history that you could taste," he says.

The Cognac tasted incredible, in fact, and when Calabrese sold off the entire bottle in one week, he knew he was onto something. His general manager then gave him an actual budget to find more bottles.

Starting in 1984, Calabrese quickly began amassing a collection of Cognac and Armagnac that stretched back to the eighteenth century. No one else cared at the time, so he got these bottles for a song. They weren't put on display at the bar but locked in Dukes' basement, known about only via word of mouth. A lot of mouths were apparently offering those words, however, and there were many customers who would gladly be up-charged to taste what Calabrese dubbed "liquid history."

"Uncorking them is always an emotional experience," Calabrese writes in his 2001 book, *Cognac: A Liquid History*. In it, he recounts the story of Winston Churchill opening a Bual 1792 Madeira and being awestruck upon the realization that it had been produced when Marie Antoinette was alive.

Calabrese intentionally linked all his vintage bottles to the past, offering a Cognac from the year Lord Nelson was slain at the Battle of Trafalgar (1805) and one from the year Napoleon invaded Russia (1812). For American guests, Calabrese might pull a bottle from 1865, the year the Civil War ended.

"I always associate the age of the spirit with something happening in the world," Calabrese explains.

He would acquire a bottle of Hine 1815 Cognac, inspired by a portrait of the Duke of Wellington hanging in the bar; the duke had commanded the coalition armies that defeated Napoleon at the Battle of Waterloo that very year. It sold for £250 a glass, a huge figure for the day.

Calabrese recalls serving the last pour of a Cognac from 1802 to a customer curious about it.

"I walked away, and after a little while I went back to him to see if he enjoyed it. And I saw that he had tears in his eyes," recalls Calabrese. "I thought, Christ Almighty, I hope he's not thinking about what it's costing him. So I lean over to him and say, 'Is everything okay?'

"He picks up the balloon glass and says, 'I'm sad because when I finish this sip, no one will ever be able to taste this spirit again.'"

With that stark thought, Calabrese quit selling the last measure of any bottle, comparing it to losing a child.

Quickly, Dukes Bar had gone from making £400 to £500 a week to bringing in up to £10,000 a night—and, in a way, Calabrese had created a new kind of model for drinking. It was a model that was too difficult, though, for other London bars to copy; Calabrese did so much research (in these days before the internet) and had much better sources for bottles.

Despite his romance with the past, Maestro Calabrese—as he now goes by—is very much in tune with the present and the future. And he's still obsessed with vintage spirits—his "greatest pleasure," he writes on his website—even as he enters his septuagenarian years.

"I can't stop," he tells me of his obsession, though his wife thinks they have more than enough dusty bottles in their home.

In a recent Instagram video, Calabrese eagerly opened a package to find a 1955 bottle of Kina Lillet. He thought it would be perfect to pair with some 1950s-era Gordon's Gin and Smirnoff Vodka to create a Vesper the way James Bond would have drunk it back then.

Calabrese currently curates the beverage list at the Donovan Bar in Brown's Hotel, London, with a menu offering seven pages of vintage spirits of all categories plus two additional pages of vintage cocktails.

"It is the tremendous, tingling excitement and anticipation that I try to pass on to a guest when I open a bottle of vintage Cognac at the bar," he says. "For me, the magic never fails to work. It is as if it is a part of the spirit itself."

PRE-PHYLLOXERA 'GNAC

For Calabrese, as with many other collectors, finding and tasting vintage spirits aren't only about a remembrance of things past. They are also about tasting a flavor profile that will never ever exist again, for a variety of reasons we'll get to as we look at different spirits categories.

In the case of Cognac, that never-to-taste-the-same-again flavor profile is due to something called phylloxera, microscopic sap-sucking aphids that destroyed most of France's vineyards in the nineteenth century.

Thus, any Cognac produced before or shortly after the 1872/73 season is known as pre-phylloxera Cognac, and highly coveted. (No shit, you say.) Of this category, 1869, 1871, 1874, and 1875 are known as particularly stellar years. These Cognacs would have been made with grape varieties such as Folle Blanche and Colombard, some of which had originally been planted by the Romans.

"You think back to Roman times. They love to drink. They love to drink wine," says Calabrese. "But those wines, those styles of grapes, were completely destroyed. So when you try a pre-phylloxera Cognac, it's just a different feeling, a different journey."

(Believe it or not, it was a horticulturist and grapevine expert from Denison, Texas, of all places, Thomas Volney Munson, who would help save and rejuvenate the French wine industry by sending Lone Star State grapevine cuttings that were disease resistant.)

According to Calabrese, who estimates that by now he's tasted more than one thousand bottles of pre-phylloxera Cognac, they are the pinnacle of spirits, way more intensely aromatic and flavorful than modern Cognac vintages.

"I've sat there with people tasting super-super-old Cognac, and they go, 'No, I don't like it. I prefer this newer one,'" says Isabel Graham-Yooll, a longtime vintage spirits expert in the United Kingdom. "Well, yes, you might be right, and in that case, it's not worth it to you.

"But if you're trying something pre-phylloxera and it makes your heart sing and you get slightly tearful and you feel like you're the most privileged person on the face of the earth . . . then it really is something truly special."

Shockingly, as I write this, pre-phylloxera Cognac is still somewhat undervalued. In early 2023, I can go online and see bottles available for as low as $800. But demand is beginning to increase, and by the time you read this, tasting this sort of liquid history may be out of reach for most drinkers.

Calabrese was so far ahead of everyone else in the vintage spirits game that it would take another couple of decades for the hobby to jump the pond to America.

It would likewise take a different, uniquely American form. Instead of being mostly set in auction houses and high-end hotel bars, the arenas would be seedy liquor stores and the internet. Instead of mustached Italians in white dinner jackets, it would be white dudes in band T-shirts. Instead of Cognac, bourbon would become the American dusty hunter's fixation of choice.

While it's virtually impossible to determine who the Neil Armstrong of dusty hunting was—the first man who took one small step into an off-the-beaten-path liquor store and emerged with decades-old bottles—the first famous one was probably Mike Jasinski.

Forty-five miles outside Philadelphia, in what he knowingly calls the exurbs, Jasinski has long worked in an environmental laboratory that tests drinking water and wastewater. Like most other dusty hunters, his job has nothing to do with, as Jasinski puts it, "my weird obsessions about trying to go out and find and buy things."

He'd gotten into bourbon at the perfect time. In 2010, bourbon was a $1.9 billion industry in America; today it's worth more than $9 billion. In 2011, living in a control state like Pennsylvania was also ideal for booze hunters.

The liquor in control states, which total seventeen, is sold strictly by the government. Most of these states, even today, helpfully offer online databases that allow one to look up what bottles are available at that very moment and even what stores currently stock them. In 2011, really not that long ago, Jasinski was able to look up new releases of high-end stuff like Pappy Van Winkle and have it shipped straight to his front porch.*

---

* For what it's worth, today the seventeen states that have government-controlled liquor stores seem to have such strict inventory protocols that finding a vintage bottle there is literally impossible. "Everything's all very neat, clean, and the idea of dust would be anathema to those control states," one dusty hunter told me.

As he was living in the exurbs, a lot of Jasinski's hunting in those days was online. He'd spend most of his time on Straightbourbon.com, perhaps the internet's earliest bourbon forum, which Jim Butler, a Silicon Valley programmer, had first put online in 1999. Remarkably, that forum still has online archived discussions of dusty hunting going as far back as a 2000 thread in which bourbon historian Chuck Cowdery mentions that you might still be able to find Henry McKenna bourbon distilled at the Fairfield distillery in Kentucky (where it was produced until 1974) as well as "pre-Beam Old Taylor" (produced until 1987) in certain liquor stores.

That site also has arguably the first-ever reference to a "dusty hunter," in a 2008 thread where a user mentions being aware of a liquor store that still has bottles of Suntory Royal, a Japanese blend that first hit the market in 1960 to commemorate the distillery's sixtieth anniversary. The second appearance of the term on the site would find "the lamest dusty hunter ever," as he labels himself, snagging a bottle of A.H. Hirsch 20 Year Old, something that might be worth about $15,000 today.

Sitting in on conference calls at his day job, Jasinski would bide his time by obsessively reading any and all dusty-hunting threads on the forum. One day he told his wife, Claire Doordan, a vintage clothing dealer, about the practice. If dusty hunting has always predominantly been a male avocation, it would be a woman who laid the cornerstone for this country's dusty GOAT. While her husband worked that day, Doordan hopped into their old Jeep CJ7 and went around to all the crappiest liquor stores in Wilmington, Delaware, the closest decent-sized city to them; she came home with forty dusty bottles.

"And that's where the madness started," says Jasinski.

He set his sights on a bigger city, Baltimore, which, on the heels of *The Wire* running from 2002 to 2008, had garnered the sort of reputation that scared off most other suburban, middle-class white guys. Jasinski believes that from 2012 through 2014 he must have visited every single liquor store in the inner city, skipping the ones in more gentrified areas like Fell's Point. Back then, you could simply email Baltimore County and someone would send you back a list of every single liquor retailer.

He'd input these addresses into MapQuest—Google Maps didn't yet have this technology available—and press "optimize," and the program would create a multi-stop route for him. Jasinski would hit the road in the morning and keep going until he ran out of cash. In one "blown-out" neighborhood, there was a block entirely of vacant lots, except for a single *Addams Family* kind of row house standing in the middle of the cracked pavement, litter, and street weeds. It looked like yet another unoccupied house, yet in the front window, a vintage Old Grand-Dad 114 glassware snap case was on display. The door was ajar, so Jasinski walked in to find a foldout table with miniature bottles placed on it.

"That was the entirety of the liquor store," says Jasinski.

In those days, he found innumerable cases of coveted bourbons from the past, many produced by Stitzel-Weller, the distillery run by the literal "Pappy" Van Winkle, and Old Grand-Dad when it was made by National Distillers. An all-time great score landed him twenty bottles of 1973 Old Weller Original (Stitzel-Weller) and some late 1960s Laphroaig 10, some of the earliest single malt to hit the United States from the Islay distillery, off the Scottish coast. The mostly Korean liquor store owners in the city would always be confused by this burly white man in vintage concert T-shirts, hair cascading down his face with a big bushy beard, willing to fork over $1,000 in cash for liquor that looked like total garbage to them and their normal, everyday clientele. The owners would react in different ways.

"It runs the gamut where you have everybody in the store cheering that you're going to have this huge party, because you just bought forty bottles, to the proprietor not wanting to sell it to you because they think that you're up to something, that you're scamming them. And then others are so happy, they invite you into the back so that you can see if there are any more bottles you want to buy."

He recalls liquor store owners at the time telling him that ten years earlier, a sort of ur–dusty hunter had come through these same stores clearing the shelves of 1940s-era Maryland rye, a style that, by then, no longer existed in America.

Jasinski was also early in bidding on and acquiring bourbon via the Buyee Yahoo! JAPAN Auction website, a treasure trove of Japanese exports. (eBay had banned liquor sales by 2012.)

In the early 2000s, there was still so much dusty bourbon out there that Jasinski couldn't buy everything. He began to leave behind the 80- and 86-proof bottles in favor of strictly bottled-in-bond (100-proof) offerings. Mind you, a lot of this stuff wasn't wildly valuable just yet, and there was very little mainstream chatter about it. Even if the liquor store owners had known exactly what to google, they wouldn't have found anything that alerted them to the fact that their dusty booze was soon to be worth way more than the $8 a pop Jasinski was paying for it.

Of course, the price wasn't a big deal to Jasinski either, because he wasn't in the game simply to make money; in fact, even to this day he rarely sells these bottles. He and Doordan would open this dusty booze to try and determine what they actually enjoyed drinking; he was also extremely generous in sharing bottles with other enthusiasts.

By 2013, Jasinski had already developed a reputation as America's dusty hunter par excellence. On Instagram, when he changed his regular handle to "Bourbon Turtle" (@bourbonturtle) to share his best vintage finds, he amassed ten thousand new followers in a half year. (His friends had called him "Turtle" ever since a high school football game when he intercepted a pass and his less-than-fleet-of-foot return reminded them of the slow-moving reptile.)

Joshua Feldman, a fellow vintage enthusiast who blogs about whis-key under the name *The Coopered Tot*, wrote the first online post about Jasinski in 2013. In it, the longtime network administrator at the Morgan Library & Museum in New York details traveling to Jasinski's Penn-sylvania home to swap some bottles and drink some of his collection, notably some 1936-distilled Old Ren, a bonded bourbon from Rockford, Illinois. My friend Susannah Skiver Barton wrote the first print article about Jasinski in a 2018 *Whisky Advocate* story in which he was labeled "the Whiskey Whisperer."

On April 29, 2015, Jasinski cohosted a vintage tasting at Jack Rose Dining Saloon in Washington, D.C., along with owner Bill Thomas and celebrity chef Sean Brock, who was such a big fan of vintage Stitzel-Weller at the time that when he appeared on the Charleston, South Carolina, episode of Anthony Bourdain's *Parts Unknown* that same year, he carried along an unlabeled jug of 1991 bourbon all evening. (By 2017, though, he had gone sober and was having a fire sale on his massive Stitzel-Weller collection.)

Jasinski's Jack Rose event would offer pours of many legendary Stitzel-Weller bottles like Old Fitzgerald 1849, W.L. Weller Special Reserve, Old Weller Antique, and Weller 12 "Paper Label," along with "VIP" pours of 1940s Old Overholt Bottled-in-Bond, 1940s Baltimore Pure Rye Bottled-in-Bond, 1940s Mount Vernon Rye Bottled-in-Bond, 1940s Old Taylor Bottled-in-Bond, 1950s Wild Turkey 101 (back when it was listed as coming out of Brooklyn, New York), 1950s Double Springs 12 Year Bottled-in-Bond, and 1950s Old Sunny Brook Bottled-in-Bond, as well as two more super-primo Stitzel-Weller offerings in 1950s Old Weller Original 107 proof and 1952/1964 Very Very Old Fitzgerald.

Tickets were $150, and $250 for the VIPs.

"I poured bottles that night that I acquired for $300, that were worth $3,000 by then, and are now worth $30,000 today," Jasinski tells me.

He can only laugh at stories like that, and ones like the time he unloaded one of his two bottles of Red Hook Rye for dirt cheap—he didn't like the first bottle he had opened and had been mixing it with ginger ale. It's one of the most coveted unicorns in the game today, worth more than $50,000.

"It makes me giggle. It's ridiculous," he says.

For the most part, Jasinski quit full-time dusty hunting that same year. On April 19, 2015, ten days before the Jack Rose event, and just thirty-nine miles away, the Baltimore Police Department had callously killed twenty-five-year-old African American Freddie Gray, leading to an uprising in the city; even liquor store owners Jasinski had become friendly with over the years told him it was now too dangerous for a exurban white guy to be going into inner-city liquor stores unannounced.

Of course, similar to Calabrese, an inveterate collector like Jasinski can never fully stop. He'd still pop into liquor stores when he traveled and occasionally find crazy things, like fifty bottles of Wild Turkey's "Cheesy Gold Foil" at a spot in San Francisco. But for him, the glory days of dusty hunting ended in 2015.

"I had left a bunch of bottles on the shelves, and one day it was just gone," he recalls. "It was just the weirdest thing. Like stores that I would have left fifty or one hundred bottles of 80-proof whiskey on the shelves, and it was now suddenly all gone."

IF IT WAS done for Jasinski in 2015, however, many people online were finally hearing about dusty hunting by then, myself included. The first article I ever wrote about dusty hunting was in the early fall of 2015 for First We Feast, a food website better known today for its popular *Hot Ones* YouTube show. A new friend from Los Angeles, Josh Peters, author of the blog *The Whiskey Jug*, might have been the first person I ever heard use the term "dusty hunting," as he regaled me with tales of finding and tasting bottles of vintage Ardbeg single malt and Wild Turkey's "Cheesy Gold Foil," a late 1980s release, so dubbed because of its garish packaging. Even then, as I published that First We Feast story in 2015, I felt I was reporting on a past phenomenon. And yet, if I had just started dusty-hunting right then and there, I would have probably done pretty well for myself. Alas, I thought the party was already over.

Brad Bonds, a Verizon sales rep from Cincinnati, thought differently.

Around the turn of the 2010s, Bonds had been nothing more than a Maker's Mark or Crown Royal drinker when his fiancée, a dental hygienist, relayed to him that she wanted to get her boss some Pappy Van Winkle, but unfortunately, she couldn't find a single bottle.

"I was just blown away," he recalls. "I'm like, you can't find *a bourbon*? Bourbon is not even popular, you know what I mean?"

Then and there, Bonds became obsessed with locating this supposedly best-tasting bourbon in the world. Coincidentally, his grandpa passed away right around then, and Bonds looted the old man's liquor cabinet. There was some old Seagram's and other blended Canadian whiskies and Scotches, but there was also a bottle of Rebel Yell. Bonds's dad assumed it was swill, what with that silly (and problematic) name, but recently Bonds had noticed people in a Facebook bourbon group talking about vintage Rebel Yell, which was actually Stitzel-Weller distillate from the 1960s through the '90s.

"That's old 'Pappy,'" someone informed Bonds, being that Julian "Pappy" Van Winkle Sr. had, in fact, owned the distillery.

Not quite, but Bonds did think it tasted incredibly good and was instantly hooked. He began searching for more old bottles. "I'm like, I'm chasing my tail out here buying these new bottles when the best bourbons have already been made. It was an 'aha' moment."

One of the better, and more varied, dusty hunters of this land grab era was Seth Weinberg. He had started working at Chevys Fresh Mex, a chain Mexican restaurant, in the early 2000s when he was still underage, and he began to develop a deep knowledge of tequila. By the time he'd graduated Mizzou with a degree in hotel and restaurant management, he had become an educator on spirits in an era when few people could talk about the subject with any familiarity. Amassing valuable bottles would inherently follow.

"I was kind of a collector by nature in the first place," says Weinberg.

His mom was into antiques and would drag him along to garage and estate sales from a young age. Weinberg gravitated toward PEZ dispensers, however, which he loved to buy, sell, and trade with other collectors. Weinberg even penned a "Pez Head Diary" for the *Los Angeles Times* in 1999, writing about attending the second annual PEZ Convention at the Manhattan Beach Marriott, where he celebrated scoring a Bicentennial Uncle Sam dispenser for $100, something he thought was underpriced at the time.

I would laugh at the folly of a child, if I didn't have this same collector's mentality inside of me from a young age as well.

I began collecting baseball cards during the 1987 season, when Topps offered its iconic (though not particularly valuable) wood-paneled set, which kind of looked like the sides of your mom's station wagon back then. I gravitated toward comic books during that early 1990s era when upstarts like Image and Valiant were shaking up the scene. I collected Kenner Starting Lineups and Marvel action figures; Olympic Dream Team cups from McDonald's (the Clyde Drexler and Christian Laettner were the rarest) and unopened Wheaties boxes. I even had a sad little period when, for a few weeks in 1994, I pursued Pogs. Remember Pogs?

And, yes, for at least a summer, I had my parents stop at every single drugstore we passed so I could sprint in and rifle through the candy aisle in the hope of finding a rare Incredible Hulk PEZ dispenser, which I finally did on a family vacation to Dallas, of all places.

"The PEZ market peaked well before the whiskey market did," Weinberg laments, with no irony in his voice. And he would know. (In a bit of foreshadowing about the murkiness of the vintage spirits world, Weinberg would eventually get cited for selling a PEZ dispenser without a license, something I didn't even know was a crime.)

After inadvertently getting to try a dusty bottle of Ezra Brooks 15 Year Rare Old Sippin' Whiskey, Weinberg shifted his collecting compulsions toward vintage whiskey and other spirits. I, too, would eventually come to see spirits as the culmination of my collecting career, and the world's best collectible, not just for its ability to be consumed, but for its ability to be shared with friends and other collectors.

By the early 2010s, Weinberg was working at City Grocery, chef John Currence's landmark restaurant in the town square of Oxford, Mississippi, when he was clued into the value of rare whiskey. Weinberg's brother-in-law, famed sports scribbler and Van Winkle enthusiast Wright Thompson, furthered his education.

Weinberg began buying old bottles and any liquor artifacts he could find on eBay in the final few months before it shut down sales in 2012.

"I mean, if I had a billion dollars back then, being a collector, I probably would have bought everything in sight," says Weinberg.

Still, he was able to score plenty of Pappy Van Winkle and early bottlings of Black Maple Hill, a somewhat mysterious release said to be Stitzel-Weller stock. He bought gins, rums, tequilas, liqueurs, empty bottles, old magazine ads, and any and all spirits memorabilia.

Like many collectors then, as now, he'd post these finds on Instagram, offering a little research on the bottle if he had uncovered anything interesting about it. Because Weinberg was in the hospitality world, he had a different sort of Rolodex compared to other hobbyist dusty hunters.

"So people started reaching out to me in the industry and saying, 'Hey, I found this. Do you know what this is worth? Do you want to buy this?'" says Weinberg. "I guess it gave me a bit of a competitive edge in acquiring some of these bottles."

A community was finally beginning to form online. There were people like Chuck Cowdery and Joshua Feldman blogging about the vintage possibilities out there. As mentioned, Straightbourbon.com had become the connoisseur's online town square. There was also Facebook, of course, which launched its private groups feature in 2010. Then there was Drinks Planet, a website launched in 2006 that even today looks like a time capsule from that era.

That site attracted people like Walter C. Hurst and James O. Ely, who became vintage spirits autodidacts—remember, there was no "official" resource to educate yourself—and could soon assist nascent dusty hunters in those earlier, friendlier days of the hobby, both at tracking down bottles and at figuring out what they had scored and whence it came.

Yet, even as early as 2014, Hurst, by day a commercial over-the-road truck driver, was posting blogs on the site with titles like "Is an Older Bottle Really Worth More???" Even at this point, he realized the hobby was dividing into two factions: the *consumers*, who actually cared about the bottles and might want to drink these interesting liquids from the past one day; and the *collectors*, who cared only about an old bottle's rarity and potential worth.

The longtime prevailing rumor among vintage collectors—pretty much everyone I talked to—was that Drinks Planet was ingeniously started by a Boston-area man, Eric Witz, as a sort of search engine optimization (SEO) casting net to haul in all Google searches for vintage bottles on planet earth. Kevin Langdon Ackerman called him the "mastermind" behind the site.

And I'd once called him "the most well-known dusty hunter today" in an article for the *New York Times*.

After that mention, Witz received a bunch of cold emails from randoms asking him to assess and/or buy their dusty booze. One guy sent him a photo of a Baltimore rye bottle that was circa 1900. Fellow dusty hunters were angry, however, saying Witz was a preeminent vintage collector, yes, but he had never pounded the pavement, hitting the inner-city liquor stores like they had. In their opinion, he had yet again gotten lucky with good online SEO by being handed such a superlative in my article.

Witz, for what it's worth, claims he has been to every single liquor store in Massachusetts at least once, and dusty-hunted most of Connecticut and Rhode Island too. During the pandemic, as a senior production editor at the MIT Press he was able to work from home full-time, so he moved in with his sister, who lived farther out in the suburbs and had more space. Even there, he began steadily accruing so many bottles that by the end of 2022, he had filled up an entire room in her basement.

Unlike most vintage collectors, Witz has always had an interest outside of the standard bourbon realm and more into the odd, historical fringes of alcohol's past, posting his remarkable finds on Instagram (@aphonik).

Witz admits that Drinks Planet's SEO usually has it (and, in turn, *him*) coming up first on Google whenever anyone searches for information on old bottles, and that has indeed led to his making many great scores over the years.

And though Witz admits to being an early *user* of the site, he tells me he has no idea who created Drinks Planet. He thinks it's some Israeli guy.

Indeed, the "About the Company" section of the website notes that it is owned by Ta Keo Ltd., a privately held Israeli company based in Tel Aviv. The supposed creator of the site, Michael Mokotov, does not have any sort of online footprint, however, and I couldn't track him down. It's possible he created the website and its user contributor-based interface morphed it into a dusty-hunting website. It's also possible "Michael Mokotov" is an alias for some dusty hunter out there and he has a better bourbon collection than any of us. But who knows.

In the world of vintage spirits collecting, there are a lot of mysterious figures looming large. The eventual professionalization of the hobby would shake out some of them, however, and lead to a fame and notoriety that perhaps they didn't always want.

———⌒———

"THERE'S A FINITE amount available of these types of whiskey in the world, and the minute you take a sip of one, there's that much less on the planet."

That was bar owner Bill Thomas speaking in 2014.

The mainstream press wrote their first article on dusty hunters that year; in a *Washington Post* article, restaurant writer Holley Simmons followed Thomas for seven hours as he and his then girlfriend drove around the District of Columbia to fourteen different spots, plucking old bottles, like a 1988 The Macallan 18 Year Old, out from under the hands of unaware liquor store owners.

Thomas, today a youthful fiftysomething with shaggy hair and stubble, would use these scores to stock his Jack Rose Dining Saloon, which had become perhaps the best whiskey bar in all of America by this point. Even then, though, Thomas, like his buddy Mike Jasinski, was claiming that dusty hunting was already on its supposed last legs.

"Back in the day, when you went hunting you expected to find something," he told Simmons, who has since left journalism to run a flower shop. "Nowadays, it's not guaranteed. You don't have to know your craft anymore. Anybody can find an old bottle and Google it, and those are the people draining the market."

Thomas came from a family that had been in the restaurant business since the turn of the nineteenth century, running an Irish bar in Washington, D.C., back then. Raised in nearby Prince George's County, Maryland, Thomas could legally drink by eighteen, and he had been illegally hitting the bar scene since age fifteen.

The 1990s were still an era of blended Scotches, and that's what Thomas drank before he tried his first bourbon and liked it a whole lot better. He was particularly drawn to any Old Forester he could find from the 1970s and 1980s—"brown cinnamon bombs," he calls them. The industry had just begun to start leaning into the small-batch and higher-end products inspired by forays into Japan: Blanton's, Elmer T. Lee, and BTAC.

When it was finally his turn to get into the hospitality game, Thomas and his partners knew they wanted to focus on a uniquely American spirit. Thus, they would name their bar in the Adams Morgan neighborhood Bourbon when it opened in 2004. That same year, the Old Rip Van Winkle 15 Year Old was discontinued and replaced by the Pappy Van Winkle Family Reserve of the same age. Certain the defunct version would become a collector's item in the near future, Thomas scoured liquor stores, stocking up on all that he could find; he recalls locating a pile of the squat bottles selling for $22 in a bargain bin at one shop. He brought them all back to Bourbon, where he charged just $9 for two ounces. Today, if he had any left to sell, he could reasonably charge more than $500 an ounce.

By the end of the 2000s, Thomas had another location of Bourbon in the Glover Park neighborhood and needed more shelf space. He was by then spending two months per year dusty-hunting in Kentucky.

"Once you start diving into bourbon, you realize how many hundreds and thousands of expressions have been distilled over the last 120 years," he recalls, saying he wanted "a place you could have all those bottles front and center for people to geek out over."

His answer was the Jack Rose Dining Saloon, opened in 2011—a block from where Reagan had been shot in 1981, Thomas always likes to point out, between Adams Morgan and Dupont Circle, about a mile from the White House. With his bar in the center of this international city, tourists, business travelers, and diplomats from all over the world would visit when they were in town. In the early days, though, most of the customers filling the nearly seven-thousand-square-foot place every night were hardly bourbon enthusiasts.

You see, for Thomas, it wasn't just about having tons of bottles; he wanted bottles that would attract the kinds of people who could and would chew the fat over these esoteric pours. It wasn't always easy. Thomas recalls comping customers' entire checks if he found someone to talk and drink bourbon with. No bottle was sacred to him.

"It's all meant to be drunk eventually," he claimed. "The collection is a library, not a museum."

All the while, Thomas was continuing to build this massive inventory, more than twenty-five hundred unique bottles, which today takes up around seventy pages of his menu. He was focused on a collection for the long haul, imagining a future where people could come to the Jack Rose and drink expressions in their fifties that they had once had while visiting the bar on the night they turned twenty-one.

Besides dusty-hunting, Thomas would hit auction sites: Sotheby's, Christie's, ones in Germany and Japan, overseas eBays. If someone died in the DMV area, a collection might be unearthed, and Thomas would try to buy it at estate sales.

For the earliest owners of vintage spirits bars, like Thomas, it wasn't purely a monetary endeavor.

"I'm not maximizing my time by doing all of this," he told the *Washington Post* back in 2014. "I'd be better off at Jack Rose pushing whiskey. But sometimes you don't want to do that. You want solitude. To me, this is relaxation."

Along with Thomas, there were several other bar owners who afforded consumers the opportunity to sample America's lost whiskey history. In the middle of the country you had Mike Miller, who opened Delilah's in Chicago back in 1993. This was so long ago, at the tail end of the glut but before the bourbon boom, that there weren't yet what you would call categorical bars—for example, "craft beer bars" or "neo-speakeasy mixology bars" or certainly "bourbon bars."

Though he would soon offer customers more than one thousand bottles of brown spirits, Miller considered his spot in the Lincoln Park neighborhood more of a rock and roll den, a dark and moody pseudo-dive with beat-up barstools attracting locals who might range from bikers and punks to goths and emo kids onto craft beer nerds and college students from nearby DePaul and Loyola Chicago, almost everybody tattooed, almost everybody with enough free time to drink on weekday afternoons, often during standard work hours, all the better if a local band was blasting music in the corner.

"We're not a whiskey bar, just a bar that has a lot of whiskey," Miller has said repeatedly.

He was so far ahead of the game that simply by existing for as many years as he now has, "new" bottles he had acquired in the 1990s were considered "dusties" by the time people started caring about vintage spirits in the 2010s. For instance, Miller recalls being maybe the first person in America to buy an entire barrel of Blanton's, which he did in 1998, direct from legendary master distiller Elmer T. Lee, stamping his bar's name on the bottles. Miller showed that a bar need not be snooty to attract whiskey drinkers deeply interested in the history of these magical bottles.

Chicago would, in fact, become the big-city epicenter of both the bourbon boom and vintage spirits fascination. There, in 2010, a nearly straight shot west and three miles from Delilah's, in the Logan Square neighborhood, four partners opened Longman & Eagle with the motto "whiskey for your mouth, not for our shelves."

From the get-go, Longman & Eagle's design was meant to hearken back to a past era when inns were a social hub for urban travelers. ("The sort of place where a man can get a shot with breakfast, where local politicians might trade votes for whiskey, and one that reflects Chicago's unique neighborhood-based diversity," read its website.)

The first floor was the public space where chef Jared Wentworth offered esoteric dishes like buffalo-style frog's legs, while bar manager Phil Olson's well-curated whiskey list included dusty options like National Distillers–era Old Grand-Dad and Jim Beam from the 1960s. At the end of its first year, Longman & Eagle got a Michelin star.

Just across Logan Square Park there was Matthias Merges's Billy Sunday, which opened in 2013, and Paul McGee's vintage spirits tasting bar The Milk Room, which opened in the Chicago Athletic Association Hotel in late 2015. Customers could book two-hour drinking slots using an online reservation system, though getting into the eight-seat micro-bar was always a challenge.

Chicago also had The Office, a VIP speakeasy (that was initially invite-only) tucked behind a locked door underneath The Aviary, the molecular mixology cocktail bar owned by Grant Achatz and Nick Kokonas of Michelin three-star Alinea fame.

Across the country there was canon in Seattle, a whiskey and bitters emporium, lowercase spelling intentional. Owner Jamie Boudreau entered the service industry the day he turned sixteen, working as a dishwasher at a fish-and-chips joint in his hometown of Vancouver, British Columbia. He slowly edged his way into the city's bar firmament before he headed across the border to Seattle to open his own bar, Vessel, in 2006.

By then, Boudreau had begun to purchase vintage American whiskey at various auctions and through eBay, mostly out of pure curiosity. It was still pretty cheap—especially compared to single malt—since no one was collecting it just yet, and it made some handsome decor for his bar. One day, just for the heck of it, he tasted a bottle and was blown away.

"I realized that these were secret treasures, and people didn't know what they actually had," he thought.

These secret treasures included "medicinal" whiskey, which few people in the 2000s would have even known had ever existed, and which even fewer of these earliest dusty hunters would have ever come across. For one reason, these bottles wouldn't have been found gathering dust on store shelves because they never were sold in actual liquor stores—they were sold at pharmacies back during those terrible nearly fourteen years of Prohibition.

For whatever reason, they long flew under the radar for vintage collectors, and even until recently, bottles (with few exceptions) could be found well below the cost of similar whiskeys packaged immediately before and after Prohibition. Maybe people thought the liquid was actual medicine and not just whiskey?

Of course, even many knowledgeable collectors today worry about the integrity of medicinal whiskey—smaller bottle sizes, poorer closures, and questionable storage practices often led to a higher likelihood of oxidation and the whiskey taking on mothball notes.

Nevertheless, when Boudreau landed a case of Prohibition-era medicinal whiskey, he finally decided to start sharing finds with his guests at Vessel. Then, as now, Boudreau's barman philosophy is that you absolutely need something to set your place apart from the thousands of other bars out there—and this dusty booze could be it, he thought.

"Why would a person choose your establishment over another that has been there for decades if you're not offering something different or unique?" he told me.

By 2011, Boudreau had taken over a 450-square-foot, pink-walled cocktail bar in the hipster-beloved Capitol Hill area and turned it into canon, a compact little cocktail bar with seven tables, seating for a mere thirty-two customers, and a twelve-page menu listing many of his vintage finds. (By 2023 canon's menu would be a startling 184 pages long and on leather-covered iPad menus.)

He would soon have more than seven thousand bottles on a large wooden armoire and soaring shelves with library ladders, in hallways and the bathroom—really, anywhere he could find room for it. The place had so much vintage whiskey ("hardcore porn," it was jokingly labeled on the menu) that Boudreau claimed there was more of it stored in lockers in the bathrooms than 90 percent of other whiskey bars had in their total stock. The bathrooms also included vintage radios broadcasting 1930s radio plays.

"We have more vintage than the Bourbon Museum in Kentucky, and many of their bottles are empty," Boudreau often joked, while seriously laying claim to the largest collection of American whiskey in the world, a veritable history of this country's distilling life span, as operations moved from rye distillation on the East Coast to bourbon production in Kentucky and on to Prohibition and thereafter.

At canon, Boudreau offered single-ounce pours from bottles like an 1880s Westover Maryland Rye and 1905 Allegheny Pure Rye from Pennsylvania, a Cedar Brook Sour Mash produced in Kentucky in 1880, and Old Overholt "medicinal" whiskey flasks bottled between 1921 and 1932. It would additionally stock one of the largest collections of vintage Chartreuse around.

Really leaning into the shtick, canon didn't just offer vintage spirits but also vintage glassware, a gramophone, an entire copy of the seminal 1934 *Harry Johnson's Bartenders' Manual* shellacked under the bar, and a 1919 cash register, which had apparently been owned by chewing gum hotshot William Wrigley Jr. Checks were presented to customers in vintage cigar tins.

By 2017, Boudreau estimated that he had $1.5 million in dusty inventory. With the way the secondary market has boomed in the last half decade, that same collection could be worth $5 million today. For the most part, Boudreau has quit acquiring bottles; the prices are too insane these days, and he has enough dusty bottles to stock his bar for the rest of his lifetime and beyond.

Despite being in early in the vintage spirits boom, even back in 2017 Boudreau realized that it was highly unlikely he would ever sell it all, ever get all his money back. And, crazily enough, he didn't seem to care, claiming that most guests came to canon not just for the great cocktails, but to be surrounded by such liquid history, even if they couldn't necessarily afford to drink any of it.

Which was kind of a funny thought.

As the only reason vintage spirits still exist today is that someone chose not to drink them in the past.

3

MR. DEMILLE, I'M READY
FOR YOUR BOOZE STASH

KEVIN LANGDON ACKERMAN got the tip one quiet Tuesday morning in August 2020. He pushed aside his mug of black coffee and threw on some clothes as fast as he could, then hopped in his car and headed toward an address he had just scrawled on the palm of his hand.

From Ackerman's apartment in the Beachwood Canyon neighborhood of Los Angeles, it was an eighteen-mile drive northwest on the 210 to Sylmar, California. He guided his metallic black BMW through the twisting, winding roads to the top of Little Tujunga Canyon: on the right side, Middle Ranch, an equestrian facility and popular wedding venue; on the left, multimillion-dollar estates, everything surrounded by the mountains of the Angeles National Forest. Eventually, amid this 650-acre property, he reached his destination, a Santa Fe–style home built in the early 1900s.

There he met his contact, a rare wine importer who just so happened to be riding her horse, Fuego, on the ranch one day when the new owner of the house mentioned that upon taking over the property, he had discovered a dank basement that still had some bottles in it.

She'd already staked a claim on the wine, including a rare bottle of 1947 Château Haut-Brion, but had left the spirits for whatever dusty hunter got there first.

The winner was Ackerman, and the wine importer led him around to the back of the property. There a modern lock code opened the swinging cellar doors, and the two descended a flight of concrete steps to the bunker.

One entire wall had built-in wine turrets, with dusty bottles of wine and champagne lying on their sides. Another wall acted as a liquor cabinet, with bottles of bourbon, Irish whiskey, and rum that had apparently sat there untouched for more than a half century.

It was the booze collection of Cecil B. DeMille, the legendary movie director and producer, and the former owner of the house.

"Holy hell! I want this, and I need to get this," Ackerman told himself.

In his mind, he had finally reaped the fruit of a near decade of tireless dusty hunting. He had come to the hobby in its infancy. Ackerman, coincidentally a filmmaker just like DeMille, who has worked in development for both Roger Corman and the late George Hickenlooper, took up the quest in 2012 after coming across an online article about a group of friends who had flown to Kentucky specifically to search liquor store shelves for old bottles from the Stitzel-Weller Distillery.

"There were these funny photos of guys standing in front of their cars, holding up dusty bottles as if they were trophy fish they had just caught," he told me. A neophyte whiskey drinker at the time—"I had only had Jack and Jim," aka Daniel's and Beam—he was intrigued.

Seeking the rare and unusual was already in Ackerman's blood. He had long been a high-level collector of movie memorabilia and ephemera, specifically the artifacts of Billy Wilder and Orson Welles. He'd always had a fascination for objects from a bygone era.

One Monday morning, in the cigar-shaped, eight-by-twenty-five-foot office in the Taft Building that he shared with an intern, Ackerman couldn't concentrate on the script he was supposed to be writing. He feigned writer's block, took $300 out of the ATM, and drove as far south as Long Beach, with a goal of visiting one hundred liquor stores that day. He hit only about half that number but still managed to find twenty-three dusty bottles, including decades-old gems like Ancient Age, Old Charter, brown-label Wild Turkey from the 1980s, and five bottles of Old Grand-Dad from back when it was produced by National Distillers and considered superior in taste to its modern incarnation.

That night before he went to bed, Ackerman put one of the bottles up on something known as Bourbon Exchange, a buy/sell auction group that had been set up on Facebook (and which I'll detail more in a few chapters). When he woke up the next morning, the highest bid was already at $100.

He was hooked.

For the next several years Ackerman would go dusty-hunting several times per week, alternating between working on a film project one day and driving around the Greater Los Angeles area on the next. If the city has more than fifteen hundred liquor retail outlets, he figures he has hit most of them.

"The old sort of fun, which has always been my favorite part of the game, is what I call 'free-balling,'" says Ackerman. "You get in your car and you drive far enough out of the city to a place you don't know, then start working your way back home," visiting every liquor store along the way.

Like Jasinski and Thomas, Ackerman had gotten in at a perfect time, once easily finding bottles for $15 that were then worth $75 (and then, eventually, worth $500) on the secondary market. Ackerman believed that dusty hunting was certainly a more fun way to invest his money and time than buying a municipal bond from the Los Angeles water department.

Ackerman, a MENSA member, was more cunning and strategic than most dusty hunters. He would often use a tactic called FOAFing to unearth bottles. As in telling random liquor store owners that a "friend of a friend" (a FOAF) had mentioned they had old bottles in the back storeroom. Even if the proprietor didn't, what would they care, and who was this friend?

And if they did have those dusty bottles, they might pull them out and sell them to Ackerman. I mean, he was a FOAF.

"But why do you want these old bottles?" they sometimes asked him with suspicion.

Living in Los Angeles was the perfect place for someone with interests as varied as Ackerman's, and he used them all: He'd tell them he was once a fashion photographer (true) but dusty bottles were now his preferred subject, or that he was an artist who liked to paint old bottle still lifes. He'd claim he was a set dresser for the movies and needed bygone booze for a period piece about to go into production (in fact, he had been the one to provide that bottle to Sean Brock when he appeared on Parts Unknown; he'd also supplied whiskey props to Mad Men). He'd "adjust chiropractically," he told me, using whatever story would keep these store owners off Google and away from learning the real value of the bottles.

It often worked, but by 2020, this "free-balling," this FOAFing, had quit yielding the true superstar bottles from the past as the West Coast's liquor stores had been completely picked over by people like him.

As I've mentioned, it takes a certain amount of skill to dusty-hunt: an awareness of shuttered brands from the past; the ability to read esoteric laser coding and to notice bottle sizes, like quarts, that no longer exist. But the internet has made it easier for everyone. When Ackerman started hunting, he had only a Razr flip phone; now anyone could use a smartphone to quickly call up Facebook, Reddit, or bottlebluebook.com, an online pricing guide, to see the value of whatever oddity had just been stumbled upon.

That was why people like Ackerman had begun to get craftier with their hunting, making contacts, cultivating sources, and following way-out-there tips, in the hope of stumbling across buried treasures like the one in front of him at DeMille's old house.

If happening upon a great score at a liquor store or estate sale typically involved a snap judgment calculus of how much cash to offer, Ackerman was given a little more time to assess the DeMille collection: twenty minutes or so to catalog what was there. He held the bottles up to the light to see their clarity (if the liquid appears milky, it is usually no good), to examine their "fill" levels (how much liquid is still in the bottle), and to see if the tax stamps and bottle cap seals were still intact.

It was a stunning array of some of the greatest bottles in American whiskey lore.

These are all unicorns, Ackerman thought to himself, using the parlance of collectors who have come across something they never expected to see.

There were ten bottles of Old Overholt Rye barreled in 1936, five bottles of 1930s Belmont Bottled in Bond, bottles of Kentucky Tavern, J.W. Dant, and Old Taylor bourbons, some 1930s Jameson Irish Whiskey, Veuve Clicquot Ponsardin champagne from 1929, and a nearly flawless case of extremely rare Green River Kentucky Straight Bourbon Whiskey from 1936.

The funny thing was, DeMille wasn't considered much of a drinker. Unusually health-conscious for his era, he had a mere ounce of bourbon in his nightly Old Fashioned, according to his biographer Scott Eyman.

What DeMille was, however, was a serial philanderer; after purchasing the seven-hundred-acre secluded ranch that he would eventually dub Paradise, he used it to host devoted mistresses like Jeanie Macpherson, Gladys Rosson, and Julia Faye. His wife, Constance, older than DeMille and very much a Victorian lady, preferred not to deal with the snake-riddled outdoors and a ranch that lacked electricity and creature comforts. The director of *The Ten Commandments* and *The King of Kings* also frequently hosted his silver-screen friends for bacchanalian bashes attended by Charlie Chaplin, Charlton Heston, and their ilk.

DeMille died of a heart attack in 1959 at seventy-seven, having found piety late in life, and in 1963 his family bequeathed the ranch to the Hathaway Foundation, which turned it into an orphanage for abused children. Separating themselves from DeMille's sordid behavior, his family sealed off the basement until 2018, when its current owners bought the house for nearly $5 million.

As not just a dusty hunter but a lifelong lover of Hollywood history— he rents an apartment at the Villa Monterey once inhabited by Marlon Brando—Ackerman, overcome by the discovery, made an offer in the five-figure range. The homeowners relayed that they wanted twenty-four hours to think about it, to do their own research, to maybe even receive further bids. If the early days of dusty hunting often involved bilking an unknowing bottle owner, everyone is a lot savvier these days. In fact, with just a little research the owners would have noticed that a similar collection had been discovered just a few years earlier.

DeMille's longtime neighbor in Little Tujunga Canyon was Jean-Baptiste "J. B." Leonis, a banker and liquor importer who founded the city of Vernon. Sensing that Prohibition was on the horizon as the 1920s approached, he began to stash booze in a ten-bolt bank vault behind a trick bookcase. In 2017, upon the death of Leonis C. Malburg, Leonis's grandson, the collection was finally unearthed, featuring numerous pint bottles of Old Crow distilled in 1912, Hermitage Bottled in Bond whiskey distilled in 1914, and rye bottled specifically for the iconic Biltmore Hotel. It had sold at Christie's Auction House for a startling $640,000 in 2018.

Despite such possible competition, Ackerman's offer was accepted the next day, and he spent several days maxing out withdrawals at the ATM as well as migrating the collection back to his apartment and the various storage units he rents specifically for his vintage finds. He'd been told that all the good stuff was already lined up on the bunker's concrete floor and that everything else was junk—cheap dessert wines like Blue Nun—but, eventually, Ackerman got his hands on the crown jewel of the collection.

It was something dusty hunters typically don't like to find and certainly never pay good money for: an empty. But the filthy bottle of De Goñi sherry was signed and dated by DeMille.

At the bottom, on a hand-attached label, scrawled in the great man's cursive, it read:

"This bottle of sherry was bought in New York City the day Constance and I were married, Aug. 16, 1902. We decided to keep it until the wedding of our first born—we did open it then because the cellar was full of soldiers."

It was not just the provenance that provided a sort of "certificate of authenticity" for the collection; it was also proof of perhaps simpler, happier times in the DeMilles' lives.

And now, a century later, Ackerman had captured all the epic director's remaining soldiers.

REMARKABLY, THE FIRST-EVER mention of "dusty hunting" in the *New York Times* was not courtesy of my article about Ackerman's DeMille haul. It actually occurred in a March 2014 article on collectors of rare nail polish colors, who are also known as dusty hunters.

The funny thing about being a collector is that it's easy to look at what you and your cohort pursue as normal, but what other people collect as strange. Like, why wouldn't you collect dusty old whiskey? It tastes great and is valuable. But paying $250 for a discontinued bottle of Essie Starry Starry Night colored nail polish? Come on. Grow up and find a real hobby.

And yet, if you truly have the collector's mentality, you get it.

"It's a treasure-hunt feeling. It's got a lottery kind of effect," one such nail polish dusty hunter told the *Times*.

Ackerman liked that feeling too, liked that potential for hitting the lottery every time he went hunting.

His DeMille score, with its dozens of bottles of Prohibition-era bourbon, rum, and champagne, was certainly a jackpot. It was the best find of Ackerman's decade-long dusty-hunting adventure and one of the more intriguing finds in *public* dusty-hunting history.

But Ackerman was certain that the supposed collection, currently under probate and kept in a padlocked storage unit somewhere in Los Angeles, that he was telling me only a tantalizing amount about, had the potential to be an even bigger score. Even if the actual bottles weren't of a better quality, the score would still be far more valuable because, as Ackerman told me, the celebrity was far more famous than DeMille.

And yet he wouldn't tell me who it was.

Of course, Ackerman only even knew about this A-list collection because of my *New York Times* article about him. (Then again, I only knew of the DeMille score because of Ackerman reaching out to me.) Dusty hunting may have made countless casual appearances in mainstream media before it appeared in print, but once there's a twenty-five-hundred-word article on the subject in the *Times*, things are taken completely to another level in the public consciousness.

The comments section of the online version of the article—did you know the esteemed *New York Times* has a comments section?!—blew up with readers sharing stories of their own finds and pondering the dusty bottles they had lying around the house.

They told tales of finding their late grandfather's sealed bottles of Scotch and Canadian Club, of owning bottles of 1933 Gordon's Gin that had been poured at their father's bar mitzvah so long ago, of stumbling upon a stash of unopened whiskey bottles in an abandoned cabin while backpacking in the woods, and of ancestors who had hidden bourbon under the kitchen floorboards and then forgotten about them for eighty years.

"The apartment building is still there and as far as I know, so is the unopened bottle of bourbon," wrote the commenter.

And, apparently, so was this amazing celebrity booze collection. Instead of commenting on it for the entire internet to see, though, one man had privately reached out to Ackerman and told him about what he believed to be this even better score.

Before I sold this book, as part of my book proposal, Ackerman had agreed to eventually tell me who the celebrity was, and to let me follow along as he tried to locate the treasure. I even signed an NDA with him, so worried was Ackerman that my reporting on this book would inadvertently find me mentioning the hidden treasure chest to Mike Jasinski or Eric Witz or Seth Weinberg or some surely conniving, upwardly mobile figure who, all of a sudden, would swoop in and steal it out from under him.

Ackerman was still smarting about a past incident when, he claims, one dusty hunter swooped in and nabbed a cache of unopened cases of Old Overholt, J.M. Douglas Canadian whisky, and some rye from the 1940s, from a northern New Jersey location where he had been planning to acquire it.

The more and more I pushed Ackerman to tell me about who this celebrity was, though, the more and more he pushed back at me, trying to get me off his case.

"From what I can tell, it doesn't exist anymore," Ackerman told me in July 2022.

As Ackerman understood it, this legendary person supposedly had the most amazing bar, a "monster" bar he used to booze and schmooze the ladies with, as he did not really drink the hard stuff. When he died, it all got boxed up and put into storage with his numerous other personal effects.

"And I haven't pursued it too hard because it's apparently pretty *unpursuable*. The minute you even would get close, if this Holy Grail did exist, you'd be shut down by lawyers, apparently, because everything's tied up still to this day."

"OK. So then tell me. . . ."

"But who knows if it even exists?"

"You're right. So tell me!"

Surely frustrated after being on the phone with me for yet another one of our hourlong conversations, Ackerman got silent for an interminable amount of time.

The smartest thing to do when this happens, when you're interviewing someone, is to not say anything. That's an old Robert Caro trick. But few journalists have such restraint, and I certainly didn't. I started rambling.

I assured Ackerman that the absolute earliest the book would be on shelves was 2024. So no matter what he told me, he had at least two years to find the collection before the general public would even know about it, not like anyone was even going to read my silly book!

"I'm really nervous about doing this," he kept repeating.

"At the least, if you told me, I could use my own reporting and investigative skills to help you out. . . ."

That seemed to work.

"All right, here we go. . . ."

"The one thing I hold closest to my chest. . . ."

I finally shut up and sat in silence at the little desk in the corner of my bedroom, staring at my iPhone sitting on a brown leather blotter, set on speaker, right next to my recording device, both slowly ticking off the passage of time.

00:41:52

00:41:53

00:41:54

"It's Howard Hughes."

DESPITE HIS ECCENTRIC nature, despite his well-known addiction to prescription drugs, it is often repeated that Howard Hughes never drank.

Still, even if he didn't drink, it would only make sense that when Hughes died, there should be *some* booze left around. When Charles Foster Kane died, there were surely lots of quality bottles of booze left throughout the studies and barrooms and pool houses and the cellars of Xanadu. Unlike the fictionalized Kane, however, Hughes seemingly had a lot more residences, spending his final years in the Bahamas, Nicaragua, Canada, England, Mexico, and Las Vegas, where he famously lived in the Desert Inn, a luxury hotel.

It's not even that hard to research whether these homes had liquor collections in them at one point. Hughes's Samuel Wacht–designed mansion in Beverly Hills' Trousdale Estates was known as a party pad for Hollywood glitterati during his tenure, according to neighbors. His Palm Springs house—which Hughes owned from the 1960s until his death—had a stylish bar. As did his Spanish Colonial hacienda in the Hancock Park section of Los Angeles. The decade or so when Hughes lived there was a pivotal time in his life and career: He produced the film *Hell's Angels*, set a transcontinental airspeed record, and romanced Katharine Hepburn for eighteen months.

Hepburn, it should be pointed out, was known to be fond of Scotch, with Famous Grouse being her brand of choice. Had Hughes at one time stocked up on it so it was always around for her? (For what it's worth, I have rarely seen any dusties of late 1930s Famous Grouse on the open market, so it's hard to estimate how much a vintage bottle, especially one linked to Hughes and Hepburn, would fetch.)

The most amusing story concerning Hughes and booze comes during Prohibition, when apparently he did some bootlegging, despite producing the anti-bootlegging film *Scarface* in 1932. According to Charles Higham in his book *Howard Hughes: The Secret Life*, Hughes used his yacht to run liquor up and down the West Coast. Later, upon learning that the Rice Hotel in Houston had never disposed of its cellar of fine wine once Prohibition began, Hughes hatched a scheme to get it all back to Los Angeles.

His idea? Smuggling the thousands of bottles, for which he had paid several hundred thousand dollars, to Los Angeles in an armored freight train car marked "Unexposed Film." His right-hand man, Noah Dietrich—known as "Noah can do it"—was tasked with picking up this contraband, but, once at the train depot, inspectors wouldn't let him take his shipment. The inspectors wanted to open the film canisters to look for boll weevils, a major problem at the time. A frantic Dietrich begged and pleaded to no avail, claiming that opening the canisters would expose the film. Eventually Dietrich had no choice but to pay off the inspectors to the tune of $700.

"The bootleg liquor made its way to Hughes's house," writes Higham. "When Hughes had drinking associates in for dinner, they found themselves enjoying 100-year-old French champagne."

So even if Hughes didn't drink—a fact very much up for debate itself—he almost certainly owned a lot of booze, vintage booze even.

But where did it all go after his death?

Hughes was thought to have had a stroke but was later learned to have died of kidney failure, on April 5, 1976, aboard a private Learjet flying from one of his homes in Acapulco, Mexico, to Houston, where he was going to seek medical treatment.*

Estimates of the value of Hughes's estate ran from as low as $168.8 million by Merrill Lynch, Pierce, Fenner & Smith—hired by the executors of the estate, for whom a low valuation would mean lower federal

---

* A conspiracy theory claims Hughes faked his own death and would live until 2001.

estate taxes—to $465 million by the IRS to $1.1 billion by the State of California, much of it contingent on some undeveloped land he owned in Los Angeles and Las Vegas.

Whatever the value, upon his death,† there was one major problem: Hughes had no direct descendants or immediate family, and he died "intestate," meaning he didn't leave behind a will, or at least a will that anyone could legitimize. Several wills appeared, including a liquid-stained one found in the offices of the Mormon Church in Salt Lake City, but these were all eventually declared forgeries.

It would take until 1981 for the initial fate of the billionaire's estate to be determined. Inside a small Harris County, Texas, probate courtroom, it was ultimately divided among sixteen first cousins, three fiftysomething granddaughters of Hughes's uncle, and his eighty-year-old stepdaughter, while, according to the *Washington Post*, "More than 600 alleged wives, sons, daughters, first, second, third, fourth and fifth cousins lined up in [Probate Judge Pat] Gregory's small courtroom on the fifth floor of the family law center on the north edge of downtown Houston with their hands out, trying to claim a share of the Hughes fortune."

This was hardly the end of things. In fact, the divvying up of Hughes's estate dragged on until at least 2010, when General Growth Properties Inc., a developer of planned communities and the nation's second-largest shopping mall operator, which had fallen into bankruptcy, finally agreed to pay Hughes's heirs $230 million for their interests in a Las Vegas residential development called Summerlin ("Be part of something beautiful").

The *Wall Street Journal*, in reporting on this, called it "the final asset of the eccentric billionaire's estate."

Yet Ackerman's source was certain that wasn't quite true. He had been part of a job some years back at 7000 Romaine Street—Howard

---

† Or faked death.

Hughes's former headquarters in Los Angeles—and had remembered seeing some old bottles still being stored there, under lock and key, despite the building having a new owner. That building still stood just three miles from where Ackerman lives.

"I don't know what's there, but it's apparently a shitload of stuff," Ackerman told me.

Of course, his random source's recollection was from twenty years ago. In the last two decades could the stash have been parceled out, or even thrown away? Ackerman remained hopeful.

"I'm told there are, to this day, legal entanglements over this property of his, and so the alcohol is still stuck in storage and is potentially still in those boxes," he claimed. "But people cannot get into those. They can't get through the storage doors. They can't get through the legal tape because it's been going on since his death. *Apparently*. It's never been resolved."

To a certain extent, this was a completely believable story. When Charles Foster Kane died, how much booze would have been left over and ignored? How many first cousins and middle-aged granddaughters of uncles would be fighting over Xanadu and his art and wild animals and where did that fucking sled go, without giving a second thought to the cellar full of dusty bottles of pre-Prohibition whiskeys and rums.

Of course, I feared, this could also be a *Mystery of Al Capone's Vaults* situation too and I could be your Geraldo Rivera, wanting to blast open a storage unit only to find bupkis and have egg on my face, live on Fox. Though, to be fair, there were, in fact, several bottles of gin inside Capone's vault when Rivera pulled his own stunt back in 1986. Then again, they were empty.

Ackerman knew that, he realized that, but he didn't care. Because for him, as he continually mentions, a lot of the fun of dusty hunting isn't in the score at all—it is in the hunt. The "free-balling." It is in taking a small tip, pulling at the threads, unraveling a mystery, figuring out who to talk to, and negotiating a deal, all to finally taste that sweet liquid history.

And this seemed like a hunt worth pursuing to him.

"It's history. It's a billionaire. Maybe it's now gone, or it's been drunk, or it's tied up with legal, I don't know. There's a super far-off chance of it coming to fruition, I know," said Ackerman.

"But if anyone's going to get it, it will be me."

Though the last decade had created an entire underground marketplace that would surely also be interested in this potentially lucrative score.

4

THE RISE OF THE SECONDARY MARKET

OWEN POWELL MIGHT have been the only MBA working
the register at a liquor store.

Like many Kentuckians, he'd first tasted bourbon early in his life, in
just seventh grade, and fell for it, then had a bad experience and swore
off it, then grabbed some Elijah Craig 18 Year Old on a whim while in
college at Sullivan University and got back into it. When a friend of his
started working to launch a bourbon brand, Prohibition Craft Spirits,
Powell decided he, too, wanted to professionalize his passion.

And that's how he found himself starting from the ground up,
working at a liquor store, on his phone during the endless downtime
reading about bourbon, learning about bourbon, and stalking Facebook,
where the rarest bourbon, the "allocated" stuff as they call it—Pappy
Van Winkle, George T. Stagg, and the like—was being bought, sold,
swapped, auctioned, and raffled on private groups with names like
Bourbon Exchange (BX), Whiskey Exchange, Strong Water Showcase,
and Phil's Basement. These groups could be very insidery, full of lingo
and jargon and obscure references, and had little tolerance for newbies
looking to join in on the fun.

Because of that, one morning in 2014, Powell decided to start Facebook's first *public* bourbon marketplace, Bourbon Secondary Market (BSM). With eBay and Craigslist no longer allowing liquor sales, Powell wanted to offer something more egalitarian. While more discreet people wheeling and dealing in this modestly illegal gray market were certain Powell was going to topple the entire hobby, BSM immediately blew up, eventually reaching a membership of well over fifty-five thousand users.

Powell would also become a sort of guru of the vintage bourbon marketplace.

There's the paradoxical fact that the hardest place in America to find rare bourbon at retail is probably where it's produced—Kentucky. But even as late as 2014, 2015, it was still one of the best places in America to find dusty bourbon.

Then, as now, there are tons of little mom-and-pop shops located off dusty roads in the most rural of places. Powell would drive to liquor stores in the middle of nowhere and immediately go to the pints section. Pints are not a size that legally should have existed in America by this point in time. He found tons of Heaven Hill products distilled before its Bardstown campus had a massive fire in 1996. Deeper in flavor and richer in mouthfeel than post-fire Heaven Hill, it immediately became his vintage collecting passion.

Because he was the admin of BSM, Powell would get numerous private messages each day.

"Hey, man, I found this bottle. What is it?"

Back at his day job at the liquor store, in between stocking shelves and waiting for delivery trucks, he would educate himself about defunct distilleries, old brands from the past, and the little tricks for dating bottles. He'd PM back to the person and, now with authority, tell them everything he'd just taught himself.

It's not as hard as it seems.

HOW TO DECIPHER AND DATE OLD BOTTLES

On December 23, 1975, America went metric. President Gerald Ford thought getting our measurements on track with the rest of the world was critical in keeping us a global power. Earlier in the year, Congress had passed the Metric Conversion Act, making metric the preferred measurement system of the United States. A U.S. Metric Board was even created to oversee the conversion.

I can easily imagine all the dumb protests today—all the Ted Cruz tweets smugly showing him holding a ruler with *inches*—if an unpopular president took away our beloved gallons and miles. Then again, many people weren't thrilled with it back then either. There were anti-metric parties held across the country. Eventually Congressman Chuck Grassley—who, as I write this, is improbably still in office, now in the Senate, at nearly ninety years old!—was able to kill these federal regulations, and by the time of Reagan, metric was kiboshed.

Except in the beverage industry.

By 1979, American brands had completely switched over to eight standard sizes: 50 milliliter (mL), 100 mL, 200 mL, 375 mL, 500 mL, 750 mL, 1 liter (L), and 1.75 L. With just a few additions, those metric sizes still prevail today.

Meaning: If you find a bottle measured in imperial units, you know you've scored a dusty from back when 'murica didn't let the French dictate how we boozed. In fact, in the 1960s and 1970s there were dozens of different-sized bottles. Pints and quarts and even gallons.

Pints were often offered in flat packaging, like a hip flask. And as early as the 1950s, distilleries like Jim Beam, National Distillers, and Stitzel-Weller produced remarkable gallon-sized bottles—that's 128 ounces—so large and unwieldy many came packaged with a wooden "swing," allowing one to pour a bottle without actually having to lift it.

Ever wonder why a standard 750 mL bottle is called "a fifth"? Because before the metric system, it was indeed labeled one-fifth of a gallon (or sometimes four-fifths of a quart).

If some booze has that oh-so-scary government warning on it— "According to the Surgeon General . . ."—it was bottled after 1989. But if it lists just the proof (and no ABV percentage), it's probably older than 1990.

Another key signifier of vintage is the tax stamp—in essence, a cheap strip of paper tape across the bottle cap. From 1897's Bottled-in-Bond Act until 1985, the government mandated that distilleries include these to assure both customers and, more importantly, tax inspectors that no one had opened the bottle and futzed with its contents in this era before tamper-proofing.* Thankfully, most tax stamps will list both the year the liquid was distilled and the year it was bottled, making dating easier. (Look for a green tax stamp for bonded bourbons and red for all others.)

Of course, sometimes tax stamps can be hard to read; sometimes they may lack dating information; other times the vintage spirit may be from a category that didn't have as strict regulations. In that case, things can get tricky, and you might have to pull out the magnifying glass.

Occasionally, the last two digits of a bottle's bottling year are embossed in the bottom glass. By scrutinizing a vintage bottle's

---

*   Though the act was initially introduced to guarantee quality in the whiskey industry, any American spirit can theoretically be bonded—today that includes a few brandies and rums.

barcode, specifically the first five digits, you can often tell who bottled a given whiskey, something critical with bourbon brands so often changing hands while labels so often remain mostly looking the same.

For instance, Jim Beam, the current distillers of Old Grand-Dad, will have a UPC prefix of 80686 on all its whiskeys. If the bottle has 86259 on it? That would mean you've lucked into some vastly better National Distillers supply from before 1987.

You can likewise look for the DSP number, which is almost always on bottles of bonded whiskey. Standing for "distilled spirits plant," the code tells you where a particular bottle was distilled. Stitzel-Weller, for instance, was DSP-KY-16, meaning if you discover a bottle with that code on it, you're in for a treat.

And when all else fails, when you can't figure out who distilled your bottle or what year it's from, many people just message bourbon historian Mike Veach at his website (bourbonveach.com) or DM Eric Witz (@aphonik) on Instagram.

"So how much is it worth?"

If many early dusty hunters quickly became self-taught at dating bottles and determining where the "juice" came from, calculating the worth of these bottles—which sometimes still had old $4.99 price stickers on them—was a lot more difficult. Especially if it was a bottle that had no recent history of ever having been sold.

So what Owen Powell would often do is suggest that the person have an auction. In other words, post a photo of the bottle on the Bourbon Secondary Market Facebook group and ask for bids to come in over the next twenty-four hours or so, then take the highest one. In turn, all these auctions that began happening in the mid- to late

2010s started building the market prices of so many bottles from the past.*

At the same time, literal pricing guides had just been launched on the internet in the hope of monitoring the volatile market prices of top bottles. There was Bourbon Blue Book, started by John Bull, then a VP of sales and marketing for a manufacturing company out of northwest Arkansas who had also started BX back in 2012, and Bottle Blue Book, created by Justin Sloan and Dan Donoghue, two Lexington, Kentucky, firearms dealers by day and bourbon collectors by night. ("Somehow we need to work with tobacco to hit the trifecta," Donoghue joked to me when I first interviewed him.)

If it was now harder to manipulate the value of bottles, it wasn't impossible, as both Bourbon Blue Book and Bottle Blue Book used self-reported data. For bottles with tons of transactions and dates, like the Van Winkles, it was easy to get a fairly accurate value. For older or more esoteric bottles, it was a little trickier. Eventually, however, most collectors could recite the "actual" price of dozens of bottles at any given moment off the top of their head.

To some, however, these price guides just made it more desirable for people to buy underpriced bottles for the pure purpose of flipping

---

* There would also arise something called razzles, essentially raffles in which sellers would offer a bottle and then provide a number of "slots" to potentially win it. OK, say someone had a bottle of George T. Stagg or whatever. The owner would like to get $800 for it, but there's no guarantee that a single person will pay that much. Instead, the seller offers ten slots at $80 each. Many collectors not willing to pay $800 would be more than willing to pay $80 for a one-in-ten chance at winning. Once the slots are filled, the seller looks to the next drawing of the Illinois Pick 3 plus Fireball Lottery—held twice daily, at 12:40 P.M. and 9:22 P.M. CST—and uses the last number of that drawing, which will be between 0 and 9, to determine which of the ten slots has won. Yes, this is definitely gambling, and yes, some bourbon collectors also happen to have gambling addictions as well, which is perhaps why these "Fireballs," as they are sometimes known, worked out so well. They also worked well to drive up prices and manipulate the market.

them at their current secondary price. Suddenly, finding a case of $5 Old Grand-Dad pints from 1975 was like finding gold. It wasn't something to potentially drink; it was an asset. In fact, it's hard to think of any other consumer product—save maybe sneakers—that could so easily be found at retail and then quickly sold for more money.

"We don't like to consider ourselves a 'Flipper's Handbook,'" Donoghue told me back then. "Our guide is for collectors who want to know how much it may cost them to acquire a bottle not found on the shelf at their local liquor store. Unfortunately, [flippers] exist, but we do not advocate that people clear the shelves simply to make a profit off of the bottles they just picked up."

By 2016, however, that was just what was happening.

DID IT REALLY USED TO BE BETTER?

With dusty drinking becoming mainstream, with prices soaring, and with more and more vintage bourbons and ryes making their way onto bar and restaurant menus (sometimes at several hundred dollars an ounce), a debate would eventually emerge for those wondering if the time, effort, and price were truly worth it.

Was American whiskey really better back in the day? And, if so, why?

More than any other spirit, American whiskey, especially bourbon, has long had incredibly strict regulations. The Bottled-in-Bond Act, introduced by the federal government in 1897, was designed to combat underhanded adulteration and ensure quality and integrity in U.S.-made spirits. It meant that for more than a century, pretty much the entire history of bottled bourbon, you could be assured that the liquid in the bottle was made mostly of corn, always aged in newly charred

THE SPIRIT OF TODAY

oak barrels, and 100 percent devoid of any sort of flavoring and coloring that so many other spirits still suffer from today.

And yet it's so hard to fairly compare the past to the present. Old Rip Van Winkle Old Time Rye was produced by the much-ballyhooed Stitzel-Weller. That distillery is now defunct, and today's Van Winkle rye comes from Buffalo Trace. Same name, completely different product made at a completely different location. (And the Stitzel-Weller Distillery is now owned by Diageo, which makes the Blade and Bow and Orphan Barrel brands.)

Likewise, dusty Old Grand-Dad may have that same orange bottle/elderly visage as today's juice, but previous to 1987 it was made by National Distillers; today it's distilled by Jim Beam. The current product is fine; the former is a whole lot better. Truly the only legitimate past-present comparison is Wild Turkey, which has pretty much always been distilled by Jimmy or Eddie Russell in Lawrenceburg, Kentucky. While modern Wild Turkey remains beloved, dusty Turkey is absolutely deified.

But why?

"I just think it's just more of what your palate likes," says Mike Jasinski. "I just happen to like funkier, weirder stuff because I've just tasted so much of the, quote, unquote, off-the-shelf spirits.

"Once you start going down the rabbit hole, your palate tends to skew toward the weirder stuff. You've tasted all the more normal stuff; now the more esoteric stuff appeals to you."

There are countless theories as to why dusty bourbon tastes better to people like Powell, Jasinski, and me too, and here they are, which I've roughly put in order from the least to most likely to be true, in my humble opinion.

BOTTLE MATURATION

To many drinkers, it's self-evident that whiskey stops aging once it has been removed from the barrel. You'll continually hear people call dusties "drinkable time capsules." But the most out-there theory goes, what if something *does* happen in the bottle? Maybe not aging per se, but perhaps something else. As early as 2010, blogger Oliver Klimek was writing pieces on the subject, believing oxidation might play a role. (He cites how many fruit brandies improve and get rounder even when merely aged in a glass vessel.) Or could decades of UV light affect a bottle? There is a small contingent of collectors who are absolutely dead certain that liquor continues to mature even once bottled. "Bourbon is brown because charred oak has essentially dissolved into the liquid," explains Powell. "I believe when bourbon sits in the bottle, that dissolved bourbon char continues to age the alcohol on some level. Take that minuscule aging process and multiply it by the years it sits in the bottle, and we can assume taste would improve." The great thing about this theory is that it is virtually impossible to study or analyze in any way.

THOSE TASTY
CANCEROUS CHEMICALS

David Jennings, a Wild Turkey superfan and the author of *American Spirit: Wild Turkey Bourbon from Ripy to Russell*, thinks the lowering of urethane levels (by law) in 1989 might be a critical factor no one considers. Urethane is a cancer-causing crystalline compound formed naturally during fermentation, found in particularly high levels in older bourbon, and said to produce a bitter flavor. "I'd imagine [urethane] to be part of the old bottle taste, or mouthfeel at the least, but no one's talking about urethane levels," notes Jennings. "It's apparently second only to alcoholism in spirits industry taboo."

CONGLOMERATION

I'm not going to completely bash big business, but when just about every major Kentucky producer is owned by some multinational conglomerate, it becomes hard to imagine that decisions are being made by the artisans on the ground and not some board of directors in Italy (the Gruppo Campari–owned Wild Turkey), Japan (the Beam-Suntory-owned Jim Beam and Maker's Mark, as well as the Kirin-owned Four Roses), or countless Manhattan towers where MBAs ruin things.

THE GRAIN

I'm likewise not going to go on some anti-GMO rant, but you can't help but wonder if it has also made bourbon worse and more homogeneous, especially compared to a past era when a variety of heirloom corns reigned. Today's corn is genetically modified to grow bigger kernels. "But did the sugar content increase proportionally with size?" wonders Powell. "If not, wouldn't that affect the mash?"

THE WOOD

It's a fact that the oak trees being chopped down to turn into barrels were significantly older some sixty to seventy years ago. Flavor-producing oak lactones and vanillin reside in the tree's rings. The older the tree, the more growth rings, the more flavor inherent in them. Like everything within this now wildly popular industry, cost-cutting measures see today's cooperages (barrel makers) harvesting oak at much younger ages, with far fewer rings and, yes, much less flavor for the white dog to extract. (We'll encounter a similar problem when it comes to agave maturity and modern tequilas.)

ENTRY PROOF

The highest proof that bourbon can legally be distilled to is 160. The highest proof at which bourbon can enter a new charred oak barrel is 125. In 1974 the *Journal of the Association of Official Analytical Chemists* found that a bourbon's congener concentration—in other words, its flavor and complexity—*decreased* as this entry proof increased. Distilleries used to add their bourbon to the barrel at a lower proof, but over the years most major distilleries have continually upped it; notice Wild Turkey raising its entry proof from 107 to 110 in 2004 and then to 115 proof in 2006. (Back in the day, Old Grand-Dad was said to have one of the higher entry proofs at 112. Today many distillers go with the maximum 125 proof, as it's the most economical move. The lower the entry proof, the more water is added to the liquid, the more barrels are needed, and the higher the production costs.) It's impossible not to notice that dusties have a much richer nose and a much thicker body than their contemporary counterparts. This is best exemplified by Heaven Hill of yore, which has an incredible aroma and texture despite a lower bottling proof. "It's why so many guys like high proofers today," believes Powell, referring to the "barrel-proof" or "cask strength" whiskeys that have become de rigueur among drinkers. "It's because it's just concentrated bourbon, and they can actually get a better taste from it, even though it's blowing out their palate."

THE EQUIPMENT

Visit a major bourbon distillery today and you'll notice how gleaming all the equipment is, how automated and computerized the production is. But back in the day, you had distilleries like Wild Turkey and Maker's Mark using cypress fermentation tanks. It's impossible for me to believe that, much like Belgium's lambic breweries, a certain house microflora didn't live in the wood. (Wild Turkey's tanks had been in use since 1925!) Likewise, back in the day, you had an actual man making the mash and then distilling it. "Like there was just some dude sitting in the distillery deciding when to cut the heads, and when to cut the tails, and now everything is automated," says Jasinski. "So you're losing that kind of crafty aspect."

THE AGE

Since demand for bourbon dropped considerably from the late 1960s through the 1990s, many distilleries had no need to immediately dump barrels and thus aged them longer. Likewise, when it was time to put together batches of, say, Wild Turkey 101 8-Year-Old, what was the harm of sneaking a few 13- or 15-year-old barrels into the mix? There was nothing else to do with it. And that's probably the most reasonable explanation for why these standard shelf bourbons from the past are so damn good.

Then again, not everyone believes dusty bourbon is better. Of course, those who believe *today's* bourbon is better typically have a vested interest in it being better. I'm not sure I've ever met any active distillers who believe they produce lower-quality product than their brethren did in the past.

A few months before his death in 2019, I was fortunate enough to connect with Al Young, the legendary Four Roses Ambassador who served in the industry for fifty-two years. "You know, everyone is different in terms of their interpretation of what 'good' means," Young told me. For him, the overall quality and consistency of bourbon had greatly improved in all aspects. "This results in cleaner, more defined bourbons that have benefited from the data collected from less controlled production and aging methods in the past."

Which was probably true. Even the most mediocre bourbons today are well-made, taste decent, and, at the least, aren't off-putting. The state-of-the-art distilling equipment and multimillion-dollar labs at these conglomerate-owned distilleries make production flaws a near impossibility.

The earliest vintage whiskey collectors didn't care about predictability and consistency across an entire industry, though—they cared about taste. And the best of the best bourbons from the past are far better than the best of the best stuff being released today. I'll say it.

Unfortunately, however, there had emerged a whole new breed of collectors who didn't care about taste either—they simply had dollar signs in their eyes and saw yet another emerging hobby that could be exploited for a quick buck.

In the summer of 2016, at a bartender trade show in Baltimore, Matthew Landon, a Louisville bar owner and noted dusty collector, presented a seminar about bourbon vis-à-vis Facebook titled "Underground Whiskey: How to Navigate the Collectors Market for Fun and Profit." Though Landon claimed it was just a coincidence—"I'm surprised they're not blaming me for the tobacco trade and gun trade," he later joked— Facebook shut down several bourbon groups within hours of his talk.

BSM was by now averaging more than one hundred transactions per day, with an average price of $200 a bottle. Powell had seen transactions as high as $100,000. Some members had even begun to trade guns for bourbon, something Powell tried his best to quash.

Just as with gambling, there's a weird correlation between bourbon collectors and lovers of guns (along with sports cars and luxury watches), all of which often appear in social media tableaux of rare bottle scores. One private bourbon group I belong to even celebrates this fact, noting in its group description:

"[We are all] about American freedoms!! Bourbon, Guns, Cigars, Hunting, Fishing and any American freedoms you really love!! We are not a PC group. If you are sensitive this will not be the group for you. Post away and enjoy your freedoms!!"

Anyhow, as you can imagine, eventually a hundred-billion-dollar company, constantly examined in front of the Senate, is going to start paying closer attention to the questionable practices it is hosting on its site (the amplifying of *Daily Wire* articles excepted).

On June 13, 2019, at 1:45 P.M. EST, BSM was shut down by Facebook administrators. Some people would claim it was the Van Winkle family that pushed for this to happen. Pappy's great-grandson Preston Van Winkle told the *Bourbon Pursuit* podcast that a "lot of [legal] dollars" had been thrown at just that.

"Good riddance," wrote one person on a Reddit r/bourbon thread discussing the shutdown. "Too bad the rats are just going to flee from one burning building into the next."

He was completely correct. The groups moved to private WhatsApp groups and other harder-to-monitor locales, but eventually they began to reappear on Facebook. As of this writing, it is still relatively easy to buy, sell, auction, and razzle bourbon on Facebook.

BSM is still shut down, and Powell no longer works at a liquor store, though his role in the vintage bourbon industry has only grown. As the decade came to an end, he didn't need that MBA to know that dusty spirits were now booming and people were going to need a legitimate outlet to easily buy them.

"I fall back to Econ 101," he told me. "The demand dictates everything."

KEY BOURBON DUSTIES

As with any breed of collector, there's a certain hierarchy to the collectibles that are pursued. Within American whiskey dusties, a few key distilleries dominate the conversation and marketplace unlike any other, for a variety of reasons detailed below. Just remember, though, that the most pursued collectibles do not necessarily always correlate with those that are the highest quality—in this case, meaning the best tasting.

TIER I

ANYTHING STITZEL-WELLER

Started by the actual "Pappy," Julian Van Winkle Sr., in 1935, Stitzel-Weller became famous for its wheated mash bill, an anomaly then as it mostly remains today. Thus, collectors can't help but think of Stitzel-Weller (or SW, in collectors' parlance) as a sort of ur-Pappy. And indeed, most of it is quite tasty, as typically seen in bottlings of Old Fitzgerald and W.L. Weller, and the older the better, or at least more pursued. But there are plenty of more esoteric Stitzel-Weller bottlings like Rebel Yell and Cabin Still, not to mention tons of gimmicky, ceramic decanters from the 1970s shaped like Rip Van Winkle, a hillbilly, and other "fanciful characters from the Kentucky bluegrass where great bourbon was born" (according to the label), which Julian Van Winkle Jr. and eventually Julian Van Winkle III had to shill in order to try and fight their way out of the glut. Today dusties that were once produced at the distillery are incredibly pricey, whether sold as entire bottles or by the pour at vintage spirits bars. But despite being so coveted, some Stitzel-Weller secrets are still out there, like a circa late 1970s 10-year-old that Owen Powell poured me in early 2022. The fact that it was bottled under the Old Commonwealth label—and packaged in a cowboy boot decanter (see Loredo Pass in "Key Japanese Export Dusties," page 20)—meant that only those truly in the know *knew* what they would be getting, and thus a one-ounce pour was a relative steal at twenty-five bucks, compared to the $100 or so most Stitzel-Weller of that age was fetching at the time.

TIER 2

WILLETT FAMILY ESTATE

Known to collectors as WFE, Willett is a brand nearly impossible to parse for neophytes. Unlike Stitzel-Weller, it is still very much active today, releasing bourbons and ryes in elegant, Cognac-style bottles with subdued white labels, often differentiated only by small, handwritten details near the shoulder noting age, proof, and barrel number. These current releases, which the company distills itself in Bardstown, Kentucky, are generally pretty good, but they aren't the releases the true diehards lose their shit over. Like many Kentucky brands, the roots of Willett go back to the nineteenth century, but we mostly only care about it since 2006. That's when Drew Kulsveen began releasing cask-strength, non-chill-filtered single barrels from what he thought to be the best tasting of the company's glut-era stock sourced from producers like Heaven Hill, Bernheim, Four Roses, Jim Beam, and perhaps even Stitzel-Weller. (Quite a few of these single barrels were selected by Bill Thomas for his bar Bourbon.) Look for any bottles with wax tops, even better if "WILLETT" is written on the label in a block letter font and not the expected script, a change that happened around 2011. Of course, the best of the best vintage Willetts are the private label releases from a decade and a half ago, like Red Hook Rye (2006–2008), Speakeasy Select and Rathskeller Rye (2007), Rogin's Choice (Japanese export, 2007), and The Bitter Truth (German export, 2009) (see "Private Labels and Personal Bottles," page 207).

TURKEY FOR ME?

Wild Turkey remains the only still-active distillery with a massive following for the older bottles it also distilled. That's because the dusty Turkey flavor profile is truly one of a kind. Though drinkers will endlessly debate why exactly it tastes the way it once did—cypress fermentation tanks? a secret change in yeasts? higher urethane levels? lower entry proofs? crumbling cork closures causing oxidation?— vintage collectors are obsessed with dusty Wild Turkey, often citing how much they love its indelible "funk." Maybe it's simply because, due to the glut, master distiller Jimmy Russell had no choice but to use much older bourbon in his standard Wild Turkey 101. Limited releases from the past, with silly nicknames coined by the modern cognoscenti—"Donut" (Wild Turkey Kentucky Legend, late 1990s), "Pewter Top" (Wild Turkey Kentucky Spirit, mid-1990s), and especially "Cheesy Gold Foil," a 12-year-old from the late 1980s, so dubbed due to its garish, cheap-looking packaging—are some of the most valuable dusties that can still be found.

NATIONAL DISTILLERS OGD

It's 1985 and bartenders in Wayfarers are standing on top of the bar at your local nightclub reciting bawdy poems, then throwing shaker tins behind their backs before whipping up another batch of Sex on the Beaches. And that must have been the reason Jim Beam paid $545 million to National Distillers in 1987 to acquire DeKuyper Peachtree Schnapps, incredibly the ninth-best-selling liquor overall at the time, and the critical component in of-the-moment drinks like the Fuzzy Navel and the Redheaded Slut. Tossed in as part of that deal? The woefully unhip and stuck-in-a-glut "Olds"—Old Grand-Dad (OGD), Old Taylor, Old Crow, and Old Overholt (a rye?! in 1985?!?!?!). Today Old Grand-Dad in particular, from the 1960s through the Jim Beam acquisition (look for DSP-KY-14 on the bottle), remains extremely coveted. "If the UPC code starts with 86259, it surely has sweet caramel notes all over it," one collector told me.

TIER 3

FOUR ROSES

Much loved today, the fact that vintage offerings from the Lawrence-burg, Kentucky, brand look so similar to modern bottlings leads some greener dusty hunters to assume they've made a big score. But much vintage Four Roses—despite the cool labels—is swill, especially post-1950s Seagram's-produced products, which were all blended whiskeys. But yeah, the bottles look cool.

BROWN-FORMAN

Jack Daniel's is the world's best-selling whiskey, and maybe that's one reason no connoisseurs really collect examples of it from the past (with one exception; see page 93). Most of it is decent tasting; little of it is particularly exciting. Nor do dusty hunters really collect Jack's Brown-Forman stablemate Old Forester, even if vintage versions of it can, in fact, be quite tasty.

SLEEPERS, IN YOUR HUMBLE AUTHOR'S OPINION

PRE-FIRE HEAVEN HILL

Like Wild Turkey, many vintage drinkers are certain that dusty Heaven Hill is simply better than its modern incarnation; unlike Wild Turkey, it's easy to find the demarcation between the modern and the old— namely, the 1996 fire that destroyed ninety thousand barrels as well as some distilling operations. "Pre-fire HH," as it's now known, is simply more flavorful and richer in mouthfeel despite the lower proof. This is evident in numerous Heaven Hill brands unknown today, with names like The Yellow Rose of Texas, Anderson Club, Mark Twain, Virgin Bourbon, Old Kentucky Rifle, and others, some of which were sold only on the Japanese market during the glut. If you stumble on a bourbon of strange origins that is shaped like today's boxy Evan Williams bottle, you're in for a treat and, most likely, a decent price.

SECRETLY OLD BLANTON'S

You don't have to convince anyone that Blanton's is hot these days. America's first commercial single-barrel bourbon has gone from a reliable, always-available, semi-luxury brand to being impossible to find. Something that makes true connoisseurs roll their eyes, as the 6-year-old liquid really isn't that great. But savvy collectors know that Blanton's released between 1991 and 1993, back when it wasn't selling well—1991 may have been the worst year for bourbon sales in America since Prohibition—was composed of much older barrels; reportedly, 16-year-old juice in 1991, 13-year-old in 1992, and 11-year-old in 1993.

MAKER'S MARK

A reliable stalwart that has never been much of a collector's item means vintage versions of it are also under-pursued. And yes, the similar packaging and mostly similar production processes mean you really aren't going to discover how the longtime Loretto, Kentucky, distillers "used to" make its bourbon. But vintage Maker's is nevertheless an economical treat.

BOURBON AND RYE BRANDS YOU HAVE NEVER HEARD OF

I swear, any time someone hands me a glass of some rye from the past, often produced in Pennsylvania, Maryland, or Ohio—with names like Harvest King, Old Quaker, or Hannisville Rye—it is no doubt delicious. The same holds true for many defunct bourbon brands like Meadowlawn Distillery's Distillers Pride and anything from General Distillers out of Louisville.

5

CHANGING LAWS SPAWN A NEW INDUSTRY

THIS IS THE point in my story where I break the fourth wall and, looking directly into Marty Scorsese's camera, with those hypnotic blue eyes of mine, rhetorically ask the audience:

"The real question is this: Was all this legal?

"*Absolutely fucking not.*"

But since this is not the *The Wolf of Wall Street* and I am not Leonardo DiCaprio as Jordan Belfort and this is mostly a story of obsessives buying and selling and drinking dusty bottles of booze, there's perhaps not quite the legal implications of the financial world. Though, to be clear, by this point in the vintage booze story, the buying and selling of vintage spirits had mostly been an under-the-radar practice since its onset, save the weird District of Columbia.*

That is, until Gary Crunkleton, a burly bear of a man and a

---

* As the only federal city in the United States, there is no county or state to make liquor laws for Washington, D.C. So someone like Bill Thomas could buy whiskey from anyone, any bottle ever legally sold, and, since it had already been federally approved, he needed only to fill out an application form, pay some additional taxes on it, and it could be on the shelf of Jack Rose the next day.

self-described "hillbilly" bar owner originally from rural North Carolina, found himself in Portland, Oregon, for its Cocktail Week. He was drinking at The Woodsman Tavern, his bespectacled eyes staring up in awe at a wall of Very Old Fitzgerald, Very Very Old Fitzgerald, and Very Xtra Old Fitzgerald. This immense stock of vintage Stitzel-Weller juice was such a beautiful sight to Crunkleton, and yet he was confused. He politely asked a nearby bartender:

"Hey, how are you guys allowed to sell all this?"

"Because it's a gray area," the barman replied. "There's not a law for it, but there's not a law *against* it."

Though Crunkleton didn't realize it then, the wheels were now in motion and he would eventually find himself making the first law *for* it.

Crunkleton had opened his eponymous bar in Chapel Hill in 2008. North Carolina then, as now, was a government control state with very slim pickings for what bar owners could stock. There were maybe only thirty different bourbon labels available in the entire catalog. Crunkleton wanted to set The Crunkleton apart from his peers, however, and figured out a loophole that would legally allow him to order whole cases directly from distilleries and distributors and get them specially coded for sale in North Carolina. Early on, because of this, he was able to get most of the Van Winkles as well as coveted early offerings from Kentucky Bourbon Distillers.

By 2013, other Carolina bars were beginning to get into the bourbon trend, and they, too, wanted Pappy and Willett on their shelves. So they started complaining about Crunkleton and then got the state involved.

"I'm pissed because I'm a business owner and I was able to, you know, navigate the system and figure out how to get product," Crunkleton recalls. "And now that I've done all that and gotten the product, other people want to complain about my inventory."

It didn't matter; he would no longer have these rare releases all to himself. Orange County, North Carolina, even sent him a taunting, Soup Naziesque email: "No more Pappy for you!"

Crunkleton's wife, Megan, told him to quit bellyaching and figure out the next big thing, the next "Pappy."

"And I said, well, the best bourbons in the world are from the 1950s, but I can't sell those because they're not available through the three-tier system," recalls Crunkleton.

He refused to exist in a gray area like some of these other bars across the country. The Crunkletons are moral Southerners. They go to church. They have little children. They live and work in a small college town with his name on the bar. He knows he can't do anything shady or the family name will be mud in Chapel Hill.

By that point, Crunkleton had been acquiring vintage spirits for his own edification for a few years, mostly scoring them via online markets from out of Europe that were still undervaluing American vintage. The shipping charges over the pond often cost more than the bottles, in fact. He soon had dusty whiskeys ranging from Prohibition-era pints to four-fifths of a quart from the 1940s to the '70s. He estimated the collection was worth $100,000 or so by then.

"Anything produced before 1982, it could have been called Ass-Lick Bourbon, and I'm still going to buy it, and I'm certain it's going to be better than what's being made today," jokes Crunkleton.

On one fortuitous day in late February 2015, the Atlantic Coast Conference basketball schedule put North Carolina State on the road against its in-state rivals, the University of North Carolina Tar Heels. That morning, Crunkleton got a call from the North Carolina General Assembly. Newly assumed Speaker of the House Tim Moore wanted to set up a private bourbon tasting for his cronies before the game. Crunkleton, in his signature blue button-up and big, black bow tie, played the perfect host, serving the pols pours of Pappy, of course, along with some other, lesser-known gems.

Before heading to the Dean Dome for the game, Moore told Crunkleton if there's anything his office could ever do to help him out, just let him know.

This was Crunkleton's big chance.

He had a sealed pint bottle of 1917-distilled AMS Special Old Reserve, a 15-year-old "medicinal" whiskey that could legally be sold during Prohibition. He passed the ornate, diagonally ribbed glass flask to the muckety-mucks, who gingerly studied it, cradling the bottle like a baby. Crunkleton gave them his spiel.

"Most people don't even know this stuff exists. And if they did ever come across it, they would probably think, oh, it's probably rotten, it's no good. Now, at this bar, which I pride myself on, which has my name on it, I would love to be able to offer my guests some of the finest whiskey ever made, like that bottle there, but I can't because these aren't made anymore."

As these tough-to-sway politicians stood listening, Crunkleton continued, a regular Jimmy Stewart in *Mr. Smith Goes to Washington*.

"You know, sometimes when I drive on the highway, I'll see these old cars and they'll have an orange-colored license plate that says 'Antique Auto.' Y'all have given a special waiver to these antique cars to allow them on the road, even if they don't meet modern specs and regulations.

"I'd like to have the same kind of waiver from the great state of North Carolina so that I can offer these antique spirits to my guests."

Moore was moved. And maybe the Republican was just a bit buzzed. Because he slapped Crunkleton on the back and told him he would get this done for him.

(The funniest thing is: Crunkleton was pretty sure that beautiful 1917 bottle he used as a prop would have tasted like motor oil if he had opened it for them.)

A few months later, perhaps having forgotten about that conversation, Crunkleton was driving to the Blue Ridge Mountains on Easter weekend when he got a phone call from Moore's office. It was the Speaker's attorney who composes all his bills, telling Crunkleton that they were actually going to put together an antique spirit law.

After some political jockeying, the General Assembly passed House Bill 909, which added an "Antique Spirituous Liquor" section to its alcoholic beverage control (ABC) laws:

> *"Antique spirituous liquor" means spirituous liquor that has not been in production or bottled in the last 20 years, is in the original manufacturer's unopened container, is not owned by a distillery, and is not otherwise available for purchase by an ABC Board except through the special order process.*

In February 2016, The Crunkleton unveiled its "Antique Spirits" menu, separated by distillation decades—from pre-Prohibition up until the 1980s—and then sorted by distillery. Crunkleton charged a pour price based upon what he had paid for the bottle, not what it was now worth in secondary circles. Bourbon historian Mike Veach joined Crunkleton to discuss what was being opened on the first day the menu was available.

In 2018, Crunkleton opened a second namesake bar in Charlotte, a city that would become a mini-mecca of vintage when a second location of Billy Sunday, a vintage amaro bar, also opened there in 2020.

IN 2017, KENTUCKY would have its own "Vintage Spirits Law" take effect when Governor Matt Bevin signed HB100. Unlike North Carolina, there was no twenty-year minimum of dustiness—literally any bottle that was no longer in regular distribution counted as vintage.

The Bardstown Bourbon Company (BBC), a sort of distillery/
amusement park for bourbon geeks, was one of the first to take advantage of the law after it was signed. The facility's bar and restaurant,
then called Bottle & Bond, hired Bill Thomas as well as bourbon
author Fred Minnick to help source a world-class collection. Minnick described it as building his personal dream bar "with someone
else's money."

He first set his eyes on acquiring an entire set of Old Crow Chessmen, what he has long claimed is the finest bourbon he has ever tried
("some [decanters] taste like sublime blissfulness and others taste like
shoe leather"). Around this time, Thomas thought there might be
only fifty full sets still left in the world—complete with the carpet
chessboard—but this law would cause a ton of sets to come out of the
woodwork, or Grand-pappy's attic, and into the open.

But for Bottle & Bond, it wasn't just about having an immense
collection; BBC wanted vintage bottles that told stories about the past.

"We asked [Thomas and Minnick] to find bottles that had a unique
history and something to say," claimed Dan Callaway, the company's vice
president of hospitality, "instead of just having a unicorn to have a unicorn."

The first menu would offer bottles that Callaway believed could teach
drinkers about the industry's illustrious early years, like a Cedar Brook
Hand Made Sour Mash Whiskey dating back to 1892, a pre-Prohibition
Old Overholt Rye, or a Prohibition-era "medicinal" flask of 1929 Old
Oscar Pepper.

In Lexington, a few blocks off Main Street, you also had Justins'
House of Bourbon—apostrophe in the correct spot—opened in 2018
by Justin Thompson, cocktail bar owner and copublisher of the *Bourbon
Review*, and Justin Sloan, our old buddy who had helped launched Bottle
Blue Book back when dusty bourbon was still trying to set a market.

Kentucky's unique law would allow them to legally ship their selection of uber-rare bottles like Corti Brothers 19 and 20 Years Old—the

first-ever private label Stitzel-Weller Van Winkles from the 1980s—to any number of other states. (Sloan claims that 75 percent of his business is from out-of-state, actually.)

By the end of 2019 the Justins had a second location in Louisville, along with an actual staff whiskey historian, Caroline Paulus, a former archaeologist who had first come to Kentucky "to dig holes on the side of the road" for $13 an hour. A life in bourbon seemed a lot more appealing than spending nights covered in dust and sleeping in a hot tent.

New York's little-used and rarely discussed vintage spirits law would see a second location of The Office, The Aviary's upscale dusty den, open in the ritzy Mandarin Oriental in the fall of 2017. Pours were prohibitively expensive—I only went if someone with an expense account treated me—and, for the most part, New York has remained a not particularly great vintage spirits city during this legalized boom. As this book was going to print, Texas would also legalize vintage spirits—Houston's Reserve 101 would be the first bar to capitalize.

The messed-up thing is that in early 2023, the Kentucky Alcoholic Beverage Control raided both Justins' locations, claiming they had committed eleven interstate code violations, most notably transporting cases of Blanton's into Washington, D.C. The charges were quickly dropped, but this just proved to many that when it comes to alcohol in the United States, you can still get in trouble for dealing in supposedly legal things.

And the feds are always watching you.

THE JACK DANIEL'S COLLECTOR LOOPHOLE

There is one other state that merits mention for having a vintage spirits law on the books, though one few people are aware of.

That's the great state of Tennessee, which is home to the best-selling whiskey in America, and perhaps the most beloved too. I'm talking about Jack Daniel's, of course, which has a rabid fan base that will take frequent pilgrimages to the Lynchburg distillery, tattoo their biceps with the Old No. 7 logo, swathe their children and pets in the brand's gear, and, in some cases, stockpile dusty bottles from the past, all while existing in a space siloed from other vintage whiskey collectors who mostly have no interest in old bottles of "Jack."

In October 2007, the sheriff's office raided two Tennessee warehouses owned by Randy Piper, a local plumber who had amassed twenty-four hundred bottles of Jack Daniel's, some of it nearly a century old and perhaps worth millions in total. The Alcohol Beverage Commission (ABC) fined Piper $15,000 and claimed it had no choice but to pour these vintage bottles down the drain, causing Kyle MacDonald, a Canadian Jack Daniel's obsessive and blogger, to give an all-time great quote:

"Punish the person, not the whiskey. Jack never did anything wrong, and the whiskey itself is innocent."

By 2009 officials had somewhat relented and returned the collection to Piper. And with so many other Jack Daniel's collectors in Tennessee wanting to legally build, thin out, or sell off their collections, eventually the Senate snuck a small ordinance into its state laws in 2010.

Tennessee Code § 57-3-209 was enacted for "Alcoholic beverage collector[s]," meaning "an individual who collects commemorative bottles containing alcoholic beverages." If said collector was willing to *display* the collection in a location available to the public, either by appointment or on a regular schedule, then this individual could actually apply to the ABC for a license as an alcohol beverage collector, something that would grant the right to purchase and sell "collectible alcohol . . . without the intent that the collectible alcoholic beverage be consumed."

As far as Seth Weinberg, who by 2023 was living and bartending in Nashville, knows, only a few private Jack Daniel's collectors currently have this license, maybe six or seven. Piper would display his collection at a gift shop he owned in Lynchburg, which is paradoxically a dry county.

"It's kind of a weird law the way they have it," says Weinberg, who hopes to exploit this loophole one day to open a legitimate vintage retail shop in Nashville. "So my goal is to have the law adjusted over the next few years where it's more open to do what I want to do and really mimic what Kentucky has already done."

That's not to say this second breed of vintage bars was happening only in these three newly legalized locations either.

Pablo Moix was a would-be actor and part-time bartender at a Pizzeria Uno in Queens during the mid-1990s, mudslide-slinging, late-stage fern bar mixology days. He went to the liquor store once to grab some smokes, saw a dusty bottle he thought looked cool, and grabbed it. It was 1940s Bénédictine; Moix didn't know it at the time, but this was one of the better vintage liqueurs one could find. Soon he began accumulating any weird old bottles he saw on the shelf.

Initially, Moix found himself particularly in pursuit of tequila; a lot of great brands had gone defunct, or changed their production processes, and he yearned to find them and taste them.

By now, Los Angeles was in the nascent days of its own cocktail renaissance that New York had already gone through. Moix got a gig at La Descarga, a Cuban-themed speakeasy with a hidden cigar lounge that was owned by twin brothers Mark and Jonnie Houston. Steve Livigni was the GM.

Working behind the stick, shaking up rum drinks, Moix and Livigni bonded over the notion of liquor bottles as time capsules, stashing away finds for special occasions. They helped set up the beverage programs at other Houston brothers bars: Pour Vous, a Parisian-style cocktail lounge, and Harvard & Stone, a Rosie the Riveter–inspired blue-collar bar with some of the most inventive cocktails in the city. Regulars would also sometimes gift Moix and Livigni with interesting old bottles.

As Moix and Livigni became more intentional in their dusty hunting, they began spending ten hours a day, every day, searching stores throughout California and Mexico's Baja Peninsula to score old bottles of Herradura and El Tesoro tequila. On one road trip they visited nearly every single liquor store between Detroit and L.A.

"We later learned we were apparently hitting liquor stores in neighborhoods that are essentially considered war zones," says Moix, one of the fastest talkers I've ever met, bursting with knowledge as he passionately bounces from subject to subject. They'd also visit forgotten hotel bars and estate sales.

By 2011 the partners had shifted their focus to American whiskey, with sights on one day opening their own space. The men began stockpiling cases of well-aged Rittenhouse ryes, Vintage Bourbon 17 Year Old, and Stitzel-Weller-distilled Old Fitzgerald Bottled in Bond. They'd speculate on new releases too, like Black Maple Hill, which was selling for only $19.50 wholesale at the time.

"It reinforced this idea that you have to prepare yourself for the future," Livigni explained. "This will happen with other spirits besides whiskey. If you want to carry these products in the future, you need to start changing the way you purchase."

———

BY THE LATTER half of the 2010s, with so many bars now wanting to offer a "vintage program," no longer could they simply rely on having an owner who'd done a little dusty hunting back in the day. More often than not, when I found myself in a bar or restaurant anywhere in

America—some place like Fausto, a sophisticated Italian wine restaurant near my apartment in Park Slope, Brooklyn—that just so happened to have a few vintage amaro bottles on a special menu, I'd ask where they got them, even though I already knew the most likely answer.

Raised on Chicago's Gold Coast, Alex Bachman had first fallen for the beauty of vintage spirits while working as an assistant sommelier at Charlie Trotter's, Chicago's Michelin-starred tasting menu restaurant, in the late 2000s.

"These rich regulars would come into Trotter's: 'Hey, I've got this bottle of Napoleonic Cognac we gotta open.' 'I've got Amer Picon from the '30s,'" Bachman told me back in 2018. "It was very obscure shit they were genuinely curious to taste."

Sensing an opportunity, the sommeliers started curating a small collection of off-menu vintage spirits—mostly Cognac and single malt Scotch—for wealthy regulars and rock star chefs like Joël Robuchon who Charlie Trotter wanted to wine and dine.

"That was the first time I really saw people enjoying vintage spirits in a service environment," says Bachman.

After leaving Trotter's, Bachman began to immerse himself in the vintage spirits world, working under Christopher Donovan, proprietor of House of Glunz, Chicago's oldest liquor retailer, which his great-grandfather Louis Glunz Sr. opened in 1888. The store still had bottles purchased by Glunz Sr., like some Napoleonic Cognac—meaning it was distilled during the emperor's lifetime, 1811 in this case—purchased for sixteen bucks back in 1934. A history major in college, Bachman was inspired, and he started building his own vintage collection.

In 2013 a longtime Trotter's chef de cuisine, Matthias Merges, opened Billy Sunday,* an avant-garde cocktail bar in the Logan Square

---

* Named after a former Chicago White Stockings baseball player who became an anti-alcohol evangelist in support of Prohibition.

area of Chicago, with a specific focus on amaro. Bachman would be the head bartender, not only building the cocktail list but beginning to focus on sourcing vintage spirits and vintage glassware.

Bachman was fascinated that even the most astute American drinkers knew only of the few big Italian amari—Campari, Aperol, Averna—when so many others had been produced in the past, in numerous tiny Italian villages most people had never heard of. Though the bar had more than six hundred different amari, Bachman would often note that was a small fraction of what had been produced in the last century and a half.

At the end of an evening, Bachman would often recommend that guests try a glass of vintage fernet, often from a producer besides the now-ubiquitous Fernet-Branca, explaining that fernet is a category, not a brand. He loved what it revealed about its production area.

"There are not a lot of distillates in the world where you can really talk about terroir and a sense of place, and fernet does that in my opinion better than [anything]," he claimed. "Herbalized or botanical spirits that have organic compounds macerated in them change over time—they age. So it's an exciting thing to see a current-release Fernet-Branca, say, versus one that was bottled in the sixties and has a good fifty-plus years of bottle age on it."

Going to off-the-beaten-path liquor stores in Baltimore or Kentucky wasn't enough for Bachman. He began visiting Europe and Asia to dusty-hunt, tracking down shuttered bars, restaurants, and warehouses. He also began developing relationships with locals around the world, creating a team of semiprofessional dusty hunters.

There was a former distillery manager in Rome, a father-and-son team in Northern Italy, a Spanish man who had a knack for finding old Chartreuse, a Cognac hunter from that region, several contacts in Germany who could snag export bourbon, a Japanese restaurateur, and various chefs, liquor store owners, and even booze writers (though not me).

These contacts, in turn, had their own networks of former employers of now-defunct distilleries, liquor distributors, and restaurants, as well as access to local estate sales and auctions. Bachman would never share the names of any of these people with me, no matter how much I prodded. I always wondered who they were; I always wanted to interview some of them.

By 2015, Bachman had enough dusty-hunting freelancers that he was able to found a company, Sole Agent, in order to source and sell vintage spirits and liqueurs to bars and restaurants across the country that were now clamoring for it, places like canon in Seattle; The Milk Room, Longman & Eagle, and Lost Lake in Chicago; and Smuggler's Cove in San Francisco. He had more than three hundred clients at one point, and his team was finding dozens, if not hundreds, of cases' worth of vintage bottles per month.

Every month, the booze would be put on a container ship that traveled from Livorno, Italy, to Newark, New Jersey, before passing through customs, then driven to Bachman's climate-controlled storage facility in a northwest Chicago suburb. Bachman had likewise navigated the tricky laws for importation and label approval.

Though quiet and soft-spoken, a baseball cap often pulled down low on his head, the tall, athletic-looking Bachman seemingly knew every spirits collector of importance around the world. Like the most famous bourbon collector of modern times, Heinz Taubenheim, a German who had begun collecting American whiskey at the end of its golden age, in the late 1960s, while enlisted in the army.

BY THE EARLY 2000s, Mr. Bourbon, as he was often labeled in the press, lived on what had been officially renamed Bourbon Street, in Griebelschied, a small village near Kirn, in the Nahe wine valley of western Germany. There an American flag flew from a pole, and he had turned a meat-curing cellar (really just a garage) into a home bar with the largest collection of American whiskey in the world.

It was such a big collection, in fact, that connoisseurs would travel to Taubenheim's home just to see it; American army generals stationed nearby would pop in; famous American distillers like Jim Beam's Booker Noe came to see Taubenheim's thousands upon thousands of bourbons, ryes, and Tennessee whiskeys, dating as far back as an 1855-distilled Golden Wedding rye. Modern distilleries that Taubenheim favored, like Willett, started producing special private bottlings for him.

On February 8, 2016, Taubenheim died at age sixty-eight after a serious illness. Though the world whiskey community mourned his death, many were also champing at the bit to acquire his collection. No less than a former governor of Kentucky, Paul E. Patton, had once made Taubenheim promise to will his collection back to the state it had come from.

Ultimately, one of Taubenheim's friends, Sebastian Renner, produced one hundred copies of a book detailing Mr. Bourbon's entire collection of bottles, from the Golden Wedding rye up to 2015 releases he had acquired in his final months on earth. In the intro to the book, the final line reads:

"In the sense of Heinz Taubenheim the collection should be kept together."

Despite all that, Mr. Bourbon's widow, Edith, let his longtime friend Thomas Krüger auction off the collection of twenty-five hundred bottles, some of which he acquired for his own Whisky Krüger Museum, which he had opened in Holzbunge, Germany, in 1995.

⁓

ALEX BACHMAN WAS able to buy one of those mere one hundred copies of *The Bourbon Collection of Heinz Taubenheim*, which clued him in to a rare Japanese export, Willett Single-Barrel 24 Year Old. He bought it for Matthias Merges, who was in the process of opening a new place called Mordecai in 2018.

Located across the street from Wrigley Field and named after former Chicago Cub Mordecai "Three Finger" Brown, the high-end bar would focus mostly on vintage whiskey. (Taubenheim's 24 Year Old Willett went on the opening day menu for nearly $300 an ounce.) Merges tasked Bachman with assembling a full vertical of Pappy Van Winkle 15 Year Old from 2004 to 2018, in less than two months. Since the bar had the backing of a private equity firm run by the billionaire owners of the Cubbies, this was not a particularly daunting task for Bachman. By this point in time, deep pockets had in many ways replaced skill in finding dusty bourbon.

But Bachman did, in fact, have a unique set of skills more important than any blank check: an immense knowledge of obscure amaro producers from the past and an incredible ability to find their bottles.

"His world is now a lot less Indiana Jones and much more *A Beautiful Mind*," his friend, and client, Paul McGee told me back then. The two men had even traveled to Tokyo together, back when it was still a dusty wonderland, finding a shelf of rare Japanese-only Ancient Ancient Age 8 Year Old in a Ginza liquor store. They imported it all back to its native land.

Though we weren't exactly friends, I'd always had a good relationship with Bachman, even visiting Chicago to spend a day dusty-hunting with him (sorta—he wouldn't exactly show me any of his best-kept secrets or sources). I found him a shy, reserved guy who seemed to like being out of the limelight, or even barroom conversations, but one who would immediately light up and talk your ear off if certain esoteric subjects came up, especially terroir in the amaro world, whether discussing the role of saffron in fernet production or how Chinese rhubarb became a critical macerate for Northern Italy amari.

Even other vintage experts would concede that Bachman knew more than just about everyone out there.

"It's not just buying everything under the sun for the sake of buying everything under the sun," he once told me. "Every bottle [I buy] is specifically chosen for a reason—what it represents for a certain distillery, or a period of distillation history."

Bachman had been discussing opening a showroom, a retail space in Chicago, so individual customers would have access to these great vintage spirits without needing to trek to a canon or a Milk Room or get hit with massive auction house fees. Instead, one Friday in May 2019, Bachman sent a final email from his Sole Agent account, before shutting down his company's website and social media for good.

I'm not exactly sure what happened, why Sole Agent folded up shop, but I'd heard a few rumors I couldn't confirm.

By the start of the pandemic, it seemed that Bachman had given up on spirits totally, and most of his Instagram posts were now focused on a new obsession: bonsai trees, something I also have a bit of an interest in. As I followed his Instagram, it seemed he was amassing rare and beautiful bonsai trees like he had once done for vintage amaro. In a way, it was just a different form of collectible terroir, I suppose.

We would still occasionally chat on Instagram through 2021, usually about bonsai, but eventually he closed his account, and he never responded to my requests for an interview for this book.

MOIX AND LIVIGNI, meanwhile, would open a string of popular bars and restaurants at the end of the 2010s: The Chestnut Club in Santa Monica, Black Market Liquor Bar in Studio City, and an Italian restaurant on Venice Beach named Scopa. In 2016 they opened a reservations-required, phone-checked-at-the-door, flip-flops-prohibited, pseudo-speakeasy in the back of Scopa, called Old Lightning. It was, in fact, the anti-speakeasy—a "California speakeasy," they dubbed it—light and airy, instead of dark and brooding like you might find in Manhattan.

Old Lightning offered twelve hundred bottles of vintage spirits, a "liquid Fort Knox" as Garrett Snyder of *Punch* described it, though it seemed like Moix and Livigni didn't want anyone to know about it. Old Lightning had no sign, no marketing, no information on its website, no social media; they seemed to eschew press until they had no choice but to talk to journalists—their bar had become one of the hottest spots and toughest reservations in the city.

I'd interviewed Moix a few times over the phone, but I finally met him for the first time in the early fall of 2019 when the Old Lightning team loaded up a U-Haul and drove a massive cache of vintage bottles across the country in order to hold a series of pop-up events in New York City. There, at Peppi's Cellar in SoHo, Moix poured me a finger of my longtime white whale: Red Hook Rye.

It was merely a white calf back between 2006 and 2008 when Brooklyn "likker" store owner LeNell Camacho Santa Ana (née Smothers), purchased the first of four different barrels of well-aged rye from Drew Kulsveen of Willett. In total, these produced fewer than a thousand bottles, all privately labeled with an illustration of a flexing arm with a cursive "LeNell" tattooed on the bicep.

Put on the shelves at her Red Hook, Brooklyn, retailer for $75 each, they sold so slowly that some bottles were still available in 2009 when real estate issues forced her to close up shop. (She now owns a liquor store in Birmingham, Alabama, also called LeNell's.)

If I had just been aware of this bottle's existence in 2008, if I just had a crystal ball too, I could have walked from my apartment to LeNell's and loaded up. Of course, that was ten books ago, back when my savings was usually in the three figures, and I could hardly afford to spend $75 on a bottle of whiskey, much less numerous bottles. I certainly wouldn't have kept them as a sealed investment back then either.

(And did I even drink rye in those days? I think I was mainly into West Coast IPAs.)

By 2019, Red Hook Rye was pouring for $500 an ounce.

As I sat there alone at Peppi's Cellar, finally sipping on Red Hook Rye, something I never thought I'd get to try, thinking about my life back in 2008, I recalled enjoying that year. I was completely single for the first time in three years, working on a novel, watching a lot of college basketball with friends at East Village dive bars—but I had to admit I was sure glad to be in the present, in 2019, with both a new book and a new son about to enter the world in the next couple of months.

Hype and history and coulda woulda shouldas can fuck with the palate, and that can be a good or bad thing, but I still think that the glass of Red Hook Rye was the best American whiskey I've ever tasted.

I will never forget it.

PART II

SPIRITS FROM THE PAST

6

DUSTY HUNTING MOVES BEYOND BOURBON

DEALING WITH DUSTY hunters over the years, I've come to realize they can be a solitary, often secretive, and unusually competitive bunch. Maybe all top-level collectors are. To a certain extent, it's necessary when you're searching the world for scarce items. (How cutthroat were those PEZ conventions back in the nineties?)

Thus, rather quickly I think, Ackerman grew to regret telling me the little information he knew about the Hughes collection. I promised him that he was my guy and that I would not take any of the tips he told me and then mention them, accidentally or otherwise, to other dusty hunters I would be interviewing. And I certainly wasn't going to jump the line and make a middle-of-the-night land run on the collection myself.

But Ackerman continued to fret that I might let something slip and he'd lose out on a potentially all-time great score.

I understood.

Ackerman finally shut me down completely one day when I told him I would really like the contact info for the guy who had given him the initial Hughes tip.

"Tough shit," he responded.

He then told me that he had actually been developing a reality TV series of his own for the past two years. Called *Dusty Hunters*, it was already being pitched around town by his reps as a sort of *American Pickers*, *Storage Wars*, *Pawn Stars* for the elite dusty-hunting game. He would be the star and his triumphing by ultimately finding Hughes's booze would be the perfect culmination for the final episode of season one. I had to admit, that would be a great TV show.

And now I could fully understand why he didn't want to share intel with me any longer. I mostly quit pressing him.

Over the next year, Ackerman would remain friendly with me, nonetheless, continuing to send fire emojis after I Instagrammed rare bottles and DMing off-color memes he found funny. But we rarely talked about my book anymore. We still have a solid relationship today and I hope he invites me to the *Dusty Hunters* premiere.

IN A WAY, this was a gift. I'd been resting on my laurels, waiting for Ackerman to fully uncover my story for me. Now I was forced to use my own investigative skills, forced to report and figure out this shit myself.

So I started nosing around, seeing if anyone knew of a collection of this sort (while never breaking my NDA and actually uttering the name "Howard Hughes"). I hit up Salvatore Calabrese over Zoom. He'd dealt with many famous people's collections over the years. Famous people were also usually rich people who also usually liked to entertain at home as opposed to going out. He recounted one story for me—a woman who reached out to him because her A-list husband had just died.

"He was a famous person, a very famous person, *an icon*, and he was a collector and loved these old spirits that he had," recalls Calabrese. "But he never had the courage to open his incredible collection. He was always waiting for a special moment that never came."

The woman didn't want the collection, but she likewise didn't know what to do with it. She didn't want to just put it up for auction, because she wanted the collection to be shared with people who might love it the same way her late husband had. Calabrese bought it all, telling me he nearly needed to remortgage his house to afford it.

"His wife made me promise I would never, ever mention him when selling the bottles because it was his secret, it was his secret hobby," says Calabrese. "So I've kept the promise. But it was very good stuff."

Calabrese may have never met the man, but he still owns some of his bottles.

I THINK ANOTHER reason Ackerman was a bit stressed out about the supposed Hughes stash was because primo scores like this had become increasingly rare. As we headed toward the end of the 2010s and entered the 2020s, the days of major dusty hauls were dwindling. You certainly weren't going to just wander into a liquor store and find tens of thousands of dollars of vintage bottles of bourbon anymore.

Many of the more serious dusty hunters, like Ackerman, had begun to get more clever with their searching, following rumors and folklore for bottles that may not even exist, like career burglars looking for one final, legendary heist before they got out of the game for good.

Many other collectors had given up on dusty bourbon altogether—too hard to find, too overvalued—and began to branch out to other spirits categories, which still offered potential for exciting finds.

"I'm a little jaded, I guess. Very Very Old Fitzgerald 8 Years, I look at bottles of that every single day. Three times a day someone tries to sell me one," Brad Bonds told me. "So those might get everybody else excited. But me? I'm just like, eh, I've seen thousands in my life.

"Now? I love finding things *other* than bourbon."

When I started this book, my plan had been to almost exclusively write about the dusty bourbon that had started and then fueled America's twenty-first-century vintage spirits craze. But as I began to casually dig into other vintage categories—Chartreuse, rum, tequila, and more—and the collectors who pursued these dusties, I found them, in many ways, even more interesting.

"I feel like if you kill a cow and you're only using the filet mignon, like, what the hell are you doing?" says Bonds, referring to collectors who acquire big dusty hauls and then ignore or even toss the liqueur, rum, tequila, and other non-bourbon bottles.

Now, after delving into these categories over the past couple of years, I'd dare argue that they, in fact, are the filet mignon of the vintage spirits cow, not dusty bourbon. And many are still priced like ground beef.

For one, the flavor profiles of these non-bourbon spirits from the past are radically different from the present, for a few reasons.

Say what you will about the bourbon industry, but it's always made its whiskey with incredible integrity and strict production parameters—it's legally had to since 1897.

Bourbon is always predominantly corn juice, always aged in newly charred oak barrels. Freshly charred oak is a powerful force, packed with complex flavors that are easily extracted by the bourbon as it ages. You're not going to taste flavor profiles that no longer exist by drinking old bourbon. You're going to taste the common notes of oak, namely, caramel, toffee, vanilla, maybe some coconut and baking spices. Older bourbon may be better in many people's opinion, mine included, but it was pretty much made the same way today's stuff is and will have a recognizably similar palate.

Bourbon is the one category where the past tastes most like the present.

The same can't be said for many of these other categories, which offer a doorway to a past more artisanal and handcrafted, a past of mom-and-pop distillers not yet ruined by multinational conglomerates and worldwide distribution (and sometimes, even, electricity!), a past where tradition and quality were what mattered most, not efficiency and making a buck.

Bourbon is also, of course, an exclusively American product. America has been a mostly stable and mostly wealthy country for the last century and a half. That's not to say that bourbon history and this country's distilling history are uninteresting; it just doesn't exactly serve as a microcosm that can teach us a ton about the world "back then."

Delving into tequila and rum and weird European liqueurs, however, can teach us so much about the past. It can teach us about religion, world economies, geopolitical issues, colonialism, labor, government persecution, and man's thirst for power. It can teach us about agriculture, industrialism, globalism, technology, and gustatory heritage. It can force us to examine the ways more powerful nations have often used and abused those peoples they saw as beneath them.

It can teach us that while we may like to romanticize the past, it's probably better to be drinking it in the present.

THE ONE AND ONLY DON HENNY

If Cognac starts the vintage spirits hobby for Calabrese, if Cognac is the early vintage spirit that American restaurateurs like Charlie Trotter were serving as we entered a new millennium, today vintage Cognac is pretty much ignored by modern collectors. As I mentioned earlier in this book, you can still often find pre-phylloxera Cognac bottles for less than a non-acclaimed bottle of 1970s Stitzel-Weller bourbon.

But there is one man who still collects Cognac: They call him Don Henny.

Back in 2019 he cold-emailed me, brashly claiming he was the world's greatest Hennessy collector. When I clicked on a link he included in the email—surprisingly, not a phishing scam—I encountered a nearly nine-minute-long video of a man in a tilted Los Angeles Angels fitted cap and baggy Hennessy T-shirt. In the video, standing behind a table covered with hundreds of Hennessy bottles, he spoke in a hard-to-place European accent with an Ali G–like cadence. "Wassup, Henny fam?" he says. "This ya' man, Don Henny."

"My collection, it really started by accident," Don Henny, whose real name is Olivier Cocquyt, eventually told me over a WhatsApp call. He was nineteen at the time, out drinking with a friend in Aalst, just outside Brussels, where he lives. "One night I saw it at a bar. I remember having heard it in songs from Mobb Deep, Snoop, Capone-N-Noreaga. I saw it and I thought, 'I know this. I know this Hennessy.'"

He tried it and immediately loved it. When he went to a liquor store the following day to buy his first bottle, he encountered a special release listed for 120 euros and pulled the trigger. The flavor profile was unlike anything he had encountered in a spirit before. He became obsessed, to the exclusion of any other brand of Cognac, and of work—rarely going to his job at a medicine factory so he could instead spend time on his collection.

"No brand can touch my soul or spirit like Henny," he says.

Don Henny, now in his forties, owns three handblown crystal carafes of Hennessy Richard Extra Cognac, made of one hundred eau-de-vie (brandy distillates) aged from forty to two hundred years. The $5,000 "prestige" product is displayed in his TV cabinet. He has a Hennessy First Landing 1868, an Asian-only export. He has five uber-dusty bottles of Hennessy 3-Star from the early twentieth century. He even has a hand-labeled "Cognac-Hennessy" he dates to the 1890s.

If you guessed that a small Belgian town doesn't exactly get a ton of rare Hennessy, you'd be right. Most of what Don Henny buys comes from other foreign collectors in what he calls his "worldwide Henny network." He used to have a "Russian guy," before the war against Ukraine started, who visited him five times a year with a haul of bottles. He once purchased a 1920s VSOP from a collector in Guatemala, which cost about $90 to ship to Belgium. He's visited the brand's headquarters in France, twice, and shopped "like a boss" while he was there.

Still, despite having one of the largest private Hennessy collections in the world—a collection so unreasonably large he began to thin it out a bit during the early days of the COVID-19 pandemic—there are a few bottles Don Henny doesn't own, like the Hennessy 8, which was released only in a 250-bottle run, and which Don Henny claims was presold to "rich guys." He also covets, but unfortunately can't afford, the Beauté du Siècle, "a very cool bottle" that comes in what he describes as a "huge coffin" and costs around $200,000.

Don Henny has bottles worth as little as $5 and as much as $10,000, though he has no idea what the entire collection would be valued at. But the last time I spoke with him, he told me with a lament that many vintage collectors must also think on occasion: "If I would calculate how much I've spent on Henny in my life, I could probably have bought myself a fucking Ferrari."

7

THE SEARCH FOR OLD MONK JUICE
AND TRAGIC WISDOM

IF COLLECTING VINTAGE spirits mostly seems like a new phenomenon, there were a few people from the past who collected vintage liqueurs.
As early as 1950, the *New York Times* wrote a "who's who" about one
Clifford T. Weihman of Pelham Manor in Westchester County, New York,
who had begun collecting vintage Bénédictine, a French herbal liqueur, some
twenty-five years earlier. By the time of the article, his vintage collection
was estimated at five thousand bottles, including a Clos de Griffier Vieux
Cognac bottled in 1788—the very same vintage that Salvatore Calabrese
would deploy for a record-breaking cocktail in 2012, which I'll get to in a bit.

"It has a penetration both in bouquet and flavor that is indescrib-
able," wrote the paper's longtime food editor Jane Nickerson. Weihman's
story of landing the Bénédictine was not much different from that
of many dusty hunters of the twenty-first century. He had stumbled
upon it in the cellar of Paris's Tour d'Argent, the restaurant famed for
its pressed duck. It took three visits to finally talk its proprietor, André
Terrail, into parting with the bottle.*

* Yet another 1788 Clos de Griffier would be auctioned off by Christie's in 2017 for $46,500.

In 1956 the *New Yorker* offered a hilariously pretentious article about a vintage tasting surrounding another French herbal liqueur, Chartreuse, conducted on Manhattan's Upper East Side that year.

"We were disconcerted recently to find ourself the sole acolyte at an exceedingly esoteric alcoholic ceremony—a comparative tasting of post-Expulsion and pre-Expulsion Chartreuse," the piece began.

It was held at the Hotel Westbury, on East 66th Street and Madison Avenue, and the writer joined two New York importers of the monk-made libation along with a local wine expert, William Massee, to taste modern versions of the "supreme contemporary cordial," according to the article, as well as versions of the green and yellow herbal liqueur that had been produced sometime between 1878 and 1903, right before the Carthusian monks who produce the elixir were briefly expelled from France by an anticlerical government. The article notes that, even in 1956, these rarities were selling for $150 apiece (about $1,700 in 2023 dollars).

None of this troika of experts thought the dusty Chartreuse would taste much different from what they could have gotten at the corner store at that time. Massee dismissed it as "an old gourmets' tale" that the liqueur would have somehow evolved, stating that anything more than 15 proof was incapable of changing in the bottle.

Of course, if we can debate whether dusty bourbon changes in the bottle, it quickly becomes self-evident to anyone who tries it that Chartreuse absolutely transforms in the bottle, and even Massee would immediately realize that as well. The pre-expulsion liquids had become paler in color, less sharp, more delicate, drier, and even more herbaceous.

"The pre-Expulsion Chartreuse," claimed the writer, "has all the delightful qualities of the new, plus tragic wisdom. The difference resembles that between *As You Like It* and *The Tempest*."

If Chartreuse would mostly fall out of favor in America over the ensuing decades—with sales cratering in the 1980s—the modern cocktail revival of the early twenty-first century would bring it back to the forefront for bartenders, who needed this "old monk juice" to revive several classic cocktails like the Last Word. That was what initially drew Joaquín Simó into Chartreuse when he was working at Death & Co, the iconic cocktail bar in New York's East Village. A former religion major at Boston University, I have to wonder if a different form of spiritual curiosity didn't play a part for Simó too.

By 2012, Simó's consulting group, Alchemy Consulting, was set to open its first bar, Pouring Ribbons, on the second floor of an establishment at the corner of East 14th Street and Avenue B. One of Simó's partners, Troy Sidle, had recently visited The Office in Chicago and tried vintage Chartreuse for the first time. He was floored, and he immediately pitched Simó on the idea of having an entire vintage Chartreuse program at Pouring Ribbons. Since they didn't have the back bar space for an exhaustive spirits list, Simó thought focusing on an obscure niche like this would be a great idea.

This was the final year before eBay ended liquor sales, so the Pouring Ribbons team was still able to use the online auction site to begin stocking up on vintage bottlings. If today Chartreuse might be the second-most-valuable vintage category after bourbon, back a decade ago, dusty bottles could still be acquired for nothing. Since the bottle design hasn't changed much over the years, many decades-old bottles could likewise sit on liquor store shelves without proprietors even realizing how long they had gone unpurchased.*

---

* To date a bottle of Chartreuse produced since 1991, when Frederick Wildman and Sons became the importer, which it still is today, look at the six-digit number on the lower gold band at the top of the bottle. Take the first three digits of that number and add that to 1084, the year the Carthusian order was formed and the monks founded their monastery in the Chartreuse mountainside. Previous to 1991, you'll want to see who the importer is on the label: Shently from 1933 into the 1940s, Schieffelin and Sons from the 1940s until 1969, Sussex from 1969 through 1981, and 21 Brands from 1981 to 1990.

"There wasn't any real demand for it," says Simó. "We weren't competing with anyone for this stuff."

Sampling different bottles and vintages, the Pouring Ribbons crew was blown away by how massively different each was. Some were flat-out terrible, most likely stored in direct sunlight or heat, which surely cooked the sugars inside the bottle. Some had completely lost their vibrant green or yellow color. In some bottles the liquid had even turned brown.

What I personally love about vintage Chartreuse is how the sugars inside almost crystallize, creating an incredible mouthfeel; if you look at the neck of an old bottle, it will look like it's lined with rock candy. Simó, however, struggles to describe what happens to Chartreuse as it ages in the bottles, since "there's still so much that we don't actually know about what is actually in Chartreuse," he says. The monks claim that 130 plants go into making their liqueur, but they don't reveal what those are; only two living monks know the full recipe. Simó has even been to the distillery, where he was unable to acquire any further information.

"We had some bottles of green Chartreuse that had this super bright, fresh note. And you're like, this is a forty-year-old bottle. How does this still taste so fresh? Whereas a lot of others, you lost a lot of the brightness, and you had a lot more of those, like, lower notes that had come up," he says. "Some [vintages] move away from the herbal and toward the spice. And sometimes it's sweet spices like cinnamon, and sometimes it was savory spices like caraway or cumin. We had one bottle that almost tasted like a kümmel [a German liqueur flavored with caraway seeds, cumin, and fennel]. It was wild how savory it had gotten. I loved that variable of never really knowing what was going on."

That unpredictability is what excites many collectors as well.

Simó discovered he particularly loved the Chartreuse de Tarragona that the monks produced while they were in Spain from 1904 to 1989. (Some monks had been allowed to return to France starting in 1929.)

Since there have mostly been only five American releases of Chartreuse over the years—standard Green and Yellow, the oak-aged VEPs (French for "exceptionally prolonged aging") of both colors, and Élixir Végétal de la Grande-Chartreuse, a 69% ABV release claiming to be a health tonic—there are not as many Chartreuse unicorns to pursue as there are in other categories.

Yet Simó still acquired one.

Chartreuse Eau-de-Vie was a brandy distilled as the base for Chartreuse in 1941, thrown in a sherry cask, and apparently forgotten. It was finally released to market in 1990 as a bit of a historical oddity. Simó claims he has only ever seen one other bottle of it. That bottle, and everything else, was cleared out (in other words, *drunk*) by regulars before Pouring Ribbons closed in April 2022.

The bar had survived the pandemic via to-go cocktails, but like many New York bars, it couldn't survive the end of its lease.

Chartreuse, however, still marches on.

KEY LIQUEUR DUSTIES

Aside from bourbon, there's perhaps no more sought-after vintage category than dusty liqueurs. Not all of them, of course, but a wide variety, ranging from French herbal liqueurs like Chartreuse and Bénédictine to amari from various, unique Italian regions to even fernet and Jägermeister. Liqueur is the only vintage alcohol that unquestionably changes as it ages—for the better, many people would say, as time calms down any alcohol burn while concentrating key flavors.

Vintage liqueurs typically fall into two key categories: those for sipping and those necessary to make vintage cocktails, something that will be detailed further in "Key (and Necessary) Vintage Cocktail Ingredients," page 166.

KING OF THE ALPS

ALL CHARTREUSE

Pretty much all dusty Chartreuse is of great value, and worth tasting, but there are a few eras and bottlings of particular note, with the higher-proof Green almost always being more desirable than Yellow of a similar vintage. Pre-1940s and Tarragona-produced Chartreuse ("Liqueur fabriquée à Tarragone par les Pères Chartreux") is a fun, and quite expensive, curio.

TOP DUSTY LIQUEURS

CAMPARI (NOW WITH BUGS!)

Until 2006, the most famous of the Italian bitter liqueurs was colored red via bugs—more accurately, cochineals, a parasite native to the

Americas that lives on prickly pear cacti and lends color to lipstick, fabrics, food coloring, and (once upon a time) Campari. Many believe that these older bottlings have more body than current iterations, and, just like Chartreuse, the liquid most certainly ages in the bottle, its sugars crystallizing and intensifying. In Mexico and Sweden, both of which have stricter regulations on the use of artificial colorings, Campari is still made using cochineal. (I'm a little surprised "Mexican" Campari hasn't become a hot item on cocktail bar menus the same way taquerias will tout their Mexican Coca-Cola made with cane sugar.) The ABV of Campari is also different from country to country—as low as 20.5% in most African countries to as high as 28% in Brazil and Jamaica—often dependent on tax laws. While dusty, bug-included Campari is fun to drink, it's more often deployed in vintage Negronis, the most-often-made vintage cocktail. (Look for Campari Cordial as well, a white-labeled, raspberry-flavored liqueur produced by the brand until 1992.)

OTHER AMARI

Aside from Campari, other well-known amari—Italian bitter liqueurs—from today, like Cynar, Averna, and Montenegro, are likewise coveted from the past when they were simply better made, less factory-produced. They aren't easy to find in Europe per se, but for now, locals there have less interest in the category than Americans, so they can still be dusty-hunted, especially in small villages, especially in miniature form, especially of brands you've never heard of, though there is a clear starting era for what could even possibly be found. "It's rare to find anything pre–World War II as that was the turning point for amaro's transition from pharmaceutical mainstay to being consumed commercially for pleasure," notes my friend and the author of *Amaro*, Brad Thomas Parsons.

AMER PICON

Like Campari, Amer Picon is a bitter liqueur still made today. Unlike Campari, however, this French liqueur, created by Gaëtan Picon in 1837 and made of oranges, gentian, and cinchona, hasn't been available in the United States since the 1970s. That's because the liqueur includes calamus, a plant often used medicinally that is banned by the FDA. (Even in Europe, pre-1970s bottlings are at 39% ABV, while today's releases hit at a measly 18–21%, depending). It's needed for classic cocktails like the Brooklyn, so American bartenders like canon's Jamie Boudreau have tried to make their own versions of the ingredient to fill the void—his "Amer Boudreau" combines Ramazzotti, an orange tincture, and Stirrings Blood Orange Bitters.

KINA LILLET

As with Amer Picon, this is another French product no longer made in America (sorta) and, likewise, another liqueur absolutely necessary to make a period-correct cocktail, in this case, James Bond's Vesper. ("A dry martini," he said. "Three measures of Gordon's, one of vodka, half a measure of Kina Lillet. Shake it very well until it's ice-cold, then add a large thin slice of lemon-peel. Got it?") The aperitif wine originally was produced with cinchona bark from Peru, which contains quinine, an alkaloid compound that could fight off malaria. By 2006 the quinine had been removed from the recipe, as was the Kina in the name, and the far-less-bitter Lillet remains on U.S. store shelves. Salvatore Calabrese claims he might have the largest collection of Kina Lillet in the world, which he continues to use for vintage Vespers at the various bar programs he manages and consults for.

NON-BRANCA FERNET

While dusty bottles of Fernet-Branca, the saffron-packed liqueur, produced since 1845 and today's category leader, are a fun, often tasty collectible, many dusty enthusiasts enjoy finding examples of fernet from a previous non-monoculture era of the category. Fernet Stock, for instance, produced in Plzeň-Božkov (in today's Czech Republic) since 1927, was at one time a serious competitor to Branca, and considered by many connoisseurs today simply tastier. Martini & Rossi also has a great one from the past, Amaro Fernet. There's Fernet-Pilla, Felice fu Domenico's Fernet-Vittone of Milan, Cimagrappa Fernet-Milano, Fernet-Arfe, Fernet Bergia, Fernet Everest, Fernet Gambacciani, Fernet Gavioli, Fernet Luoni, Fernet Stravecchio Aquila, Fernet Vittone, and even Grandi Liquori Fernet Tonic. Many connoisseurs like 1960s-era examples of all of these, finding them drier and more refined than today's ubiquitous Branca.

OTHERS WORTH SEEKING

BÉNÉDICTINE

As mentioned, Bénédictine was one of the ur-dusties collected by a much earlier generation of vintage liqueur enthusiasts. For whatever reason, it is not as sought out as much today—the unattractive, static bottle design surely does it no favors—though, like Chartreuse, it's an herbal, French monk-made liqueur that changes in the bottle. The one negative compared to Chartreuse is the lower proof, at 40%–43% ABV, depending on year of release.

UNKNOWN ALPINE LIQUEURS

Even more off-the-radar than Bénédictine are alpine liquors that are now defunct and unknown but might be every bit as delicious. Pretty much any old amaro bottle with snowcapped mountains and/or conifers on the label will be pretty interesting. Remember, a lot of these European liqueurs were small-town, mom-and-pop-type operations, so there's plenty of good stuff from the past that never garnered any sort of fame then, or certainly today. "Some of the most interesting bottles I've ever tasted are things you've never heard of," Seth Weinberg told me. There's also vintage Braulio, of course, an Alpine amaro that remains findable and beloved today.

ANISEED LIQUEURS

Namely, old Pernod and old Ricard, which combined to form Pernod Ricard in 1975. Today the conglomerate is more known for a portfolio that has Jameson, Absolut Vodka, and Malibu Rum, among a zillion other brands. But back then, back when they were each separate brands, they produced licorice-tasting liqueur that was so much better than what you'll find today.

UNEXPECTEDLY COOL

JÄGER BOMBED

Yes, old Jägermeister! While the German liqueur has become a bro-centric dare shot in twenty-first-century America—often dispensed from Ice Kühl tap machines—old Jäger has often mellowed into something resembling a high-quality amaro or fernet and can still be found for a steal. Now, if only you had some vintage Red Bull. . . .

SOCO

Another liqueur seen as a trashy college kid drink today, examples of Southern Comfort from the past are quite tantalizing. That's because, prior to 1979 when Brown-Forman acquired the brand, Southern Comfort was actually made with quality bourbon then macerated with citrus, vanilla, and spices. Any bad SoCo you shot when you were younger was probably made from a neutral grain spirit lightly flavored with whiskey. (In 2017, new owner Sazerac restored a legitimate whiskey base.)

8

THE MONA (LISA) OF RUM

STEPHEN REMSBERG HAD been on the hunt for Mona for thirty years.

A maritime attorney living in suburban New Orleans, he was one of this modern era's earliest dusty collectors, and rum was his passion. His home had a room with each wall stacked floor to ceiling with dusty bottles: pre-Prohibition Cuban rum and pre–World War II Jamaican rum, early era New England rum, and oddball rums from unexpected places like Uganda and Egypt. But there was one bottle of rum Stephen Remsberg had never been able to find.

Myers's Mona was a 30-year-old Jamaican rum discontinued in 1947 because, thirty years earlier, in 1917, the Kingston distillery that once produced it had burned down and was never rebuilt.

And though Remsberg had searched for it his whole life, it was Martin Cate, a bar owner, rum connoisseur, and friend of Remsberg's who found it one day on a high, dusty shelf in a San Francisco restaurant that had just recently shut down.

"The label was all faded. It was just like Indiana Jones, where I blew the dust off of it. And the word 'Mona' in faded type suddenly appeared," recalls Cate. "I almost screamed. The greatest rum collector of all time has been looking for it for thirty years with no luck. So it was an incredible experience to be able to give it to him."

Unlike with bourbon, dusty hunting is not exactly something that existed for rum collectors, for reasons we'll get to in a bit.

Also unlike bourbon, which may have been better in the past but still tastes fairly similar, dusty rum can transport us to a past that no longer exists, while teaching us about previous distillation practices, cultures, and cocktail history, and even forcing us to grapple with colonialism and slavery. That whole tragic wisdom thing again.

Finally, unlike bourbon—or Scotch or tequila or even Chartreuse—rum is the one major spirit that comes from everywhere. Rum has been and still is produced in numerous countries on every continent and has been imported to and bottled in many more. That makes picking one single location to focus your dusty hunting an impossibility.

A key demarcation point, if not a tectonic shift in rum history, occurred when the University of Puerto Rico opened a $500,000 rum research laboratory and pilot distillery in 1953. Essentially, this was the point where multicolumn stills became the norm throughout the rum industry. These are two tall vertical tubes, filled with porous plates on the inside, that can continuously distill a liquid. They are great for highly efficient production—great for a post–World War II world becoming more globalized—but not necessarily great for retaining flavor, as they endlessly strip and rectify a spirit until it is mostly lacking in character.

But when Facundo Bacardí Massó first started making rum in Cuba, he was using a pot still just like everyone else had in the nineteenth century, and he was producing his rum very slowly, very inefficiently, in small batches. It's what got his rums a certain notoriety throughout the world, winning a gold medal at Philadelphia's Centennial International Exhibition of 1876—the same world's fair where Alexander Graham Bell's telephone and Heinz Ketchup were first introduced. By the early twentieth century, he had switched to a Coffey still—more efficient than a pot still, but still able to pump out very flavorful rums.

"The rums that were justifiably famous through Prohibition for Americans traveling down to Cuba are these 1930s, '40s-era Cuban rums that were all made on two-column Coffey stills," says Cate. This early, Cuban Bacardí reawakened Americans' love affair with rum—a love affair they had divorced from on July 4, 1776, when American revolutionaries immediately turned their backs on anything the British loved. This light and clean Cuban-style rum is still most Americans' preferred style of rum even today.

Other Caribbean islands didn't see as many thirsty American visitors during this era, however, forcing these distilleries to change their production plans a bit.

"With Prohibition, the Caribbean's largest market for rum was shut down," explains Cate. "So a lot of Caribbean rum really just sat in casks and got older and older and older, and in many cases, better and better and better."

A post-Prohibition world would see the rise of tiki bars, fanciful and fictionalized tropical escapes, notably from Ernest Raymond Gantt (taking the nom de guerre "Donn Beach"), who opened his Don the Beachcomber in Hollywood in 1933. Suddenly, there were willing buyers for these Prohibition-matured rums of what Cate calls "crazy ages."

Early menus would offer a full page touting "Fine Rums from Don the Beachcomber's Cellar" that, even today, would be the envy of any rum bar on planet earth: Ron el Infierno at 20 years old, Palau Cuban rum at 30 years of age, Treasure Cove Jamaica Rum at a startling 32 years old (and a buck thirty a glass!), and, yes, Myers's Mona (only 85 cents!)

"Don's mission when he launched was to try to restore in the American eye the glory of this spirit," says Cate.

It would certainly work with Remsberg, who fell in love with these sipping rums as a young man attending Northwestern Law School in

Chicago in the 1970s; he became a regular at the Beachcomber location there—by then owned by Don's ex-wife Cora—sampling from a display case that offered pre–World War II rums.

In turn, Remsberg began his own collection in 1973—his unique job would send him to countries and islands where he could stalk stores for interesting bottles. He'd vacation in Jamaica and Barbados and stuff fifteen bottles in his suitcase per trip.

In the 1990s, shopping on Magazine Street in New Orleans, Remsberg found a wooden crate in a secondhand shop. Inside it were uber-rare bottles of 1925 Bacardí, the aforementioned pre–World War I Jamaican rum, and a 40-year-old rum from Sloppy Joe's, the famed Havana haunt that Hemingway frequented—Remsberg landed them for five bucks apiece.

When eBay launched in the late 1990s, Remsberg claims he was maybe the first spirits collector around to start raiding it for all of dear old Grandpa's collections that had been thrown on the auction site after a death. At every step of the game, he was the collector ahead of everybody else.

(Unfortunately, I was never able to interview Remsberg, who developed Alzheimer's and died at age seventy-five during the writing of this book.)

The other key tiki maven of the mid-century era, "Trader Vic" Bergeron, likewise tried to offer neat pours of well-aged sipping rum to his clientele. But as Cate often points out, by the time of his 1974 book *Rum Cookery & Drinkery*, even Bergeron was lamenting that he had failed at that endeavor. He would find a ton more success, however, with an original rum cocktail he engineered in 1944.

"We talked about creating a drink that would be the finest drink we could make, using the finest ingredients we could find," he wrote in another book, 1973's *Frankly Speaking: Trader Vic's Own Story*.

Bergeron would use a half ounce of French Garnier Orgeat and another half ounce of DeKuyper Orange Curacao along with some rock candy syrup and the juice of one fresh lime. For the rum, he reached for two full ounces of Wray & Nephew 17 years old, one of those over-aged rums produced during Prohibition.

He called this drink the Mai Tai.

"The fact that he was using something so luxurious as this seventeen-year-old product for his everyday drink speaks to how cheap it was," says Cate, who quit his job in transportation logistics to bartend at one of the few remaining Trader Vic's locales in the early 2000s. (In fact, the Wray & Nephew distillery was aging rums in Jamaica for up to thirty years at the time.) "And I wish we could have stopped him and said, slow your roll."

The Mai Tai, in fact, became so popular that Trader Vic burned through Wray & Nephew's aged stocks, selling the cocktail faster than it could produce and age the rum. Bergeron would eventually be forced to swap in a 15 year old before he started stretching that out by adding Red Heart and Coruba Rum, more affordable and lightly aged Jamaican dark rums. Eventually he began to use a dark rum from Martinique.

Cate, who opened Smuggler's Cove, a rum and tiki bar in San Francisco, in 2009, has one of the world's three known bottles of 17 years old, but he has never opened it, leaving it sealed in a climate-controlled storage facility. Cate does own and has tried a slightly less rare Wray & Nephew 20 years old from the same era, giving him some unique insight as to how the vaunted 17 years old would have tasted both neat and in a Mai Tai.

Jeff "Beachbum" Berry would also be critical in researching the value of finding dusty rum to know what tiki cocktails of yore would have tasted like. A Hollywood punch-up writer (*Inspector Gadget*) who once even directed a TV movie starring Olympia Dukakis, he became a sort of hobbyist looking to create these drinks from tiki's glory days. Acquiring out-of-print recipe books and old menus, Berry kept noticing something called Dagger dark Jamaican rum appearing in the specs.

Frustrated, he scoured Los Angeles–area liquor stores until he finally found some bottles—little did he realize he'd inadvertently dusty-hunted for something that hadn't been produced in decades.

Berry, who has since written numerous works of scholarship on the tiki world, and now owns his own bar in New Orleans, Latitude 29, has helped figure out the correct ingredients and rum profile needed for many tiki classics like the Zombie. In 2007, Remsberg would even invite Cate and Berry over to his house for Zombies made with the exact same dusty rums that Donn Beach would have used in the drink: Ronrico Red Label Puerto Rican, a Lemon Hart 151 Demerara Rum from the era, and an extremely rare Lowndes London Dock Jamaican that Remsberg had found a mere mini of. Though there was only enough for the men to share a single vintage Zombie, Berry would still call it the greatest thing he had ever drunk.

Unlike other categories, however, the rum world—propelled by these modern tiki bartenders and enthusiasts—has done a pretty good job at trying to recreate the flavor profiles of vintage rums that eventually went defunct, such as the case for Smith & Cross, a 114-proof 100% pot-still-produced Jamaican rum released in 2009 that could stand in as a bit of an analogue to those legendary Jamaican rums Donn Beach and Trader Vic were pouring. When Lemon Hart 151 got scarce for a few years while in the hands of beverage conglomerate Pernod Ricard, importer Ed Hamilton created his own Hamilton 151 Overproof. Hamilton would likewise team with Berry to release Beachbum Berry's Zombie Blend rum in 2021.[*]

As mentioned earlier, there were never really glory days of dusty

---

[*] Rum nerds had long wondered why the Campari-owned Wray & Nephew refused to offer an aged version of the brand; that was until 2023, when it released, and I got to taste, Appleton Estate 17 Year Old Legend, "a re-creation of the legendary rum crafted by J. Wray & Nephew in the 1940s." Its retail price was $500.

hunting for rum like there were for bourbon. Most island nations didn't export any rum to the United States or the United Kingdom in the twentieth century, so there simply wouldn't be much dusty stuff to find, if any at all. Many experts even wonder if stuff like Wray & Nephew 17 years old was ever even sold via retail, or strictly sent to these popular tiki bars.

Today almost all vintage rum is found through auction. That was how the so-called Rum Tasting of the Century came to be on September 13, 2018. Organized by Luca Gargano, the Italian CEO of rum importer Velier and now the preeminent rum collector in the world with more than fifty thousand bottles—he would also acquire Remsberg's collection shortly before the latter's death—and held at the Four Seasons Hotel at Ten Trinity Square in London, it drew several top rum experts from across the globe to taste several unicorns.

The tasting included a bottle of Saint James 1885 (Martinique "inhabitant rum," a cane juice rum then drunk only by locals and never exported), Bally 1924 (Martinique's first vintage rhum agricole), and a Skeldon rum from Guyana distilled in 1978; one taster, journalist Jason Wilson, couldn't help but point out that was the same year cult leader Jim Jones had led his followers to drink the Flavor Aid and commit mass suicide in the nearby Guyanese jungles. Tragic wisdom, yet again.

There was also a 1780 bottle of Harewood rum from Barbados, the oldest dated rum in existence, though one that was not without its own ominous past.

The Harewood estate in North Yorkshire, United Kingdom, was built by sugar, cotton, tobacco, and banking magnate Henry Lascelles, who had arrived in Barbados in 1711 at the age of twenty-one. Three hundred years later, his descendant Mark Lascelles, brother of the eighth Earl of Harewood, found twenty-eight handblown, unlabeled bottles while doing inventory in the cellar.

These were literally the dustiest bottles I have ever seen; covered in cobwebs, dirt, mold, soot perhaps, and looking like they'd been caught in the eruption that destroyed Pompeii and coated in black, volcanic ash. But they cleaned up pretty nicely, and the wax enclosures were still sealed well. A discovery of the estate's Cellar Book found an entry from July 1805 that confirmed they were surely the oldest rums in existence ("cane spirit," they are called in the book), bottles of both light and dark rum, imported to England from the family's Barbados plantation. Today some of the plantation is now in the hands of Mount Gay, the island's most famous rum producer.

The first twelve bottles sold for a quite reasonable £8,225 each at the Christie's auction in 2014, with Gargano getting his hands on at least one of them. To deal with the fact that this rum had almost certainly been produced by enslaved people, the proceeds were donated to a local charity focused on the West Indies.

"Drinking old rum forces you to think about things like colonialism, slavery, American hegemony in the Caribbean and Latin America, and the significant disparity between the poverty of the workers who cut sugarcane to ferment and distill, and the wealth of those who enjoy the end product," wrote Wilson of the tasting.

The other tasters, including Matt Pietrek, a rum connoisseur who posts online as "Cocktail Wonk" and who has written the indispensable eight-hundred-page behemoth *Modern Caribbean Rum*, found the 69% ABV rum outstanding, with notes of watermelon juice, fried bananas, molasses, and dark chocolate—a complex beast.

"This puts to bed the notion that the rum of the past was a horrific concoction," wrote another attendee, Steven James of the *Rum Diaries* blog.

Or, as Pietrek told me of the Harewood tasting:

"For people who study rum, we can hypothesize all we want, we can read about how it was made and this and that. But the actual tasting, for that five minutes or so that the rum is in the glass and you're enjoying it, it's like you're in a little time machine. You get to go back in time, and you're frantically trying to record your perceptions of it.

"Before it's gone forever."

KEY OLD RUMS

As mentioned, most vintage rum today is only going to be found at auction. And even that is wrought with red flags to be aware of. Old rum, you will find, unfortunately, has often been stored way worse than dusty whiskey; bottles have perhaps traveled around the globe more often. The higher the proof, however, the more likely it is to be in good shape. Likewise, there are tons of dusty rums from brands few have ever heard of, making counterfeiting—something we'll get into more in a few chapters—or "what the hell is in that bottle?" more likely.

Of note: with a few vintage brands, mostly those from English-speaking countries like Jamaica and Barbados, you will see some of their exceptionally long-aged rums labeled as "liqueur" or "liqueur rum." That is not to say these are sweet or have sugar added like we might expect from a liqueur today but is more to denote to a customer of the time that the rum would have been best deployed as an after-dinner, with-dessert type of libation.

THE HOLY GRAIL

WRAY & NEPHEW 17 YEARS OLD

It was distilled during Prohibition, and the immense popularity of the Mai Tai would lead to the well eventually running dry. If Salvatore Calabrese at one time had two bottles he cavalierly used to make vintage Mai Tais, today, Martin Cate claims, there might be only three bottles left on planet earth—and he has one of them. (A partially full bottle is on display at the Appleton Estate in Siloah, St. Elizabeth, Jamaica.)

OTHER GREATS
FROM THE PAST

PRE-COLUMN-STILL JAMAICAN RUM

Jamaica literally didn't have a column still on the island until 1968, which means all rums before that era were produced by a pot still and thus fairly heavy-bodied, certainly compared to, say, the Appleton Estate we might be used to in modern times. The Wray & Nephew 17 years old wasn't the only well-aged Jamaican rum exported to the States post-Prohibition. While not cheap or easy to find, Wray & Nephew 15 years old and 20 years old from this era are a little more readily available. Cate even still offers the 20 year old for $1,250 an ounce at Smuggler's Cove, a decent price if you think about it. (Cate prices vintage pours based on what he acquired the bottle for, not as the secondary market dictates.) Somewhat more affordable is the Dagger line also produced by Wray & Nephew until 1952—One Dagger (5 year), Two Dagger (6 year), and Three Dagger (10 year), as well as Dagger Punch (8 year). "There's this misconception that they were, like, incredibly funky," says Matt Pietrek, who notes that the funkiest stuff would have been added to blends, never bottled on its own like it is today. He says dusty Jamaica rum of a pre-1960s era tastes a bit like today's Smith & Cross.

PRE-CASTRO CUBAN RUM

Fidel Castro seized power in 1959 and within a year had nationalized the island's distilleries. The Bacardí family and top company executives immediately fled to Puerto Rico, where the brand is more famously produced today. There's likewise Havana Club, created in Cuba in 1934 and still produced today and exported internationally (except to America)—the fifth-biggest rum in the world, in fact, via a joint Pernod Ricard–Cuban government venture. The pre-revolution rum is not only built with a more flavorful production methodology, it also has the advantage of feeling like forbidden fruit to an American, which can be very exciting. These vintage rums offer a slightly higher proof, slightly more aging, and little more heft in the body than today's versions. (Bacardí also makes a Havana Club Rum in Puerto Rico—supposedly from the original Arechabala family recipe—that is legally sold in the United States.)

ORIGINAL ROYAL NAVY RUM

From 1850 until 1970, the British Royal Navy rationed out a "tot" of rum (about 2.5 ounces at 54.5% ABV, "navy strength") at midday to every sailor. Over the years it was composed of various rums from various British territories—British Guyana and Trinidad, mostly, as well as Barbados and Australia—and brought back to London to be thoughtfully blended. They were sent to ships in wicker-wrapped demijohns, essentially ceramic jugs measuring about a gallon. Though the rum is quite tasty and offers a lot of mystique, it is surprisingly not hard to come by for collectors. Demijohns often appear at auction and usually go for about a grand. Older vintages of Pusser's Rum—launched in 1982 to mimic the Royal Navy recipe, using some of the same distillery sources—would be of some interest as they would include liquid from the vaunted (and now shuttered) Caroni distillery.

THE CULT GHOST

CARONI

A newer dusty comes from this Trinidadian distillery that supplied a lot of rum to the Royal Navy. Founded in the early twentieth century, by 1975 it was government-owned and losing money until it eventually closed for good in 2003. Angostura acquired the vast majority of Caroni's eighteen thousand barrels, and Italian distributor Velier, run by famed rum collector Luca Gargano, acquired the rest. In 2005, Gargano began releasing cask-strength Caroni bottlings, all distilled in the 1980s, which immediately became a sensation among connoisseurs. Like old Willett for bourbon or ghost Port Ellen in the single malt world, any and all Caroni releases—some of which are still coming out—are as sought-after as rum can get. And as tasty too, though they are often compared to a "tire fire" in flavor and aroma. You'll have to try it to understand why that's a good thing.

THE "PAPPY" OF RUM

Foursquare Distillery was started in the mid-1990s by Richard Seale, an outspoken fifth-generation Barbados rum producer, who distilled in pot and traditional column stills and began releasing cask-strength unadulterated rums in the late 2000s. For years, these Exceptional Cask Series bottlings could be had fairly easily at "better" retail shops. Once the bourbon world fell in love with these well-aged, barrel-forward rums circa 2016, it was all over. Today, just as with brand-new releases of Pappy Van Winkle or George T. Stagg, speculative collectors would rather overspend for something modern and allocated than pay less money for something vintage and never to be made again.

OTHERS

SINGLE STILL RUMS FROM GUYANA
DEMERARA PRODUCERS

Today there is only one distillery on the island of Guyana, Diamond Distillery, which uses nine different stills repurposed from other

Guyanese distilleries that have closed over the years, some of these made from wood, to produce its current rums like the solid El Dorado line. But unblended single barrels from the ghost distilleries of Guyana's past offer collectors an incredible chance to taste rums, and sometimes, a flavor profile that simply no longer exists. (Starting in 2002, Gargano and Velier began bottling single still rums like Port Mourant 1982, Diamond 1982, Albion 1984, and Skeldon 1973 and 1978.) More readily found are old bottles of Lemon Hart 151 Demerara Rum, another purveyor to the Royal Navy rum blend as well as a critical cocktail ingredient in the early tiki era. Today it is owned and bottled by the Canadian-based Mosaiq Inc.

ANY MODERN NAME BRANDS FROM THE PAST

Just as a lot of today's lower-shelf bourbons were actually great in the past, the same holds true for rum, which was often made with more flavorful production techniques. Mount Gay, for example, once had a pot still and double Coffey still before switching to a multicolumn still starting in 2010. A lot of these old rums were caramel-colored too, and not like we understand it today, where Scotches are dosed with the additive E150. Instead, these old rums would have been colored with distillery-made caramel, which means you can distinctly taste caramel in these older rums, especially those from Guyana like Lemon Hart.

LEILANI HAWAIIAN RUM

Another popular dusty score is this not particularly great Hawaiian rum that was probably not actually produced in Hawaii. But it does have an odd-shaped bottle and a fun, postcard-like label that makes the bottle look great on your dusty-hunting Instagram account ("Follow my vintage journey at @dustydan4567"). First produced by Seagram's in 1965 for Expo 67, the Montreal world's fair in 1967, it was meant to appeal to staid Canadians looking for a tropical escape, though it seems likely, despite the cool packaging, that this was never made in Hawaii and was just bulk, kinda-decent Puerto Rican and/or West Indian rum.

9

WHY IS THERE SO LITTLE VINTAGE TEQUILA?

"UNLIKE ALL THE other spirits categories, why is there so little vintage tequila?" I asked Julio Bermejo, perhaps America's preeminent tequila scholar.

"The arrogant answer," he told me, "is because people in Mexico actually drank them all."

I didn't see that as an arrogant answer at all, because he was sort of right. If America had its bourbon glut, when locals favored drinking anything but their national spirit, that never really happened in Mexico. If anything, Mexicans undersold their beloved local spirit as a bit of a peasant drink, one reason it was ripe for being appropriated and repackaged as luxury by American companies.

There's also the fact that until the 1980s, 98 percent of tequila consumed in the United States was what is known as "mixto" tequila, a usually vile distillate produced from a minimum of 51 percent blue agave combined with up to another 49 percent other fermentable sugars, often high-fructose corn syrup, along with added coloring and flavorings. While still legally labeled "tequila"—you'll rarely see "mixto" on any bottle—its harsh taste turns off so many drinkers before they can ever get into this beautiful category. And that's why few vintage collectors would ever even want dusty tequila from a pre-1980s United States.

But Bermejo isn't 100 percent right.

There is, in fact, what we would call vintage or dusty tequila in America, and he very well may have been the first to collect it.

Bermejo grew up in a family that owned a Mexican restaurant in San Francisco in those days when they weren't ubiquitous throughout America. Tommy's Mexican Restaurant, as it was called, was opened in 1965 by his parents, Tomas and Elmy (and lies just a few miles from Martin Cate's Smuggler's Cove today). In the late 1980s, Bermejo was tasked with handling the restaurant's bar program, and he immediately saw a need to change his customers' opinions on Mexico's native spirit. To show them that it wasn't simply the wince-inducing mixto shot they'd last had in a frat house basement.

Luckily, an industry-changing 100 percent agave tequila had just made it to the country that decade, courtesy of another man who had also spent some time in the Bay Area.

ROBERT DENTON IS the number one icon to a certain breed of tequila collector; to Casamigos-swilling neophytes today, however, he's less important within the category than celebrity tequila mavens George Clooney, The Rock, or Kendall Jenner.

Born in Greenwich Village, the son of an artist and concert pianist who became a photography prodigy himself, Denton spent his early career photographing in-house fashion in Paris, before returning to the United States as a news journalist covering stories like the student protests in Berkeley. By the 1980s he was in the advertising industry, doing some work with Ketel One vodka, when he was offered a glass of tequila that would change his life.

"I had never tasted anything like it—and few Mexicans had tasted it either," says Denton, who was more familiar with quality tequila than most Americans of the era. Denton's parents had long had a vacation home in Mexico, and he'd even spent a year of high school in Mexico City, tasting 100 percent agave Herradura along the way. But nothing was as good as this tequila produced by Guillermo Gonzalez Diaz Lombardo exclusively for a private gentleman's club.

Denton and Marilyn Smith, his domestic partner, flew down to Tamaulipas, in northeast Mexico, to meet with the González family, heirs of former Mexican president Manuel González, at their Tequilera la Gonzaleña distillery. They quickly struck up a deal, and starting in 1983, Denton and Smith began importing their Chinaco, the first 100 percent agave premium brand brought into a United States still mostly stuck with mixto. The Chinaco 4 Year Añejo was the first tequila with an age statement, and Smith would serve it to curious people in a brandy snifter. (Sauza would almost immediately swipe this concept for an ad campaign featuring the motto: "The tequila that belongs in a glass by itself.")

Chinaco became a sensation among Americans just discovering quality tequila, coveted by celebrities like Kirk Douglas and Danny DeVito, sold on the black market for $300 a bottle, shipments hijacked by border bandits as trucks crossed into Texas. It even inspired Martin Crowley and shampoo mogul John Paul DeJoria to go down to Mexico and seek out the González family, hoping to filch them for their own luxury brand they were starting, Patrón. They'd end up finding a different, unrelated González family at the Siete Leguas distillery.

"The big thing that we did differently than anybody today is we gave all the credit to our distillers," says Denton. "We made our distillers the heroes, not ourselves. That's very different from what they're doing today."

Eventually Chinaco wasn't producing enough for Denton and Smith to continue importing it to America, and they went looking for another tequila. (Denton reintroduced Chinaco to America in 1993.)

Their friend Nicholas Faith, a famed British journalist and spirits writer, tipped them off to a distillery in Arandas, in the Los Altos Region of the state of Jalisco, some seven thousand feet above sea level, that was also making tequila the traditional way. This was La Alteña Distillery, long run by the Camarena family.

The Americans and Mexicans quickly hit it off, and by 1988, Denton had teamed with master distiller Carlos Camarena to create El Tesoro de Don Felipe (known by collectors as El Tesoro White Label or simply ETWL). Well-aged tequila, called *añejo*, wasn't really focused on by Mexican distilleries at the time, but Denton wanted some. Carlos, with Smith at his side, would sit in the cellar and try to put together a blend. Each batch would get a little better, until it became exceptional.

There's a reason Denton's two decades' worth of imports remain highly coveted.

"When you crack one of those Denton bottles," says Kristopher Peterson, the spirit archivist at Mordecai in Chicago, "you're tasting the birth of a category which is still gaining market share in the U.S. forty years later."

Peterson first fell in love with vintage tequila via an El Tesoro Reposado from 2003, dubbed "Olive Oil" by collectors due to its tall, squared-off bottle shape more befitting the kitchen counter. He loves its unusually heavy mouthfeel at 80 proof as well as some incredible watermelon and mint notes, unlike any other tequilas he has ever encountered. It's the key reason he remains such a fan of the Denton-era El Tesoro.

Just as with bourbon, early dusty hunters, among them Peterson, Pablo Moix, and Michael "Lippy" Lipman, an artist known online as the Tequila Whisperer, were able to scour liquor stores across North America to find these desirable bottles from tequila's recent past. Particularly savvy collectors, in the days before Facebook, would talk shop on the Blue Agave Forum online.

"These were guys that knew their shit and got in so early that it wasn't that hard for them to just walk into stores and find boxes and boxes of stuff," says Ernesto Hernandez, an Arandas-born, San Francisco–based Realtor who is also a top vintage tequila collector.

"I remember when I bought my first [dusty] bottle, it was on clearance," he recalls. "The store couldn't sell it. It retailed for $129, and they had dropped the price all the way down to, like, $70."

Other collectors have similar stories, like Moix, who cleaned out Mexico's Baja Peninsula of dusty tequila bottles that would eventually appear on shelves at his Los Angeles–area bars like Old Lightning.

Denton and Smith retired from the tequila game in 1999—health issues arose and, says Smith, "We were worn out and had nothing more to offer"—and as recently as 2000, the *New York Times* reported that only two other non-Mexican companies were truly involved in the tequila industry, and just as labelers and/or distributors. You had Don Eduardo, which was being distributed outside Mexico by Brown-Forman (more famously, the owners of Jack Daniel's), and Porfidio, packaged by a fast-and-loose Austrian named Martin Grassl.

Both would be criticized for allegedly ruining tequila in various ways. But the popularity of tequila meant that was bound to happen anyhow.

"What got me started [collecting vintage tequila] was my love of Herradura and the fact that they had said that they were purposely changing their recipe," Bermejo told me.

He had learned they were switching their aging vessels from used bourbon barrels to new charred oak—which can radically affect flavor, covering up delicate agave notes and making it far more caramel- and vanilla-laden. This was back in 1992 when Bermejo was still visiting tequila distilleries every few months on his own dime. Surely not trusting that this change would be for the better, Bermejo began snatching up any cases he could find of pre-1992 bottlings.

Herradura's reputation would decline even further starting in 2001 when it installed a diffuser on-site, a highly modern machine the size of a basketball court that is superefficient at extracting fructans (fructose sugars) from agave via high-pressure water and a bath of hydrochloric acid. (Smith compares diffuser-produced tequila to "canned spaghetti sauce.") And even more so when Brown-Forman acquired the brand in 2007.

That was just the beginning of a slew of multinational conglomerates taking over labels and, well, completely fucking up tequila.

"What would piss me off, what still pisses me off today, are distilleries changing their processes and not telling the people that sell their products it's changing," says Bermejo, who, incidentally, would marry Liliana Camarena Curiel, Carlos's sister, in 2006. "Unfortunately, in tequila today, there's been no change that has been for the better."

El Tesoro, however, is admittedly still pretty damn great today, still produced at La Alteña Distillery in Arandas, still made by the Camarena family. But when it's placed side by side with the stuff from the past, anyone can tell it's simply not as good as it used to be.

"It's night and day," says Hernandez, who still greatly respects Carlos Camarena, as do most tequila nerds. "Long story short, it definitely does not taste the same."

So you have to ask why.

Most obvious is that a post-Denton, Beam-Suntory acquisition increased the brand's distribution footprint. Less obvious is what that means.

Denton sends me a YouTube link to a home-movie-quality video he made in 1992 in which Smith, with the help of Carlos Camarena, walks viewers through La Alteña's agave fields, distillery, bottling hall, and aging cellars.

"The purpose of the video was to educate distributor salespeople about this groundbreaking artisan tequila," explains Denton. "It was literally made [to] travel back in time."

Indeed, it's a remarkable look into the recent past and an era of rustic, artisan craft that no longer exists.

We see agave field workers harvesting *piñas* (agave hearts) that are eight to twelve years old.

We see these hearts ground up by a tractor-pulled tahona (an enormous, volcanic stone wheel) while a barefoot worker, essentially in his underwear, shovels the ground-up agave fibers.

We see *batador* Don Pedro Coronado, shirtless, inside a small fermentation tank, the liquid up to his chest, breaking up the mash so it doesn't form a cap.

We see a still that's fueled by an 1870s-era locomotive boiler, loaded with the mash and distilled to exactly 80 proof—Marilyn sips some served to her in a cow's horn.

We see a facility completely lacking in electricity, no different from how things were when it was founded by Don Felipe Camarena in 1937: everything done by hand, everything hauled around by hand or balanced atop one's head.

"Tell me that El Tesoro production looks similar today under Beam-Suntory," says Peterson, who also sends me a link, to a Hollywood-quality video currently on El Tesoro's glossy, modern website, and he jokes, "I sincerely doubt you'll find Don Pedro Coronado's successor partially submerged in a small wooden fermentation tank separating the tahona-ground agave fibers by hand."

Instead, an older, more camera-comfortable Carlos Camarena proudly walks viewers through a drone-shot agave field, past stainless-steel tanks and Cleaver-Brooks boilers, through an orderly warehouse with barrels stacked to the sky.

"There are certain things like using the tahona that impart a very different taste than putting it through a metallic grinder," says Denton. "But the metallic grinder to a Mexican proprietor was a sign of success."

And that's what makes it hard to fully lament the days when tequila tasted better. To that Mexican proprietor, doing backbreaking labor at a distillery without electricity, you're never going to convince him to keep doing all these things just because it makes a "better" tequila preferred by a small subset of moneyed American tequila dorks.

"It's difficult to explain it culturally to a Mexican proprietor, and not just people we work with, that the old way is the way that the flavor came from," says Denton, who begged the Camarenas to build their new, modern distillery while still retaining the old facility as a sort of working museum. "Don't put in modern equipment. Put in more old equipment!" he claims he told them.

But the multinational conglomerates don't really give a shit about flavor. They care about efficiency and consistency, and the fact is that modern equipment—autoclaves and diffusers instead of brick ovens and earthen pits—is better at both, making it far easier to create a product that can be distributed to all fifty states and every continent. Far easier to help turn tequila into the $10 billion global industry it is now.

"It's impossible to increase volume with a boutique product, a handmade product," says Smith, and the best tequila is innately a handmade product.

Yet the Camarena family is still very serious about tequila, and El Tesoro (along with their Tapatio and Tequila Ocho brand lines) is still high quality, still mostly produced the proper way—certainly no diffusers—and still made using as many artisanal processes as a Beam-Suntory can allow. But being owned by a massive company with C-suite executives in Midtown Manhattan naturally changes things.

"Mostly not for the better," says Denton, who would sell the bulk of his remaining El Tesoro dusties to tequila collector Mark Glazier, who has hosted "Dentonfests" at his New Jersey home. "There's your real villain—the big companies."*

Another villain, you'd have to say, unfortunately, is the modern American's insatiable love affair with tequila—the category on pace to overtake vodka as the best-selling spirit in the country any day now. That has forced even the most serious producers, especially those controlled by the conglomerates of the world, to harvest the agave a little earlier than perhaps they should, no different from bourbon manufacturers today no longer having the luxury of aging their liquid as long as they might have in the past.

Less mature agave is less flavorful, so this has likewise led to some brands dosing their tequilas with additives—syrups to add sweetness, caramel coloring and oak extract to create the false appearance and flavors of age, glycerin to bolster mouthfeel—all to cover up bland or flawed tequila. Any additives under 1 percent by total weight don't even need to be reported on the bottle.

Feel free to blame climate change while we're at it, with droughts and the disruption of bat populations affecting agave pollination and cultivation.

Whoever you blame, it all brings us back to the yearning, *the need*, perhaps more than any other single spirits category, to find dusty tequilas from the past.

"What all this has taught us is that if we really like a certain batch of tequila, to buy all of it," says Bermejo. "Hoard it. And I've been doing that since the 1990s."

---

* . For what it's worth, today Chinaco is produced via roller mill, high-pressure autoclave, and stainless-steel distillation and imported by Hotaling & Co.; it is not very well regarded anymore. On the other hand, Guillermo Gonzalez Diaz Lombardo's son Germán González makes the cult extra *añejo* Tears of Llorona.

Today Bermejo defines vintage tequila as coming before a change in ownership or production. He continues to acquire old, tasty stocks when he stumbles upon them, like he did when he found a fifty-five-case pallet of 2006 El Jimador Añejo in a Brown-Forman warehouse in Kentucky.

It's also why many collectors think vintage tequila could soon be the "it" vintage category.

"I think dusty tequila will be a growing category in the next five years," says Seth Weinberg, who got his first vintage tequila client in 2022.

No doubt, for people just getting into tequila today, it's hard not to think we've already missed the glory days.

But with a little guile, perhaps we can at least still taste them.

KEY TEQUILA DUSTIES

If the Bottled-in-Bond Act of 1897 ensures that pretty much any vintage bourbon you stumble upon is going to be legitimate, the same isn't necessarily the case for tequila, in which additive dosing is rampant. If old bourbons can be traced to a certain distillery by their DSP number, tequilas can be identified by their NOM (Norma Oficial Mexicana), a four-digit number that has been on the back of every bottle of tequila since 1992 and represents the distillery at which the liquid was produced. More than any other spirit, tequilas from the past can open one's eyes to how great a category it used to be. "You'll try [vintage] tequila and think, 'This is the first time I've had tequila.' It just nullifies everything you've ever tasted," says Pablo Moix.

THE "STITZEL-WELLER" OF TEQUILA

ANY ROBERT DENTON IMPORTS

Starting in 1983, Denton and partner Marilyn Smith began importing some of the first 100 percent agave tequilas into the United States. His key brands were Chinaco (1983 to 1999) and El Tesoro de Don Felipe (1988 to 1999). The earliest Chinaco releases can be identified by paper label packaging; the next iteration evolved to a teardrop-shaped bottle, which was phased out a few years ago; by then, other distributors like Fielding & Jones and Preiss were handling the brand. El Tesoro de Don Felipe (initial bottles are known by collectors as El Tesoro White Label or simply ETWL) would last under Denton's aegis until 1999, when the company that would eventually become Beam-Suntory took over. Also highly sought-after is El Tesoro's excellent "Cognac-style" extra *añejo* called Paradiso, first released circa 1994, and aged in five different barrels including Old Boone bourbon barrels supplied by Julian Van Winkle III. (A second release, Paradiso Lot B, is said to be aged in Louis Treize [XIII] Cognac casks. By the time of Lot C, quality had drastically changed.) Specifically look for anything labeled "Imported By Robert Denton & Company LTD."

OTHER COVETED VINTAGE

EL TESORO 70TH ANNIVERSARY EXTRA AÑEJO

Even if the brand is now in Beam-Suntory's hands, it is still distilled by Carlos Camarena and, often, still very good. This 2007 release remains highly sought-after by collectors (ensuing 75th-, 80th-, and 85th-anniversary releases, the latter aged in Booker's Bourbon barrels, are of interest as well). "ET70th" is marked by its incredibly unique flavor profile, with many considering it the greatest extra *añejo* ever bottled—prices have soared over $1,000.

ANYTHING FROM NOM 1079

Defunct since around 2010, vintage brands from NOM 1079 in Jésus Maria, Jalisco, are still in high demand. These include 1921, Tesoro Azteca, Aha Toro, Frida Kahlo, Don Alejo, and Oro Azul, among others. Back when the distillery was NOM 1079, it had estate-grown agave and used old-fashioned production methods. When the facility switched NOMs to 1580, supposedly for tax purposes, many of those brands were discontinued, or moved to other facilities that didn't have such artisanal methods. The most sought-after brand from 1079 is Oro Azul and its handblown, frosted-glass, wax-top bottles.

EARLY JOSE CUERVO RESERVA DE LA FAMILIA

This annual, boxed release from Jose Cuervo is coveted and pricey (a little under two hundred bucks at retail), and it always manages to surprise tequila neophytes who typically think of Cuervo as headache-inducing swill. First released in 1995 to celebrate the distillery's two hundredth anniversary, bottles from that era can easily fetch four figures. Bottles remained coveted among collectors up until around 2005, when, it seemed to many, barrel notes began to dominate and cover up the lovely agave notes somewhat. A rare exception is an oddball Rolling Stones "tour pick" bottling from 2014. Another coveted Cuervo is the 1990s handblown *añejo* bottles featuring a reusable cork "dongle" hanging from the neck.

OLDER AND ONE-OFF
LOS ABUELOS/FORTALEZA

This is a relatively new brand, started by a Sauza scion in 2005 on the family's original distilling property using traditional production methods. It was initially named Los Abuelos ("The Grandparents"), but a cease-and-desist order from a similarly named rum brand led to it being changed in the United States to Fortaleza ("Fortitude"), which is what it still goes by. Thus, any of the original Los Abuelos labels sold in America are considered unicorns, those being the Lot 5 Reposado, Lot 16 Blanco, and Lot 42 and 43 Añejo. Fortaleza remains a cult favorite and highly coveted, especially its annual Winter Blend, aged in experimental barrels and first released in 2019.

THE POTENTIAL LAND MINE

PORFIDIO

A brand mired in controversy if not criminality, with dusty bottles that can potentially be home runs . . . or total disasters. It was started by a then-twenty-four-year-old Austrian, Martin Grassl, who, in 1991, contracted local Mexican artisans to produce a sleek bottle with a two-inch-tall green glass cactus—*not* an agave plant, as you might expect—inside and stuck to the bottom. (Lore claims that the brand is an accidental misspelling of Porfirio [Díaz], the dictator overthrown at the beginning of the Mexican Revolution. Online commentators would eventually wonder if the egomaniacal Grassl was actually telegraphing that he was Perfidious.) Initial bottles were priced at a jaw-dropping $150, yet it became a hit during America's earliest fascination with luxury tequila. "Transcendent," recalls John P. McEvoy, author of *Holy Smoke! It's Mezcal!*, who first tasted it in the late 1990s. These 1990s bottlings were well reviewed by critics, but the thing was, Grassl was merely sourcing other people's distillate (perhaps it was even mezcal, McEvoy reported), rectifying it, and packaging it in those gauche bottles (which is not a crime per se). Grassl would continuously lock horns over the years with PROFECO, a subagency of Mexico's Ministry of Commerce; by 2001 it had hit a fever pitch. Government agents went around Mexico preventing stores from selling Porfidio, while Consejo Regulador del Tequila, tequila's regulatory body, would no longer allow Grassl to call Porfidio "tequila" (he must call it agave spirit). He claims this all happened because Mexico is vindictive toward an outsider like him; people like Denton have claimed it was because Grassl was, at times, simply making agave-flavored alcohol. Under fear of arrest, Grassl fled Mexico in 2005—"If I had stayed I would have been in prison for four years," he claimed in 2007—and is reportedly now back living in Austria; he may have possibly sold ownership of Porfidio to a Russian company, or he may be making a tequila-like product using India-grown agave. None of this exactly matters. Nor does the fact that he often bottled it a hair under 40% ABV to supposedly take advantage of tax codes. Nor that some bottles don't even list a NOM. Certain collectors still greatly value older Porfidio, even despite those rumors, and even as numerous counterfeits are known to be in existence, specifically the brand's iconic Royal Blue Ceramic *reposado* bottle. (In 2009 there was even a Porfidio Fest held in Seattle and put on by the Blue Agave Forum.) Guessing which tequila—great, awful, legit, counterfeit, or mezcal—was actually in a bottle of Porfidio at tequila bottle shares would eventually become a parlor game. Caveat emptor.

SLEEPERS

THE FORGOTTEN, PRE-1980S 100 PERCENT AGAVES

It's a bit of a misstatement that there was absolutely no 100 percent agave tequila in America before Denton's era. There was actually a little; it simply wasn't labeled that way. There's La Parreñita and Tequila De Antaño from the 1960s, the latter produced by Ignacio González Vargas of later Siete Leguas fame. There's Sauza from the 1960s and into the 1970s, when it was sold in odd, lime-green porcelain bottles (collectors called them "Greenies"). A lot of it is incredibly eye-opening in terms of how agave-forward it tastes.

PRE-2001 HERRADURA

If Bermejo was interested in pre-1992, it's really 2001 that is the critical demarcation line. That's when a diffuser arrived at the distillery in

Amatitán and may have been put to use for Herradura bottlings. (El Jimador is made there as well.) The next demarcation line is around 2007 when Brown-Forman acquired the brand, and another dip in quality occurred. It's still undervalued on the secondary market; collectors are most interested in pre-Brown-Forman Herradura (when the Sazerac Company was distributing), especially its 46% ABV blanco.

CERTAIN (BELIEVE IT OR NOT) VINTAGE MIXTOS

Similar to bottom-shelf bourbon from the 1970s that actually had well-aged barrels as part of the blend, mixtos from the past were often made from properly matured agave. So many are a lot better than you might think, and at economical prices too, specifically the Jose Cuervo from the era that collector Ernesto Hernandez calls a "poor man's ET70th."

AND ONE MEZCAL FOR GOOD MEASURE

WAX-NECKED DEL MAGUEY

If there are few vintage tequilas to pursue, there is even less mezcal, a category that really didn't exist in America until the twenty-first century. Ron Cooper, a sort of Robert Denton for mezcal, would launch the Del Maguey brand of single village mezcals in 1995. While not extremely valuable, early bottlings with wax-dipped necks, some in brown glass like the Santo Domingo Albarradas village, remain a fun collectible.

THE MODERN DUSTY

"I used to wonder how my ancestors would have tasted tequila," says David Suro-Piñera, the longtime owner of Tequilas Restaurant in

Philadelphia, another early champion of the spirit when it opened in 1986. In 2017 he commissioned the production of Siembra Valles Ancestral Tequila specifically using painstaking, machine-less production methods including hand maceration of the roasted agave, ambient yeast fermentation, and distillation in a pine wood still. "It was completely the opposite of the way the industry is going with mass production," he says. And completely delicious.

10

THE DUSTY MIXOLOGIST

IT WOULD GET to a point where certain collectors had so many dusty bottles around that many thought: Why not combine them? Salvatore Calabrese, too, can be credited with creating the first vintage cocktails, but unlike many made today, he mainly did it as a lark. Back in the 1980s when he was first pursuing old bottles of Cognac, he'd often end up buying entire home bar collections from people and taking all the other spirits and liqueurs that they had accumulated over the years. That's how he ended up with two bottles of Wray & Nephew 17 years old in the mid-1980s. Absolutely no one had any interest in old rum at the time—certainly not to sip neat—so he turned them into vintage Mai Tais, which he sold for £5 a pop.

That made Calabrese even more curious about tasting cocktails the way past patrons would have. He just so happened to have landed a bottle of 1850 Sazerac de Forge et Fils—the Cognac that would lend its name to the Sazerac House and in turn to the Sazerac cocktail—as well as an era-appropriate bottle of Peychaud's Bitters.*

---

* It is said that the phylloxera issue would eventually lead to the Sazerac being made with rye whiskey instead, though some historians claim this is apocryphal and the cocktail *always* used rye.

"These were more for me than actually for selling, right?" he recalls. At the time, there was no margin, because who would buy a vintage cocktail at the price it would need to cost? "I just wanted to do that. It was fun to do."

But vintage cocktails did eventually catch on. Or, at least, became an incredible gimmick for garnering press, more so than any vintage spirit by itself has ever been able to land.

In the more than three decades since Calabrese stumbled upon the value of liquid history, he has essentially been canonized as a true GOAT bartender. In the ensuing years, "the Maestro" would move to The Lanesborough in the Knightsbridge district of London and create the iconic Breakfast Martini, a deliciously bittersweet combination of gin, Cointreau, lemon juice, and thin-cut orange marmalade served in a chilled cocktail glass.

He would launch his own bar in 2004, Salvatore at FIFTY in the Fifty St. James private members' club, followed by Salvatore at Playboy in Playboy Club London in 2010.

There he would enter the *Guinness World Records* in 2012 by offering the most expensive cocktail at £5,500 a glass. (He claims he made no profit and by market price it should have been £30,000.) Called Salvatore's Legacy, it was built off a vintage quartet of 1788 Clos de Griffier Vieux Cognac, 1770 Kümmel Liqueur (a German caraway- and cumin-based liqueur), 1860 Dubb Orange Curacao, and two dashes of early 1900s Angostura bitters. Nearly 750 years in one drink!

"For me, I was more interested to make the world's oldest cocktail, something that I know nobody else would ever be able to do," says Calabrese. "But unfortunately, the *Guinness* book did not recognize that—they only recognized that it was the most expensive."

Nonetheless, he got press and television coverage across the globe.

In the United States, meanwhile, Jamie Boudreau had begun to put vintage cocktails on canon's menu.

"It started off with making an Old Fashioned, and then I began to try other cocktails with the bottles I already had in my possession mixed with newer spirits," he recalls. "The results were impressive enough that I started searching for other vintage ingredients beyond whiskey, brandy, rum, and gin."

Early on, he might sell a single vintage cocktail every month or two. Now he sells enough to dedicate three full pages of the cocktail menu to them. "It is in these cocktails that we will transport one to an era when socializing with cocktail in hand was a magical, yet everyday occurrence," reads the menu.

Today there's a Pegu Club made with 1964 Booth's Gin, Cointreau from the 1930s, and, cheekily, the menu notes, lime juice circa 2023. (As Boudreau jokes: "If I could only find vintage juice and syrups, the world would be mine!") A Sazerac can be made with 1935 Cognac or 1945 Monticello Rye. The vintage Negroni at canon uses 1960 Tanqueray Gin, 1960 sweet vermouth, and 1970 Campari.

Because of its all-alcohol specs, somewhat easily findable and fairly economical dusty ingredients, the Negroni would, in many ways, become the darling of the vintage cocktail world. Indeed, it was the first full-vintage cocktail I ever tried, in the mid-2010s at an event at Dante in New York's Greenwich Village. I enjoyed seeing how the botanicals held up in the Plymouth Gin, tasting how the Campari had deepened and intensified, and what the slightly oxidized notes of the Cinzano Rosso vermouth did to such a familiar cocktail. But I was certainly glad someone else grabbed the tab for the $100 drink.

Martinis and Manhattans would become second and third among the most re-created vintage drinks, due to their being composed of 100 percent alcoholic ingredients and no juices or syrups. Experimental Cocktail Club, across town from Dante on the Lower East Side, offered a martini "the way Hemingway would have preferred it in his day," read the menu with 1950s Gordon's Gin. Jack Rose sold a $300 Manhattan with a 2001 bottle of 19-Year W.L. Weller whiskey and Cocchi Vermouth di Torino.

A few select amateurs like Eric Witz would likewise find themselves most interested in collecting vintage spirits from a classic cocktails angle. Living on the East Coast in the 2000s, Witz saw firsthand the cocktail renaissance with the emergence of seminal bars like New York's Milk & Honey (1999), Death & Co (2006), and PDT (2007) as well as Boston's Drink (2008). Bartenders were rediscovering classic cocktails like the Navy Grog and the Aviation. The only issue was that necessary ingredients like allspice dram and crème de violette were no longer commercially available.

"So I was kind of really excited and fascinated by that historical angle," says Witz, who was already an antique collector. "And that's how I started really getting into it."

All the more so when he discovered a bottle of 1940s Forbidden Fruit, a strange grapefruit-and-honey liqueur that has not been on the market for decades.

There were a few classic cocktail scholars emerging at this time— David Wondrich most notably—but they weren't actively searching for dusty old bottles like Witz was. He had found his niche.

The amusing thing is that Witz, who started this hobby in order to learn what classic cocktails might actually have tasted like, has not opened so many of these rare finds and tasted them because they're just too valuable. "It's the collector's dilemma," he notes.

Just like Calabrese, however, Witz did once open a 1945 Wray & Nephew with the label missing, which he suspects was the 15 years old, becoming perhaps the first American to taste a "correct" Mai Tai since the Trader Vic days.

Back a decade ago, friends and fellow collectors would buy entire lots of dusty bottles, keep the whiskey, and fob off the other spirits and liqueurs to Witz. The fact that he cast a wide net for vintage bottles meant he was early into buying things like dusty Campari and especially Chartreuse, which had recently begun to explode in value, though it actually has one of the oldest histories of vintage collecting.

Of course, not all bartenders or dusty collectors have been fans of vintage cocktails.

"Master distillers are like mixologists," Pablo Moix said in 2016, as the trend was picking up steam. "A well-made spirit is basically a cocktail in a bottle. The idea of having something that's perfectly distilled is much more exciting to me than making a vintage Manhattan."

Nevertheless, vintage cocktails sold quite well in the mid- to late 2010s.

In a place like a post-recession Manhattan, many drinkers would buy them, not to learn about the past but to simply show that they could afford to ball out. But the vintage cocktail was also a great way for bartenders to introduce geekier customers to oddball ingredients and drinks from a past era. It would also lead to more esoteric dusty bottles from the past suddenly becoming sought-after, like the previously discussed case of Amer Picon, an orange-flavored bitter necessary to make a Brooklyn, and Kina Lillet, a now-defunct aperitif wine needed for James Bond's Vesper.

The pinnacle of the vintage cocktail trend might have come with 2015's opening of The Milk Room, a pricey, eight-seat bar in the Chicago Athletic Association Hotel. The intimate space, helmed by Paul McGee, offered not only vintage whiskey, rum, and amaro, but vintage cocktails like a Hanky Panky that were made using ingredients dating to the 1940s. Once a month, McGee would hold ticketed events where he would make vintage cocktails entirely from one of his favorite cocktail books of yore, like Charles Baker's *The Gentleman's Companion* from 1939, which he referenced to whip up a round of Remember the Maine, a drink that included vintage Cherry Heering and Abbott's Bitters.

"The reason why this works so well is in part because of its surroundings," McGee noted at the opening. "This hotel is from 1893, and the building has been beautifully restored."

Seth Weinberg, too, had begun to make vintage cocktails at his latest gig. Bourbon Steak Nashville. He had started solely as a dusty whiskey collector, until around 2018, when he noticed that a bottle of 1910 Weller Dry Gin sold at auction for $1,046. Sure, it had the obvious connection to *that* Weller and Stitzel-Weller and the Van Winkles, but the bottle had been predicted to fetch only around three hundred bucks. Clearly, people were now very interested in making old cocktails, and Weinberg decided to start seeking out these vintage ingredients that would be less for sipping, more for mixing.

Hunting for dusty Weller Dry Gin—Weinberg just loved the squared-off bottle and label, with a horse's head underneath a horseshoe—he eventually found an almost-full case of some. Later, at an event held with Julian Van Winkle III, Weinberg matched it with vintage Campari and Gambarotta Vermouth Chinato to make "200-year-old" Negronis.

"That gin bottle could be worth $10,000 in five years, but I just don't think so," Weinberg says. "I think the story of me using them in a cocktail was more important to the historical aspect."

The gin tasted a bit off, however—something Van Winkle noticed as well. Sipping the gin straight, they both thought it was good, but highly unusual.

"So we were both kind of wondering, like, what is this? It tastes like some sort of gin, but nothing that we'd ever tried. It was definitely the oldest gin I'd tried at the time," says Weinberg.

Eventually Van Winkle decided to take a sample of it back to the lab at Buffalo Trace. When the lab tested its chemical compounds, the results showed absolutely no presence of juniper. There were other botanicals there, but no trace of gin's most inherent botanical.

Had the juniper "dropped out," as many people think happens to vintage gin, or was it never there in the first place?

Weinberg is uncertain, which is another thing that makes drinking vintage spirits such a fun mystery to unravel.

"Maybe that was just the taste of gin in America at the time," says Weinberg.

Not quite tragic wisdom, but wisdom nonetheless.

KEY (AND NECESSARY) VINTAGE COCKTAIL INGREDIENTS

For a while, the American secondary market really cared only about vintage whiskey. Then collectors began to move on to other aged spirits as well as liqueurs that could be enjoyed as a neat pour. The final vintage boom might be in ingredients needed solely to make period-accurate cocktails.

VINTAGE GIN

ACTIVE BRANDS FROM THE PAST

The interesting thing about gin, perhaps more than any other spirits category, is that a lot of the big brands of today have been around for decades, meaning that many of the same exact brands, often in fairly similar-looking bottles, are what you'll find when you go hunting. That might mean Beefeater, Plymouth, and Gordon's—all British labels, of course. Weinberg thinks there is still great value, or at least fun, in comparing a gin cocktail made with, say, modern Tanqueray to one made with a vintage bottling. Pre-Prohibition gins from these brands show not only a good value but also cool packaging from a past era, like Booth's octagonal "House of Lords" bottling. But many collectors will debate whether gin is the most *unnecessary* of vintage spirits. "Old bottles of Plymouth Gin are not wildly different from today's Plymouth," says Martin Cate, who also owns Whitechapel, an elite gin bar that became a private event space during the pandemic. Yet other collectors note that the botanical profile greatly changes once you get to the Prohibition era, with more pointed flavors of anise and cardamom punching through.

OLD AMERICAN GIN

If most major gin brands from the past have a distinctly British tilt, Calabrese is of the belief that one should make a vintage martini using gin from America, since that is where the cocktail was created. You're going to have to go way back to find any, however; aside from Seagram's and Gordon's (produced in three U.S. states starting in 1934), there wasn't a ton of different American-made gin from after Prohibition until 1996, when Anchor Distilling launched Junipero. Weinberg, too, likes these old bottles of American gin, especially if they offer a flashy name like Weller on the label.

THE VINTAGE
VERMOUTH DEBATE

One of the greatest debates of dusty enthusiasts: Should one use vintage vermouth? Due to being a fortified wine with a much lower ABV than most liqueurs and any spirits, vermouths have a high likelihood of oxidation. That's why many vintage cocktail enthusiasts will skip the dusty stuff altogether and use modern-day vermouths in their "vintage" cocktails. Others, like Weinberg, and me for the matter, enjoy seeing what a slightly oxidized vermouth can do to a cocktail. ("In sherry and Madeira, oxidation is an important thing," notes Weinberg. "So if you like those, you're probably going to like vintage vermouth too.") Still, no one wants a vermouth so oxidized that it tastes like cardboard. Thus, when buying vintage vermouth, more than with spirits, knowing how it's been stored over the years is vital. If you might take a chance on some dusty bourbon that was in a hot attic for all these years, it's simply not worth the risk for vermouth, which can easily get "cooked." Always check the neckline for evaporation. Vintage vermouth can still be readily found in places like Italy, France, and Spain, and you'll recognize many of the same brands seen today, among them Martini & Rossi, Cinzano, Carpano Antica, and Punt e Mes.

THE VINTAGE
BITTERS CONUNDRUM

Oddly, vintage bitters are damn hard to find and superexpensive on the secondary market if you do. When I learned this, I assumed the former fact might be due to the technicality that bitters have long been sold, not in liquor stores but in groceries and supermarkets, because the FDA classifies them as a food item—and indeed, people back in the baby boomer era did use them for salad dressings. Likewise, the only mainstream bitters for much of the last century was Angostura. But no, Weinberg tells me you can't find vintage bitters, and when you do they might run several hundred dollars per tiny four-ounce bottle, because the few major collectors of bitters across the country take all of them off the market and hoard them. If you do stumble upon a vintage bitters bottle, aside from Angostura, you're mostly likely to see Abbott's Bitters, "a cocktail ingredient that has beguiled drinks fanatics for years," wrote the *New York Times* in 2007. The brand initially dissolved in the 1950s, the original recipe was lost, and thus early dusty collectors and cocktail enthusiasts hunted for ancient bottles or tried to re-create this ingredient they had never tasted. (It is said to be more intense than Angostura, heavy on the cloves, nutmeg, cinnamon, and anise notes.) Robert Hess, a director at Microsoft in Seattle who was an early devotee to the cocktail renaissance (blogging as "DrinkBoy"), acquired ten bottles of Abbott's, one of which he lent to a perfumer based in New Jersey who was able to run a gas chromatograph test on it—he found that Abbott's contained the unusual ingredient of tonka beans, which smells like vanilla and contains the blood-thinning chemical coumarin, surely why it was banned by the FDA right around the time the company dissolved. (Tempus Fugit Spirits has revived the brand today as accurately as it can, classic label and all.)

OTHER VINTAGE MODIFIERS

If dusty Chartreuse, Campari, and fernet are perfectly enjoyable on their own, other liqueurs of yore, like the previously discussed Amer Picon and Kina Lillet, are more typically coveted to be deployed in cocktails.

GRAND MARNIER AND OTHER BRANDY-BASED CORDIALS

Seth Weinberg thinks the slew of Cognac- and brandy-based cordials that were especially popular mid-century remain undervalued today. Grand Marnier, an orange-flavored Cognac liqueur produced in France since 1880, would be at the top of the heap. Like Chartreuse, it changes over time, and there have been a lot of different variants released over the years. It could also be used in a vintage Sidecar.

CRÈME DE VIOLETTE

By the 2000s, a new breed of bartenders was eager to make an Aviation, a pale-purple-colored cocktail created in 1916. The only issue was that no brand had produced the liqueur most necessary for it in many decades. Dusty brands of crème de violette include Benoit Serres, Boss, and Crème Yvette; in 2007, U.S. companies would again begin importing and making their own brands of crème de violette. Ironically, today many members of the cocktail cognoscenti have since turned on the Aviation, now considering it a bad, overly floral cocktail—if not tasting like hand soap—that should have never been revived for modern audiences.

MARASCHINO

Another esoteric ingredient in the Aviation, as well as in the much better Last Word, Tuxedo, and Brandy Crusta, maraschino, too, was little seen in America in the 2000s and early 2010s. Thus, enthusiasts might have turned to dusty bottles of this marasca cherries liqueur, which honestly tastes nothing like cherries but is more nutty and herbal; brands from the past include Drioli, Maraska, Buton, Vlahov, Stock (of fernet fame), and Luxardo, which is the industry leader in this odd category today.

FUN AND ECONOMICAL

WEIRD FRUIT CORDIALS

Since there's no way to use "vintage" fruit juice in a period-correct cocktail, some dusty mixologists have turned to fruit cordials from the past. Cherry Heering is probably the most famous, occasionally still seen on shelves and backbars today, and necessary for the rare Scotch cocktail from the past, the Blood and Sand. Jewsbury & Brown makes a key lime fruit cordial, which Weinberg notes is ideal for a vintage daiquiri. (Be careful about not accidentally consuming a nonalcoholic fruit cordial from the past, which could have gone bad.) Cuba, specifically, produced a ton of oddball fruit liqueurs like Havana Club's pineapple liqueur. Brad Bonds, in particular, thinks bottlings like True Fruit Banana Liqueur Leroux are surprisingly tasty and fun to have around. (Not the case for mint liqueurs, however, with one seller joking to me: "If you love any classic recipes with mint liqueur, you've got it made, because no one buys that shit.")

FOUR CHAMBER BOTTLES

Fruit liqueur imports were killing it in America after Prohibition, and brands needed to find a way to differentiate themselves. Enter Distillerie

P. Garnier from Enghien-les-Bains, just north of Paris, which introduced the "Flacon Quadrille" in 1933. It offered four quarter liters of liqueurs, stacked on top of one another, with four different pour stouts ascending from the side of the bottle to dispense: Abricotine (apricot liqueur), triple sec, Liqueur d'Or (a sort of ur-Goldschläger that had literal gold flakes floating in it), and crème de menthe, which, as of 1935, was "America's favorite liqueur" according to *Harper's Bazaar*. It was a successful enough ploy for other liqueur companies to follow suit. By the 1950s, Bols was offering a cross-necked two-chamber bottle and "four-compartment" bottles mostly mimicking Garnier's lineup with cherry liqueur, apricot liqueur, triple sec, and crème de menthe. Cusenier, a once-great family-owned distillery located in the Cognac region (and today a part of Pernod Ricard), similarly offered bulb-shaped four-compartment carafes. Bottlings had everything from orange and cherry liqueur alongside anisette and Prunellia (its proprietary liqueur made with sloe berries and Cognac) to ones with apricot liqueur, crème de cacao, kümmel, and Freezomint (its crème de menthe). Dolfi had a four-chamber bottle with apricot and cherry brandy, peppermint liqueur, and fraise des bois (a wild strawberry liqueur). And D.O.M. would put its iconic Bénédictine and brandy—the makings of a B&B—in "La Bouteille du Couple." These gimmicks would last until the mid-1970s.

VINTAGE VODKA?!

If, in discussing the bourbon glut era, I noted the coincidence that vodka is the only spirit without a vintage market to speak of, I was surprised to learn even that's not true. Weinberg has been acquiring dusty vodka in earnest of late.

"To me, vodka is one of the few spirits I don't care much about. But I also know that vodka sells as much as whiskey does in America," says

Weinberg. In fact, vodka sales are more than $7 billion per year in the country. "So my thought process is, if there's this many vodka drinkers out there, vintage vodka must have value. Whenever I buy something, I don't necessarily have a plan with it, but I think here's what I can do with it at some point."

With eyes on one day opening his own vintage liquor store that makes and sells vintage cocktails, Weinberg knows that vodka-drinking friends and family tagalongs will come into his business with the dusty enthusiasts who dragged them there. If the liquor law allows him to make only vintage cocktails, he wants to be able to offer that vodka drinker a vintage martini or a Moscow Mule using Smirnoff from the same year the drink was supposedly invented.

"I probably couldn't use vintage ginger beer, because I can't find any, and that might not be something you'd want to drink," says Weinberg. "But maybe some people are willing to take a risk just to say, 'I had the world's oldest Moscow Mule.'"

Another seller I spoke to sees vintage vodka becoming critical for Rat Pack cosplayers, a group I hadn't realized was so prominent and one whom I hope to never encounter.

"You got one guy who wants vintage Jack Daniel's because he's going to be Frank Sinatra, and then another guy needs vintage vodka because he's Dean Martin and is going to have his martinis. . . ."

No word on what the Sammy Davis Jr. imitator will want to drink.

Unfortunately, there's not really any sexy vodka brands from the past, or even bottles that old, out there. Remember, vodka wasn't even sold in America until 1934, and not even truly prominent until Stoli made it to the States in the mid-1960s. That's why some of the more interesting vintage vodka bottles Weinberg has found have been private labels, like one that Jim Beam, of all companies, bottled in the 1970s so it would have vodka to pour for attendees at one of its annual bottle collectors conventions.

Weinberg thinks that simply having an old bottle with a cool label goes a long way; it can even start a conversation with a customer. He certainly sees intrigue in true Russian-imported vodka from the past, especially as Russia's unjust invasion of Ukraine lingers on. (Weinberg claims that if he ever sold dusty Russian vodka, he would surely donate the proceeds to a charity for Ukraine.)

In fact, Weinberg purchased one of his earliest lots of dusty vodka from Brad Bonds who had listed them online. Bonds was so excited they had sold that he called Weinberg, who he didn't know at that point in time.

"He's like, 'I'm so happy, because I thought there was value in this stuff,'" recalls Weinberg. "'And my business partner thought I was crazy, and now I can say, "Hey, I was right!"'"

PART III

A SPIRITED FUTURE

11

THE MERCENARIES

"IT'S ALL ABOUT the bottle!

"The real value is *only* about that bottle.

"Not because it comes from a Hollywood star—that shouldn't increase the value! It's all about that dusty bottle."

Salvatore Calabrese was almost shouting at me, so adamant was his belief that linking its provenance to a famous former owner didn't necessarily make a vintage bottle any more valuable. He claims he has certainly never used that as a sales gimmick.

But I'm not sure I agreed with the Maestro.

I was certain a Howard Hughes booze collection would be a massive score, all the more so because it would be linked to one of the richest, most famous, and most enigmatic men who ever lived. How could that not stir feelings in a drinker so powerful that they'd pay more for a mere taste of it?

Others believed this as well.

Scott Torrence, who was senior wine specialist at Christie's at the time of the $640,000 Jean-Baptiste "J. B." Leonis auction, told me, "You put celebrity on top of [a great vintage find], now you're talking an order of magnitude seven times greater. That's what celebrity can do."

He recalled for me the 2004 Christie's auction of tobacco heiress Doris Duke's wine collection, which sold for an astonishing $3.7 million, much higher than he had anticipated. And no offense to the "richest little girl in the world," but Doris Duke was no Howard Hughes.

"As an auction house you really want these items that generate news," says Torrence, who today runs his own fine and rare wine dealership called Chapter 4.

Alas, I had no angles to pursue anyhow.

Since I wasn't getting help from Ackerman anymore, and since I couldn't even figure out who to contact next, or whether there was some state agency that might know who controlled the rights to something like this, I simply started reading books about Hughes, thinking maybe I'd find a clue. (I knew I wouldn't find a clue, but I had nothing else to do in the mornings before my kids woke up.)

Like any average American of my age, I, of course, already knew the basic things about Hughes. How'd he come from a Texas oil family and gotten into the movie business and dated famous actresses and recklessly flew airplanes in the early days of aviation. I thought I heard he liked golf, and was pretty sure that he eventually went crazy and let his nails and hair grow long and started drinking his urine and died in a Vegas hotel room. But maybe those were all just rumors.

I'd seen the Martin Scorsese picture as well, but *The Aviator* hardly registered with me nearly two decades later—not one of Marty's best, if I recall, despite an Oscar for Cate Blanchett as Katharine Hepburn.

I bought a copy of the definitive, posthumous biography, *Howard Hughes: His Life and Madness* (originally published as *Empire: The Life, Legend, and Madness of Howard Hughes*), by two-time Pulitzer Prize winners Donald L. Barlett and James B. Steele. It's the book that *The Aviator* was adapted from. It happened to have been originally published in 1979, my birth year.

At first I mainly read the book looking for mentions of Hughes's drinking and/or entertaining habits, as well as any information on his estate planning after his death.

Even from an early age, Hughes was cagey about setting up his will. When Amelia Earhart mysteriously vanished in the South Pacific in July 1937, Hughes was shaken. Then and there, he composed detailed instructions governing the reading of his will "in the event . . . it should be deemed that I may be dead, but not conclusively proven." In that case, the First National Bank of Houston was to keep his will unopened and not allow his estate to be probated for three years.

As for drinking alcohol, the book, early on, provided an amusing anecdote about Hughes after he had just broken the record for an around-the-world flight. Taking off from New York City, Hughes flew from Paris to Moscow to Omsk in Siberia; Yakutsk, not far south of the Arctic Circle; Fairbanks, Alaska; and Minneapolis, before finally returning to New York City on July 14, 1938, in a then-record ninety-one hours. Flying a twin-engine Lockheed 14 Super Electra, dubbed the *New York World's Fair 1939*, he had smashed legendary aviator Wiley Post's previous record by nearly four days.

Hughes, press-shy, dead tired, unshaven, and smeared with grease, offered some cursory remarks to the crowd before jumping into a waiting limousine heading toward Lower Manhattan.

En route, he sipped on a Scotch and soda.

I STARTED REACHING out to some of the more avid and intrepid dusty hunters in the game. Seeing if they had any insight, advice, or simply interesting stories to tell about their own successes.

My first call was to the first person I always called when I wanted to solve a vintage spirits mystery: Jonah Goodman.

You think it's too late to get into the vintage spirits game? Goodman was barely a bar mitzvah when people like Mike Jasinski, Bill Thomas, and Kevin Langdon Ackerman first started clearing shelves throughout the country. Today he's a prodigy of dusty hunting, able to navigate both the physical globe and the World Wide Web in search of odd bottles, better than just about anyone out there.

Goodman was just fourteen when his parents moved to Kentucky. His father loved bourbon, and Goodman thought it was pretty cool himself. A bookish kid, he started spending time on message boards and private bourbon Facebook groups, even reading my earliest articles on the subject matter.

By 2018, he was finally, legally allowed to enter the commonwealth's liquor stores in search of these vintage bottles he knew so much about but had only read about, never tasted, just seen images of online. He scored a 1984 Eagle Rare 101 decanter on one of his earliest hunts, and was hooked.

Still in his early twenties today, with no wife or kids, with no "day job" per se, with the kind of minor expenses needed to live a fun life, untethered to any particular person or city or even time zone, Goodman's become a sort of vintage-seeking nomad, traveling the globe to find bottles he can sell to a growing list of clients, some of which are famous distilleries looking to build their own museum collections. Whenever I call him on WhatsApp, or receive a text from him, I can never be sure where in the world he's going to be, what hemisphere or time zone he is going to be in.

He might be in Panama—a country that used to have a huge U.S. military population—looking for dusty old American imports that troops had left behind. He might be in Scotland, investigating a lead on some coveted bourbon barrels he'd heard were oddly aging there, and that he could nab for a good price. He'd recently found some intriguing old Thai rum in Phuket.

In China he once bought a bottle of bug repellent, and when he absentmindedly peeled off the Chinese-language label, he saw there was an English-language label underneath. From this, he realized that many distributors must be buying things in bulk at American Costcos and then sending entire containers over to be relabeled. And that was legal in China. The same thing had clearly happened with liquor over the years and was still happening today in the country. Maybe he could capitalize on it.

I thought Goodman might possibly have insight on nabbing the Hughes collection, because his biggest dusty score had also involved an enigmatic rich guy.

In 2020, the first summer of the pandemic, a former employee of Richard Mellon Scaife's Pennsylvania estate contacted Goodman. She had once worked very closely with the late billionaire—heir to the Mellon family fortune—over many years and was often tasked with organizing his cellar. In return, she had occasionally been gifted cases of Old Overholt that had been passed down through his family from Andrew W. Mellon and his brother Richard B. Mellon, Scaife's grandfather.

Goodman drove to a small house thirty minutes or so from Scaife's nine-hundred-acre Westmoreland County estate, about an hour southeast of Pittsburgh, with an unnamed friend who was helping finance the purchase. A 1911 Old Overholt quart had recently sold at auction for $12,000, but Goodman thought he could probably get these bottles at less than market price. Nevertheless, it would still be a huge financial outlay for the full lot.

If there had been around one hundred cases of Old Overholt when the Mellon patriarchs died, this former employee still had six cases left. But they were primo. Whole sealed cases of 1905 and 1908 vintages, a bunch of loose quarts (thirty-two-ounce "big boys") from 1908 and 1909, and a single bottle from 1910, a year Goodman had rarely seen an example of.

Unfortunately, this 1910 had been recently opened and tasted by the woman's just-turned-twenty-one-year-old son. He didn't find it enjoyable, so he didn't finish it.

That actually worked out well for Goodman, however, as he got to try the liquid without devaluing any bottles. Goodman, who has tasted as much dusty American whiskey as pretty much anyone out there, was blown away.

"They're, like, delicious. Like, genuinely delicious," he excitedly told me. Mind you, Old Overholt from that era would not taste anything like the Old Overholt of today, currently being distilled by Jim Beam in Clermont, Kentucky.

For one, back then it was actually being distilled in western Pennsylvania, at the Broad Ford plant. Abraham Overholt had started the brand in 1810, grinding local Monongahela rye to make the mash, and by 1919 Andrew Mellon owned the brand; he used his position as secretary of the treasury to allow Old Overholt to be sold medicinally during Prohibition. It can be assumed that Mellon stockpiled hundreds of cases for his home cellar during this time as well.

Indeed, Goodman could tell that the crates the bottles were stored in had come from a pre-Prohibition era and were once probably owned by Richard B. Mellon. They even had "R.B. Mellon" stenciled on the side of them, along with his former address in downtown Pittsburgh, today the current site of Mellon Park. The bottles, however, seemed to be from a later era than the years printed on them.

What Goodman thinks happened is that at some point, in what appears to have been the 1940s, Paul Mellon, Andrew W. Mellon's son and a noted wine collector, ordered these pre-Prohibition bottles to be rebottled because they had become incredibly brittle. Old Overholt famously used low-quality glass in the early 1900s. The best closure technology by the 1940s had become the screw cap, which is what Paul Mellon used for the rebottling; Goodman calls the seals "genuinely great" and presumes that's why the liquid has held up so well.

So the bottles themselves are not pre-Prohibition, but the liquid contents are. Make sense?

Yes, Goodman understands how odd that might appear to other collectors and potential buyers, but there are other bottles out there on the vintage market that look just like his.

"There's a lot of hesitancy around people thinking that they're fake. And I've seen other bottles where the plastic has fallen off, and people are like, 'Well, I bought it sealed,' but the plastic corroded or whatever," says Goodman.

Remember, Paul Mellon didn't rebottle these so that a century later they would be considered valuable dusties. These were simply bottles that the Mellons planned to drink themselves one day, never meant for the world at large to even know about.

"The rebottling was never meant to seal it long-term. They were for a very wealthy family that never would need to care about its provenance, and reselling it," Goodman says. "They just cared about preserving a family heirloom at the time."

As for the Hughes collection, I thought Goodman might be interested, might be able to help me, but, without a better tip, he didn't have time to jump through hoops to find another billionaire's boozy heirlooms. He had no interest in going to Los Angeles.

Instead, he was thinking about going to the Middle East. He suspected that, ever since Russia had invaded Ukraine, brands would be pulling out of the country and sending their more high-end bottles to places like Iraq, Iran, Oman, and the "Stans," former Soviet republics.

Goodman was interested, thought he could turn an easy profit, and was getting sick of hanging in Kuala Lumpur.

LIKE THOSE BOTTLES of bug spray with Chinese labels over American ones, occasionally the vintage spirits enthusiast will come across a bottle that simply does not make sense, does not match up or register with all the knowledge of the industry and its history that the individual knows to be true.

It could be the simple paradox of some Prohibition-era medicinal whiskeys listing two competing distilleries on the label, despite their being legally bottled in bond and thus, inherently, the production of a single distiller. Often, this occurred simply because companies didn't have enough bottles or labels, and they just mixed and matched whatever was around, such as in the case of a famous AMS bottling with Judge William Harrison McBrayer on the label, despite the liquid coming from Aaron Bradley Co.

"The funny thing about these labels is they create this confluence of stories," Joshua Feldman explains. "The front of the label is about one nineteenth-century whiskey person, but the whiskey is actually produced at another distillery with a whole 'nother story."

Prohibition would, in fact, lead to other shenanigans.

Such as the case of Mary Dowling, heir to the Dowling Bros. Distillery, which produced the Waterfill and Frazier brand. Angered by the new proscriptive laws, she simply dismantled her distillery piece by piece and moved the operations to Juárez, Mexico, where she befriended a local businessman who was soon elected mayor, and hired Joseph L. Beam to distill bourbon. Yes, bourbon.

How is that possible, you ask? If you know anything about bourbon, one of its most prevailing regulations is that it must be distilled in America. But that's only been true since 1964.

So Waterfill and Frazier *bourbon* was, in fact, being made in Juárez, right on the border of the United States, where someone could easily walk a few bottles across the border to El Paso on a dusty road that had no sort of customs or security at the time. Many Americans at the time, though, did the reverse, and traveled to Juárez, which had become a sort of "Little Louisville," with taverns popping up with names like the Mint Cafe, which served mint juleps for 60 cents, and the Kentucky Club, which is still operating today, believe it or not. Two other well-funded, American-owned bourbon distilleries would sprout in Juárez as well, the more notable one being D.M. Distillery.

Meanwhile, Dowling's existing American stock ended up in "Pappy" Van Winkle's hands and was also bottled by him under the Waterfill and Frazier brand name. It found itself competing against the same-named Mexican bourbon that had inexplicably (and illegally) now also found its way back into America's medicinal whiskey market. This Mexican bourbon is a fun curiosity to find, but generally regarded as swill, as it was regarded even by Van Winkle back in the day, who was angered he was getting undercut in price by the illegal import.

When Prohibition ended, Mary Dowling kept her distillery in Mexico, while opening a new one in Kentucky. Her Mexican distillery continued to make "Kentucky-type bourbon" (according to ads) until 1964, when regulations forced her to label it simply as "whiskey." The distillery remained active until the 1990s.

Surely the oddest anomaly I encountered in writing this book was that of Horse Shoe Straight Bourbon Whiskey, 10 Years Old Aged in Wood, and "Bottled in Bond Under Cuban Government Supervision."

To have the "Bottled-in-Bond" designation—created in 1897—it must have been aged in a federally bonded warehouse under U.S. government supervision for at least four years, then bottled at 100 proof. (This bottle is only 90 proof, which was actually legal for exported bourbon.) The bottle claims it came from the Berman Liquor Co. Inc. from "Habana-Cuba."

The guy who found it was Kevin Minnick, a chef and restaurant owner of the Maine Course in Quincy, Illinois, which has one of the largest whiskey collections in the state. He was another dusty hunter I wanted to speak to about Hughes, as he seemed to have an incredible knack for finding things no one else even knew existed.

One of the keys to Minnick's success is his relationships with numerous "pickers," antique hunters who scour the state for valuable items. One of these pickers has an interest in vintage signage, but not dusty alcohol—so he passes those finds on to Minnick. In Chicago this picker found a small lot of booze, and among it were two bottles of the Horse Shoe Cuban bourbon.

Minnick immediately noticed the strange packaging: an old-fashioned wine bottle with deep punting (that indentation on the bottom of all bottles), a cork covered in wax that had dripped flush against the bottle's neck, and a Cuban tax strip over the top of that. The color of the liquid was ridiculously dark. Unlike more cautious, economically minded dusty hunters, Minnick had to try it.

"I was like, fuck it, man," says Minnick. "Here's an odd bottle nobody's really seen."

He lugged one bottle to the Grains & Grits Festival in Townsend, Tennessee, a Tennessee whiskey and "Southern grub" event that Minnick has cooked at for several years. A fellow chef was Cuban and, with help from his father, identified the bottle as pre-embargo, which would mean 1961 or earlier. The second bottle Minnick took to Louisville, wanting to impress Owen Powell, who, up until then, he had yet to meet in person.

"He sat this bottle down on the bar and said, 'Let's open this and drink it,'" recalls Powell. "And I looked at it, and I knew it was going to be special."

As they sipped, the two men shared their thoughts about how the bottle might have come to be. Had a few barrels of bourbon been smuggled out of the Cincinnati-based Mill Creek Distilling Co.—"one of the largest distilling companies in the country" as of 1886, according to the *New York Times*—during Prohibition? It, too, once offered a Horseshoe (one word) whiskey. Had these barrels made the secret trek over the border to Canada—which also bottled its own "bourbon" during this time via brands like Gooderham and Worts—before being shipped down to Cuba, where it was bottled along with rum that had been smuggled there as well?

That was one story that certainly seemed like a possibility.

In fact, in 1937 one Morris Roisner, part of a known organized bootlegging syndicate, was charged with tax evasion, put on trial in a St. Paul, Minnesota, courthouse, and found to have illicitly sent $41,500 to Cuba during the Prohibition. The recipient down there? A Mill Creek Distilling Company in Havana.

Another story is that with rising anti-Semitism in both Europe and America, many Jews fled to Cuba after World War I. Some entered the cigar industry. Others started booze companies. Berman Liquor Co. (sometimes known as Berman's Distillery) was founded in 1930 in the heart of Old Havana. It sold "Famous Berman's Cordials" like peach, cherry, and apricot brandy, along with slivovitz (plum brandy) and vishnick (cherry liqueur), not to mention Old Tranquility Brand rum, in handsome gold-necked bottles, as well as, yes, straight bourbon whiskey "aged for many years in oak for half the price you would pay at home." That was also called Horse Shoe.

So was Horse Shoe distilled in Kentucky or Cincinnati or Cuba? All we know is that it was almost certainly bottled in Havana and then some of it made its way back to the States.

A 1931 article in the *Times* of Shreveport, Louisiana, details the arrest of a man when he was caught with twelve pints of Horse Shoe bourbon discovered by the cops in a hermetically sealed tin, apparently shipped to him from some great distance. And a 1933 report in the *Key West Citizen* details U.S. customs officials stopping a boat coming from Cuba and loaded with "good stuff" like twelve quarts of Hennessy, twelve quarts of Ron Caña, twenty-four quarts of 1873 Bacardí, five-gallon demijohns of gin, twenty-four bottles of Crystal beer, and yes, fifty-one pints of Mill Creek whiskey.

However it came to be, I like Powell's explanation for how it came to taste so extraordinary.

"What I think happened, because it was bottled at a rum distillery, when they bottled it, maybe in the bottling machine some of the rum was still present and got imparted into the bourbon," says Powell, who describes Horse Shoe's taste as "phenomenal," viscous with just a little sweet kiss of Cuban rum on the aroma and palate, making it just a hair sweeter than you'd expect from American oak.

Minnick left him with about four ounces of the Horse Shoe, and Powell immediately called some industry friends like Andy Shapira and Bernie Lubbers. Everybody who tried a sip was equally blown away. It's still one of the best bourbons any of them have ever tasted.

Powell, who knows what dusties are still out there as well as anyone in the industry, thinks the two bottles Minnick owned might have been the only two still left in America. And now, perhaps, there are zero left.

"It's definitely my unicorn of all unicorns," says Powell, who speculated that the bottle Minnick generously popped might have been worth $100,000.*

Powell claims that if he knew then what he knows now, he would have demanded it never be opened and instead be sent to a museum. He added, "But I'm also glad that I drank it with him."

And that's the struggle of the vintage enthusiast: Is it worth diminishing the value of something in order to know what it tastes like?

So forget about finding Hughes's stuff—Powell wanted more of that Cuban bourbon.

---

* When I passed that info along to Minnick, he was silent for a second before responding: "Well, that's interesting. I think that's kind of a crazy story. Is it far-fetched? Maybe. Is it realistic? You fucking never know what's going to happen when it goes to auction."

He's even thought about hiring a translator and heading down to Havana for a hunting expedition.

Surely there are more bottles in someone's closet, right?

Maybe there are some dusty Horse Shoes hiding in the back of a store or warehouse?

There have to be.

He knows there have to be.

But how would he even find them?

MAYBE I NEEDED help from a military man like Dan Rineer.

In the run-up to the Iraq War, he was on Operation Northern Watch, flying on an AWACS, an airborne radar system, based out of Incirlik Air Base in Turkey. Barely twenty-one at the time, Rineer and his brothers-in-arms were constantly annoyed by how much CAOC, the Combined Air Operations Center, would jerk them around. The command was notorious for telling the flight crew they were canceled for the day—in other words, not needed—and then changing plans fifteen minutes later and sending them out on a mission.

The military has a rule called twelve hours "Bottle to Throttle"—in other words, you can't have a drink within half a day of taking off on a mission. Knowing this, after the fourth time CAOC had bounced Rineer's AWACS crew around, they came up with a plan: They would start carrying miniature liquor bottles in their helmet bags. If CAOC canceled them for the day, the crew would sit down and immediately pound their minis. If CAOC came back to tell them to go fly, it would encounter a group of thirty troops with just as many bottles of tiny booze in front of them.

Military life can be boring, and it quickly became a challenge as to who could obtain the coolest, the rarest, the most obscure miniatures in the group. Rineer had an incredible knack for acquiring oddities in these early 2000s days. He'd source them from parents, from friends, when shopping on pit stops throughout Europe. It wasn't only whiskey, of course: He'd grab raki minis in Turkey, ouzo in Greece, Campari nips in Italy. A favorite of his were the airline-labeled miniatures. In his military career, Rineer traveled to ninety-one countries, was stationed everywhere from Germany to Japan, and acquired miniature booze bottles everywhere he went.

Back in the States and out of the military since 2016, today Dan Rineer lives in Clarkston, Michigan, just north of Detroit, and runs flight simulators for the Air National Guard. Rineer had been hoarding minis for so long during his service days, constantly mailing them back to America, that he now has an estimated forty thousand bottles, loosely organized (but not really) in a ten-by-thirty-by fifteen-foot warehouse with ladders and racks up to the ceiling, completely packed with teeny-tiny bottles. His wife isn't even aware of it—and I hope she doesn't read this book.

Any time something vintage becomes unexpectedly hot—say, Campari, of which he has a few hundred bottles—Rineer tracks back to his warehouse and searches through his bottles to find ones to unload, capitalizing on a dusty bull market, to help fund a restoration of his 1967 Corvette.

But this is no side hustle; Rineer is a collector, a hoarder, an obsessive, and he hasn't stopped accumulating. He had just purchased two thousand miniatures from an undisclosed location when I spoke to him in early 2023.

Rineer, like Jonah Goodman and Kevin Minnick and Owen Powell, had no insight on the Howard Hughes collection, and no strategies for how to find it either. He was more than willing to tell me about his best, or at least most amusing, score, though. It had happened the year before.

Rineer has some friends who clear out houses so real estate agents can sell them. If they hear of something that might interest him, they let him tag along. Such was the case for a "very prominent" family in the Detroit suburbs who had a basement in the neighborhood of five thousand square feet.

Opening the door to head downstairs, Rineer had to clear the cobwebs away—clearly no one had entered the space in a very long time. Looking around, Rineer immediately realized the family must have illicitly used their basement as a venue of sorts. Illegal poker games? Drug den? Key parties? Who knows?

There were round tables set up, a stage of sorts, and a commercial-quality bar with a dirty, dank liquor cellar as big as any restaurant's. He spied tons of bottles of Old Grand-Dad, Crown Royal, Chivas Regal, green-label Jack Daniel's from the 1960s, cases upon cases of "you name it," says Rineer, some boxes stuck to the floor because they'd been there so long. A lot of these bottles were in duty-free gift boxes, clearly acquired by someone crossing the nearby border to Canada, surely capitalizing on the exchange rate back then. The "newest" bottle in the entire basement seemed to be from 1988. Thirty-four years earlier.

Like finding Pompeiians still frozen in the year 79, this was when time had stopped in this mysterious, subterranean, suburban space.

Finally, Rineer found the Rosetta stone that explained what had actually been going on downstairs.

Hundreds upon hundreds of miniature bottles of 1965-distilled Seagram's VO Canadian whisky. On each, a self-applied label was stuck to the back of the bottle with the black-and-white image of a smiling tween, a shag haircut flowing down to the high gorge lapels of his checkered suit jacket.

The labels read: "Andy's Bar Mitzvah—August 19, 1971."

"I snickered," recalls Rineer. "I'm thinking, here's this teenage boy, and they slapped his face on liquor bottles and gave them to everybody."

It wasn't just Andy's bar mitzvah either, but Joshua's and Alan's and Richard's and even Sandy's bat mitzvah. From the 1950s through 1988, this was, apparently, *the* place for Detroit's suburban thirteen-year-old Jews to party. And if you did, you might just get a party favor nip to take home to Mom and Pop.

Rineer (not Jewish, for what's it worth) thought it was funny, and since 1970s Canadian whisky doesn't have much value, he started sending bottles to dusty hunter friends as a joke, a "toss-in" when he was shipping them a box of better stuff. When Seth Weinberg (Jewish but not practicing), posted Andy's bar mitzvah on his @vintagewhiskey Instagram account, it caused a bit of a stir in the community, especially from other Jewish collectors (like me), who suddenly wanted their own bottle.

"I thought it was funny because it was basically like a personalized, private label," says Weinberg. "It's one of those bottles that I definitely would never sell, because it's too cool to me."

Unfortunately, I have never been able to track Andy himself down to learn about said bar mitzvah. Andy, or surely Andrew by now, if he's still with us, is of AARP age, at least sixty-five, if you do the math. The bottle doesn't list his last name on it, and there isn't exactly a database for Michigan bar mitzvahs held on August 19, 1971.

But I think about Andy sometimes, think about that bar mitzvah party frozen in time by a miniature bottle that, improbably, has become a vintage collectible in the year 2023.

I think about a bunch of thirteen-year-olds descending the basement stairs to have the party of their so far young lifetimes. I wonder if Andy and his friends still remember that night. I wonder if any kid filched a pull from a mini bottle with their buddy's face on it.

And I think about why my parents gave out caricature portraits at my bar mitzvah, instead of 1992 nips of Wild Turkey or Old Grand-Dad.

MINIS AND MAXIS

NIPS AND AIRLINE BOTTLES

There's a weird phenomenon where some of the most prominent vintage spirits collectors today began as collectors of miniature alcohol bottles . . . sometimes even back when they were children, maybe even inspired by a bar mitzvah souvenir.

Perhaps the world's greatest collector of vintage miniatures—sometimes known as nips or airline bottles or minibar bottles—has never moved onto full-size bottles, however.

Rotem Ben Shitrit, an Israeli, became fascinated by miniatures when he was just twelve; today, in his late thirties, he has many thousands of tiny bottles, displayed on four walls of floor-to-ceiling shelving encased in childproof glass in one entire room of his house in Kfar Saba.

"The legal drinking age in Israel is eighteen, but back then it wasn't enforced," explains Shitrit of his early collecting days. His earliest acquisitions were pretty run-of-the-mill, like Finlandia Cranberry Vodka. "I found myself hitting every liquor store in Tel Aviv on my own with a Ziploc full of coins."

A post-college decade in Bethesda, Maryland, saw Ben Shitrit amass more than three thousand American whiskeys, including several examples of historic Maryland ryes like Sherwood Pure Rye, which we'll soon discuss again. He'd also be sure to hit the annual Midwest Miniature Bottle Collectors convention in St. Louis. The pride of his collection is a Glenfiddich 50 Year Old miniature he paid $2,000 for. It's easy for him to keep the collection going, as he rarely drinks.

For miniature collectors, there are many advantages: They're generally made in fewer numbers and are therefore harder to source.

Because of their shrunk-down size, they're cheaper than a matching full-size bottle, making curious collectors more apt to finally try that rare old single malt.

Naturally, they offer space-saving benefits too. But for Shitrit, the appeal of the miniatures goes beyond the practical. "I honestly find them a lot more special," says Shitrit. "Put ten large bottles in a row, and it'll look like a bar. Put ten minis in a row, and it'll look like a collection."

Unfortunately, like bourbon, tequila, and so many other categories, the halcyon days of miniatures are long gone. Most brands bottle only their lamest everyday offerings in nip form, typically now packaged in cheap plastic, destined for convenience store counters and airlines' beverage carts.

"Everything tastes like shit now," says Dan Rineer, who hates how brands have quit putting the liquid in glass. "They all taste like plastic!"

The halcyon days of *collecting* miniatures are far from over, however. In the summer of 2022, two miniatures, a 1919 Springbank and a James MacArthur's Malt Mill distilled in 1959, sold at auction for a combined £14,000.

The anonymous winner said he had no plans to drink either.

GALLON SWINGS AND OTHER LARGE-FORMAT BOTTLES

While miniatures have more avid individual collectors, no vintage bar or retail shops these days are worth their salt if they don't own and pour from oversize, large-format bottles.

"The big bottles don't really have a huge history behind them. They really were just used as a showy display," Justin Thompson of Justins' House of Bourbon once told me, after I'd encountered my first one ever in person, a 4.5-liter bottle of Four Roses made for the mid-1990s Japanese market. It was as tall as my entire torso—indeed, it was a showy, and pricey, display item.

Thompson is generally right that there isn't much history or even explicit reasoning behind these giant bottles, which have been illegal in America since 1979 when the frat-friendly 1.75-liter "handle" became the upper echelon for packaging maximums. None of the major Kentucky distilleries I talked to could even point to the first one to be manufactured, nor could the Distilled Spirits Council of the United States. Thompson's business partner Justin Sloan claims the earliest example he's ever come across is a 1957 Jim Beam, and that seems about right. Much like gimmicky decanters, also started by Jim Beam, these big bottles emerged during the glut era, perhaps in hope of moving excess product.

(However, there are also examples of giant gin and Scotch bottles from that time.)

The best of the bunch are, as usual, from Stitzel-Weller and National Distillers, both of which produced gallon-sized bottles that come in metal and/or wood pouring cradles, colloquially known as "swings" among collectors.

Getting a pour from, say, 1960s Old Fitzgerald or 1970s Old Grand-Dad Bonded as the bartender swings the giant bottle down toward your Glencairn glass is about as fun—and Instagrammable—as vintage bourbon drinking can get these days.

And we may be again embarking on a new era of gigantism.

In 2022, Lyon & Turnbull auctioned off the largest-ever bottle of whiskey—The Intrepid Macallan 1989 32 Year Old—which stood nearly six feet tall and offered 311 liters of single malt. It sold for £1.1 million.

12

YOU SHOULD DRINK A SPIRIT
OLDER THAN YOU

AS I MOVED deeper and deeper into the world of vintage spirits, though I never exactly became a full-fledged dusty hunter myself, it became impossible for me not to begin placing myself within the timeline of liquid history.

If Calabrese liked to link ancient Cognac to historic events, I eventually realized that dusty alcohol felt the most powerful when I linked it to my own life. The Red Hook Rye that made me recall my earliest years living in New York. The 1980s Johnnie Walker that could jolt me back to elementary school and the art teacher I would retroactively realize always had the smell of Scotch on her breath.

I write this chapter on my forty-fourth birthday, February 10, 2023. Forty-four years earlier was 1979, and that is the year that I have decided to collect.

I was born at NYU Medical Center in Lower Manhattan. Around the same time, some thirty-six hundred miles away, in the historical region of Gascony, France, slightly south of a town called Condom, on a small, seven-hectare vineyard, Armagnac was distilled on-site by Bernard Rozès, then put into 420-liter barrels made of French oak produced from trees grown on the estate.

When the Armagnac was 40 years old, it was finally pulled from its dusty barrels stored in a humid cellar and placed into bottles. Today I celebrated my forty-fourth birthday by drinking the Armagnac born the same year I was.

There are several ways to be a birth-year collector, of course.

Distillation year, as was the case of the aforementioned Armagnac, is one. Bottling year, which can sometimes be difficult to pinpoint, is another. Of course, if you're born before 1985, any American-sold spirit will have a tax stamp that lists both the year the liquid was distilled *and* the year it was bottled.

But by now, you've seen ample evidence that American bourbon dusties have become harder and harder and more and more expensive to source.

When I first started getting into vintage spirits a few years back, when I first decided I'd like to start drinking a 1979 something or other on my birthday every year, I was mostly a bourbon fan. And I don't want to say 1979 distilled and/or bottled bourbon was cheap in, say, 2016, but it was still an affordable luxury to a freelance writer like myself. I could treat myself to a vintage bottle once a year.

I recall buying a Wild Turkey 12-Year-Old, the infamous "Cheesy Gold Foil," bottled in 1991, and distilled twelve years earlier, in 1979. I think the bottle cost me around $400. It would go for a couple of grand, at least, today. So would a 1979 National Distillers Old Grand-Dad Bonded that I gifted myself on my birthday the next year.

Both those bourbons were incredible; they're still bourbons I think about, that I can still recall sitting in my house drinking (probably as my wife cleaned up the birthday cake detritus). But as I reached my early forties, as bourbon and dusty bourbon continued to boom, the price for 1979s just got too rich for my blood. Luckily, there was Armagnac, a still underappreciated category of well-aged French brandies. I was able to easily stock up on countless delicious 1979 vintages, most for under two hundred bucks apiece.*

By the time I reach 2029 and age fifty, who knows what 1979 spirits I will be drinking? I may have to call Seth Weinberg and see what his dusty vodka is going for.

TIME IS ALWAYS marching on. You can't stop it. You can't control it.

As one ages, as one's birth year continues getting further and further away, some are happy just to drink something older than them, regardless of distillation and bottling year. I recall my friend the great cocktail writer Robert Simonson, sitting with me as we enjoyed a sip from, literally, a million-dollar bottle of Yamazaki 55 Year Old, and him lamenting to me:

"This will probably be the last time I drink something older than me."

I imagine that for him, that dram had more potency (and perhaps pathos) behind it than it did for anyone else in the room. It goes without saying we were also lucky to be writers who got to sample this million-dollar bottle for free.

The same evening, we tasted a Yamazaki 12, 18, and 25 Year Old alongside the 55 Year Old. I honestly thought the 18 Year Old tasted best.

But, of course, if this book has taught you anything, it's that you're not drinking vintage spirits purely for the flavor. There's the liquid history, the drinkable time capsule, as we keep discussing. But there's also the philosophical nature of the beast. And that's what I actually like best.

---

* Most Armagnac and Cognac, and many single malt Scotches, will list the distillation year on the bottle.

While a 44-year-old bourbon is almost never going to be four decades more flavorful or $1,500 better than something released today, I find its power to affect the mind certainly is.

It's utterly humbling to think about what was going on in the world when the dusty Armagnac in my hand was born. What did that Gascony region look and feel like back in 1979? What was on Rozès's mind that day as he distilled the Armagnac? Was he worrying about the Ayatollah Khomeini returning to Iran? Was he wearing polyester? Was he listening to Rod Stewart's "Da Ya Think I'm Sexy?" on an 8-track in his truck?

And what does it say about me that I love having bottles with a "1979" displayed on them? I don't think I'm an egomaniac, but then again, I am an author, talking about things I assume you want to pay money to read.

So this is me telling you something you already know: Life is short.

One day you're a twentysomething man distilling an Armagnac; forty-four years later you're an old man with two adult daughters bottling up and packaging that same liquid to send to America to sell to a now middle-aged man who was days old when you first distilled it.

As the Armagnac rested in barrels for forty years, it was rotated and spun, placed on higher racks or lower dunnage, maybe even moved to different areas, anything to possibly improve the maturation of the liquid, but it never left the humid, seventeenth-century cellar. It survived history, but never affected it. Meanwhile, everyone else was living their lives, maturing in their own ways.

I moved from Gramercy Park in Manhattan to Queens to Oklahoma City when I was three. I left for college at Syracuse University when I was eighteen. By the time I was twenty-one and able to legally drink, I'm guessing the Armagnac tasted pretty good, but I know I would have probably still preferred a Vodka Red Bull. This Armagnac aged on through presidential elections, Carter through Trump, Giscard d'Estaing through Macron. Through the bourbon glut and the rise of vodka and peach schnapps and Zima and Four Loko and back again to a bourbon renaissance and a market more welcoming to well-aged "brown goods."

All this to end up in my glass in my Brooklyn apartment some forty-four years later, where I could drink the past while contemplating my future.

And I think that was why I so wanted to find these Howard Hughes bottles.

Because they wouldn't just be dusty bottles of booze, they would be liquid Wikipedia pages, filling my mind with thoughts from the past, thoughts from my own life, thoughts of my journey in writing this book, were I ever lucky enough to find one, and to drink one.

I needed to learn more about the location where I suspected the dusty booze might be.

COLLECTED IN JOAN Didion's seminal book of essays, *Slouching towards Bethlehem*, is one from 1967 titled "7000 Romaine Los Angeles 38."

The story is about (and that particular address was then) the "communications center" for Howard Hughes. Today the two-story building itself is often labeled Art Deco or "muted" Art Deco, what with painted concrete exterior walls featuring ornamental detailing based on Egyptian imagery—pyramids and ziggurats, zigzags, chevrons, floral patterns, and other geometric motifs—but Didion described it as "like a faded movie exterior, a pastel building with chipped *art moderne* detailing, the windows now either boarded or paned . . . a rubber mat that reads WELCOME."

However, as Didion notes, no one was ever welcome, because Howard Hughes didn't ever let anyone in.

Though I never spoke to Ackerman's source, I did learn that the person thought Hughes's bottles, if they still existed, had once been stored at 7000 Romaine Street.

Located in Hollywood between Orange Drive to the east, Sycamore Avenue to the west, and Willoughby Avenue to the south, the sixty-seven-thousand-square foot building—then known as 7020 Romaine—was constructed for a reported $2 million between 1930 and 1931 by Myers Brothers, a contractor specializing in structures for motion picture companies. The first year was the same one when Hughes released his iconoclastic aviation picture *Hell's Angels.*

Initially occupied by Multicolor, Ltd., the space was leased to a variety of tenants over the years, including the Hollywood Brewing Co. (maker of Red Ribbon Beer—which has no vintage value today, for what it's worth), an ammunitions plant during World War II, and a candy factory. But for most of the time, it was Howard Hughes's permanent address, save a brief interruption in the 1950s when he sold it to investors who then sold it to Eastman Kodak. It featured offices for his executives, aides, talent scouts, accountants, and other critical staff.

John William "Johnny" Meyer was hired as Hughes's press agent around 1939. A well-known man-about-town who probably had ties to the mob, Meyer had previously done publicity for Warner Bros. and owned the famous La Conga nightclub in Midtown Manhattan. If Hughes was shy, withdrawn, and often asocial, Meyer was the life of the party, an unyielding "check grabber" known for plying politicians and businessmen with booze and women to get things done.

The same year Meyer was hired by Hughes, a new liquor store opened in Beverly Hills called Vendome, offering "food and wines of distinction." Vendome quickly began catering to the Hollywood set of that era. Fred Astaire and Jimmy Stewart were regular visitors. Alfred Hitchcock purchased expensive vintage Bordeaux. The store was just around the block from the Beverly Wilshire, where Hughes frequently entertained, and a mile from where Meyers lived on Rodeo Drive.

It was also a brief drive from 7000 Romaine Street to the store at 327 North Beverly Drive, whether Meyer was doing that himself in Hughes's souped-up Buick Roadmaster or, more likely, receiving frequent deliveries of case upon case of alcohol.

If Hughes went through periods of his life when he was strictly drinking milk, Meyer was well-known for having a three-martini lunch. Meaning that many, if not most, of the bottles purchased at Vendome were surely for his own drinking and entertaining purposes. Any picture you find of Meyer on the internet inevitably shows the stocky, balding man holding a cigarette and/or a rocks glass, bottles and pretty actresses surrounding him.

In 1947, Meyer testified to a Senate committee that the year before he had spent $164,000 of Hughes's money entertaining government and army officials in the hope of winning contracts like the one for "the Spruce Goose," the derisive term for Hughes's flying boat, now known as one of the biggest flops in aviation history.

Still, I learned, quite a few of these Vendome deliveries made it into Hughes's office as well during his lifetime.

OF COURSE, IF birth eventually gives us bottles to pursue one day, conversely it is death that sometimes brings unexpected bottles back into the world and our lives.

"People would always give my father bottles of bourbon for his birthday, but he wasn't much of a drinker, and I remember [after] he passed moving a number of those bottles out and bringing them wherever I was living," Stephen Remsberg once recalled.

My grandfather Stanley Goldfarb passed on November 14, 2013, at age eighty-six. After the funeral, at the Seudat Havara'ah (first meal of mourning) in his Great Neck apartment, which he moved to in his seventies because he could no longer walk stairs, as relatives munched on deli sandwiches and bagels with lox, we began going through his final dwelling, seeing what we each wanted to keep to remember the man.

For most of our small clan, that was family heirlooms or his collection of Jewish artwork or especially Grandpa's beloved kachina dolls that he had acquired on frequent trips to the American Southwest.

I headed straight for an ornate cabinet near the kitchen where I knew he stored his booze. I didn't expect much. Grandpa wasn't much of a drinker, still stuck on the bastardized versions of tiki and tropical drinks that emerged in the postwar era of his young adulthood. I swear, the guy would order a piña colada no matter what type of restaurant we were dining at.

Chinese restaurant? Piña colada.

Family spot? Piña colada.

Steakhouse in the Theater District? Piña colada.

You'd be surprised how many places in Manhattan and on Long Island could accommodate this off-trend order.

Grandma Barbara, his wife, on the other hand, who had died three years earlier, was strictly a highball drinker, usually with Seagram's 7 and ginger ale. It was surely something she had been drinking since she had first started drinking.

As I said, I didn't expect much when I wheeled back the cabinet doors, and I didn't get much either.

Old, half-drunk bottles of Gordon's Gin and Johnnie Walker Red Label, some off-brand triple sec and peach schnapps, Bacardí, perhaps for the aforementioned coladas, and some Midori, something that hadn't been popular since the 1980s and which Grandpa had opened and then closed so long ago that the cap had been soldered on by a glowing green stickiness.

"Now *that* is a banal liquor collection," remarked my uncle Les, who had wandered over to investigate.

Indeed it was. Nothing worth drinking, nothing with any value to sell, nothing any collector would possibly want.

Yet I still took those bottles home with me. To pour them down the drain and immediately recycle them seemed a bit too cruel. Yes, they were banal bottles, but they were Grandpa's banal bottles.

That night, to toast Stanley Goldfarb one final time, I fashioned a cocktail out of the gin, peach schnapps, and Midori. It wasn't good, of course, but I enjoyed the drink just the same.

AFTER HUGHES'S DEATH in 1976, no one sat shiva at 7000 Romaine Street. The by-now-shabby "stone fortress," as many in the press labeled it, was sold by Summa Corporation—what Hughes's holding company had been renamed in 1972—to Knight Harris. His company, Producers Film Center, was already renting office space in the facility, and he had himself done some film processing for Hughes back in the day. But even Harris was unaware of what all came with the two-store property.

"A great deal of the building has been closed to us, presumably because the estate is still looking for his will," Harris told the Associated Press upon his purchase in 1977.

In fact, Summa Corporation continued leasing from Harris some of its former space simply to store items, both big and small, both important and irrelevant, that had surrounded Hughes when he had gone about his workday—movie cameras and airline maps and putters for working on his short game—back when he still went into 7000 Romaine, before he'd shifted his life to living and working exclusively out of his houses and hotel rooms.

Even as Hughes's estate was settled over the next couple of decades, I reckon none of the hundreds of his, real and purported, heirs had much interest in anything stored at 7000 Romaine, if they even knew about it, being more interested in his land or his buildings or his cold, hard cash.

So any old bottles that were there just sat there, unbothered, for decades.

Maybe they were occasionally talked about when new people were hired by Harris, when contractors or deliverymen came by the facility.

"You see the closed office there? That used to be Howard Hughes's office. There's still some of his stuff in there."

"Anything cool?"

"Naw, just a bunch of old junk."

That must have been how Kevin Langdon Ackerman's source got introduced to the collection. Did he even know it had value until my *New York Times* article on dusty hunting appeared?

I just needed to figure out a way to access 7000 Romaine Street and its treasures myself.

Harris died in 2003, and his children, Michael and Cindy, would take over both Producers Film Center and its 7000 Romaine Street space. I struggled to make contact with them.

Unfortunately, before I figured out a plan, an endgame was thrust upon me. And, much like major corporate acquisitions would ruin many modern spirits categories, a major corporation would screw up my and Ackerman's and every other vintage hunters' chances of swooping in and securing Howard Hughes's dusty booze.

In the final days of December 2021, Canadian developer Onni Group purchased 7000 Romaine Street, now known as Romaine + Sycamore, for $40 million.

If there was any of Hughes's booze still left within the 66,900 square feet of property, no one seemed to care, and it certainly wasn't reported on.

I was beginning to wonder if the dusty bottles had just been tossed.

PRIVATE LABELS AND PERSONAL BOTTLES

In a past era, back when bourbon was just to drink and not collect—or rarely drunk at all, like in the glut era—some restaurants, bars, hotels, and even private individuals were able to source and package their own whiskey. Today bars and restaurants don't really do what are known as "private labels"—depending on the state, it might even be illegal, a sure sign of what's known as "favoritism" from liquor companies that aren't supposed to influence which third-tier businesses they support. (The same is not true in Japan; see "Ken's Choice," page 23.)

While some of these private labels have become famed unicorns from the past, others aren't really known by the general bourbon-drinking public anymore—though they are major scores for those in the know. The bulk of the private bottlings from the past came from two key players: Julian Van Winkle III and Kentucky Bourbon Distillers (the ur-Willett); both specialized in this genre seemingly out of pure money-making necessity.

CORTI BROTHERS, BLUE SMOKE, OLD ADVOCATE, AND OTHER PRIVATE LABEL VAN WINKLES

In the 1980s, Julian Van Winkle III found himself with four young children, a ton of well-aged bourbon (from Yellowstone, Old Boone Distillery, and especially Stitzel-Weller), and his own bottling line. He could put some into gimmicky decanters, sure, but a few customers actually wanted their own private label bourbon. Like Corti Brothers, an Italian grocer in Sacramento, which purchased single barrels of Van Winkle Private

Reserve from 1986 through 1994; some have been hammered at auction for as high as $30,000. Probably the second-most-coveted private Van Winkle is one from Blue Smoke, Danny Meyer's upscale barbecue joint once located on Park Avenue in Manhattan—his Old Rip Van Winkle Blue Smoke 18 Year was available at the restaurant for years, and some full bottles managed to escape. One of the stranger private ones was Old Advocate, bottled by a few lawyers (their names: Messrs. Hanselman, Henricksen, Hext, Patton, and Wiethe) who ran into Van Winkle III at a liquor store in 1996 and talked him into the proposition. Another of my favorite "private Pappies," if you will, is a 20 Year bottled for *BloodHorse*, a thoroughbred racing newsletter, for a couple of dozen of their top advertisers in 1997. There were private label Van Winkles from restaurants like The Village Pub in Woodside, California; bars like the Twisted Spoke in Chicago; liquor stores like Binny's in Chicago and New York's Park Avenue Liquor Shop; and even personalized bottles with hand-scribed calligraphy ("a pain in the butt," claims Van Winkle III), which are some of the funnier dusties one can find themselves in possession of, as they wonder: "Who exactly was Deloris Wilson?"

VAN BLANKLE AND
OTHER SINGLE-BARREL PAPPY

By the early 2000s, Pappy Van Winkle was beginning to garner acclaim from early connoisseurs, and some of them wanted their own barrels of it. Randy Blank, a chemical engineer from Houston, cold-emailed Van Winkle III in 2004 and ended up purchasing his own Van Winkle 12 Year Old Lot B—"Van Blankle," which would, in turn, become a legendary bottle. Retail shop owners like Edmond Kubein, of San Francisco's Civic Center Market, and Ryan Maloney, of Julio's Liquors in Westborough, Massachusetts, and restaurants like Husk in Charleston,

South Carolina (picked by chef Sean Brock), and City Grocery in Oxford, Mississippi (picked by chef John Currence), would likewise grab their own barrels of Pappy. "There was no rhyme or reason, no game plan," Van Winkle III told me, as to who got Van Winkle single barrels throughout the late 1990s and early 2000s. He estimates it was just a few dozen retailers, bars, restaurants, and individuals in his top markets who got single barrels between that 1986 Corti's pick and the end of this program in 2011. "There were less than fifty. But more than twenty." Even in today's hyperaware collector's era, some of the bottlings have been forgotten to time, never even cataloged online. "Whenever I try talking to someone about single-barrel Pappy these days, you'd think I'm trying to find Keyser Söze—people get real quiet real quick," jokes Jamie Marcus, a Massachusetts-based collector with a specific interest in acquiring Pappy Van Winkle 15 Year Old single barrels.

RED HOOK RYE, SPEAKEASY SELECT, AND OTHER PRIVATE WILLETTS

As already mentioned, Willett Family Estate is one of the most coveted bourbon labels from the past, and still today. And the most coveted bottlings of this coveted brand are typically the private label releases done in the late 2000s. Those include the aforementioned Red Hook Rye, perhaps the whale of all whales: four 23- and 24-year-old barrels selected between 2006 and 2008, to the tune of a few hundred bottles or so. Originally priced at a mere $75, it sold so slowly that some bottles were still on the shelf in 2009 when typical New York real estate shuffling forced LeNell Camacho Santa Ana to close up shop. Today bottles go for the tens upon tens of thousands of dollars. There was also Speakeasy Select and Rathskeller Rye, bottled in 2007 by Louisville's "great hotel," the Seelbach. Rogin's Choice was 25-year-old bourbon labeled for a tavern in Osaka, Japan, and The Bitter Truth was a 24-year-old rye from two Munich bartenders that hit the German market in 2009.

BERGHOFF

Berghoff is a legendary, still-family-owned German restaurant in Chicago; the Van Winkle family began bottling private label Stitzel-Weller bourbon for it as far back as the 1960s and up until 1972, when they sold the distillery. Starting in 1992, Julian Van Winkle III regained the contract and provided the restaurant with 14-year-old Stitzel-Weller in screw-top Berghoff bottles—in fact, the restaurant was his biggest customer at the time.

STONE CASTLE

Bottled by a son as a tribute to his late father, Stone Castle refers to the historic and once-beautiful, but by-then dilapidated, Old Taylor Distillery, which Cecil Withrow purchased in 1994 with claims he had plans to turn it into a restaurant. Unfortunately, he couldn't fully renovate it before he died in 2000. Withrow had also sourced some barrels from the George T. Stagg Distillery (now known as Buffalo Trace) that he planned to bottle and export to Japan, another idea he'd never live to see. Instead, his son Michael bottled Stone Castle Special Reserve No.53 at 10 years old, exactly a year after his father's death. The bottles are similar in shape to the current Michter's Single Barrel, with a wide neck tapering down to a thick base.

13

YEARNING FOR YESTERYEAR

IN MANY WAYS, the COVID-19 pandemic would change everything about vintage spirits. Much of this was bad, but for some people, a lot of it was very good.

For one, it would bring more bottles out into the open as private collectors—who had perhaps lost their job or stopped making their usual income—had no choice but to turn dusty bottles into cash.

"It's unicorn season!" Pablo Moix joked when I phoned him up early in the pandemic, back when we could still laugh at things. He called the secondary market at the time the Wild Wild West. "Dealers you didn't know existed have come out of the woodwork."

Many liquor stores and distributors, with nothing to do for a few months, now took the unexpected free time they'd never had before to organize warehouses and back rooms—voila! Forgotten dusty bottles suddenly appeared.

Meanwhile, many great bars were forced to whittle down their massive collections by selling bottles to go—several states' ad hoc emergency pandemic laws would allow it—in order to continue paying rent and partial salaries for furloughed employees.

Jack Rose was one, and on a rainy March 20, 2020, it began offering some twenty-seven hundred bottles (including repackaged single drams from already opened rarities) to masked customers who lined up, socially distanced six feet apart, on 18th Street NW. By midday, the line had wrapped all the way around the corner to California Street NW.

Despite the tragedy of those early days of COVID, people seemed to find comfort in taking their minds off of it by trying to score Bill Thomas's dusty bottles of obscure Willett Family Estate, or maybe a 15-year-old Japanese Tribute export from Wild Turkey, or perhaps his stock of old single malt. The bar's website even crashed that day.

"When we come out of this on the other side, I want to be debt-free and get everyone back to work—that means selling a shit ton of whiskey," said Thomas at the time. "It's going to take a little creativity, a little elbow grease. We're doing everything we can."

Meanwhile, a bar owner like Moix was doing the opposite of Thomas—buying, buying, buying. "It's the busiest it's ever been, the most active I've ever seen it in history," he told me of the secondary market. He was actively contacting well-known vintage collectors and bar owners, like Jamie Boudreau, to see if they needed to let go of anything. "Everyone is selling, everyone is buying, everyone is haggling."

Yet he, too, was selling many of Old Lightning's rarest bottles, like a full lineup of The Macallan Cask Strength that had been discontinued in 2012—some at prices as high as $10,000—in order to retain staff. Neal Bodenheimer, owner of the James Beard Award–winning bar Cure in New Orleans, sold off vintage bottles from his personal stash, since Louisiana was one state that didn't allow bottle sales to-go.

"I didn't know what I'd ever do with these cool bottles; they never had an express purpose, since [Cure] has never had a vintage spirits program," he told me. "I'm not that emotionally attached to these bottles. If it gives someone else joy and helps fund our team, that's great."

What the pandemic also did was create a whole new breed of dusty hunter.

"There have been a whole slew of recent dusty finds because so many people are bored, stuck at home, and have started going around searching stores," Jonah Goodman told me in 2020.

"It was like throwing gasoline on a raging fire," thought Owen Powell. "Suddenly, everybody was collecting anything they could. Baseball cards, sneakers—it all went through the roof. They're sitting at home, working at home, and spending all day online. And they're drinking more."

By February 2022, Thomas had rebuilt Jack Rose's stock so well that he had more bottles of rare whiskey than he did before the pandemic.

"Whiskey is bulletproof, literally," he said. "The whiskey market is going nowhere but up."

Moix, too, was optimistic about his vintage bar's future.

"I'm planning when Old Lightning reopens, on day one, to have the strongest offerings you've ever seen," Moix predicted for me. "I want people to come in skeptical: 'Oh, what can they possibly have on the shelves now?'

"And then they look . . . 'FUUUUUUUCK.'"

But by 2023, Old Lighting was still shuttered, and Moix had pivoted to a completely different sort of vintage whiskey business.

───⌣───

BY THE TIME the pandemic was nearing its end (did it ever end?), a whole new breed of vintage retail and "on-premise" spots (industry lingo for bars) had arrived, many of them plotted out by people finally deciding to turn their passions into careers while bored at home on Zoom calls.

With his connections already in place, Owen Powell was able to sell enough bottles to fund his dream bar. Called Neat, it would open in the hip NuLu neighborhood of Louisville on January 15, 2022. I found myself there by March, stunned by Powell's inventory and very fair prices.

The unassuming spot is laid out with a mahogany bar, tufted leather barstools, and low-slung sofas. Red velvet curtains keep it dark and moody at all times; it looks a bit like a relaxed cigar lounge, if we were still in the era when those were popular. Vintage bourbon ads and other paraphernalia line the walls, including a particularly amusing Wild Turkey mirror from Japan hanging in the bathroom, probably not an official promotional item as it is rife with misspellings.

More than 90 percent of Neat's bottles are vintage, and it's not simply the well-known trophies like Stitzel-Weller or even Red Hook Rye, the latter of a type that hardly interests Powell. ("That's $40,000 that's going to sit on the shelf and not make me any money. I'd rather buy tons of $100, $200 bottles that I've actually vetted.") Every time I've been back to Neat over the last two years, Powell has turned me on to some hidden gem I wasn't aware of. He was the first to truly show me the brilliance of obscure label, pre-fire Heaven Hill.

Meanwhile, Brad Bonds had gone from being a Verizon sales rep to a BMW dealer, spending six years dusty-hunting, ingratiating himself with the growing community, building a collection, and tasting anything he could—he estimates he's probably consumed $5 million worth of dusty bourbon over the last decade.

One day in 2017, he saw a news report that vintage spirits dealing had been made legal in Kentucky. To him, it was like when marijuana had become allowed out in California. "Holy crap, my hobby is now legal," he recalls. "'Honey, get the kids, we're moving!'"

He would, across the Ohio River to Northern Kentucky and the burgeoning town of Covington, where he, along with partner Shannon Smith, a local lawyer and bourbon enthusiast who could help navigate this tricky new world legally, would open Revival Vintage Bottle Shop in August 2020.

Unlike Neat, Revival focuses more heavily on retail.

"People just started walking in to sell things," he told me in late 2022. A few weeks before, a guy had come in the door with fifteen Old Crow Chessmen. "It sounds cheesy, but it's kind of like *Pawn Stars*," he says, referencing the popular reality show about wheeling and dealing Las Vegas pawnbrokers. Still, Bonds says he buys from only about 5 percent of the walk-ins. There's just so much out there.

And that's why both he and Powell have little fear about building their businesses completely around a nonrenewable resource like vintage spirits. There are so many old men and women in Kentucky who worked in the bourbon industry for years, got gifted bottles, and were issued every new release off the bottling line. Powell heard a great rumor that Pappy's teetotaling secretary is still alive and has a sealed bottle of everything Stitzel-Weller ever produced during her tenure. The math doesn't completely seem feasible, but the greatest vintage bottles often seem to appear from an impossible place.

"The initial reaction is I want that shit," says Powell. "But then it's also like, fuck. I don't want to buy it. But I do want to make sure that when they sell it, they get what they should get for it, and that it goes in a museum because that kind of collection, it's probably the best collection out there."

Every year people die, and every year more incredible collections are brought out into the open. Kentucky's vintage law is written to cater to estate sale companies, which can now unload a deceased's entire collection to someone like Powell or Bonds or the Justins. But it's not really a competition.

"This vintage renaissance is just at its beginning," says Bonds. "I don't know, maybe I'm crazy, maybe I'm out of this world, but I think we have more upside than all the Fortune 500 companies combined."

AFTER SPENDING SO much time with dusty hunters, I began to wonder why vintage spirits became their particular obsessions.

Was it really because spirits from the past taste so much better? Was traveling to liquor stores where the clerk is behind bulletproof glass simply more exhilarating to them than skydiving? Was it just a weird way to turn a tidy profit?

Or was it possible that they simply yearned for the past, for whatever reason?

The rise of faux dusties and ersatz vintage over the last few years might point to this being the case.

A couple of years before he put his vintage passion into Neat, Owen Powell launched Fern Creek Bourbon, a revival of an old label that first appeared in the 1890s, probably produced by the Mellwood Distillery. When Prohibition shut the distillery down, the brand disappeared too for a couple of decades, until General Distilling revived it from the 1940s through 1950s.

Powell would source bourbon from large factory producers like Midwest Grain Products (MGP) in Indiana, blend the bourbon in small batches, and bottle it at barrel proof as is de rigueur among bourbon fans today. In a way, he was mashing the fond memories of yesteryear with the preferred flavor profile of modern day.

Of course, Michter's is the most famous modern brand based on a vintage label.

Its roots date all the way back to 1753, when Michael Shenk filed a patent for a gristmill located near Snitz Creek in what is now Schaefferstown, Pennsylvania, about seventy-five miles northwest of Philadelphia. Back then it would have been a family still house, not uncommon in the area at the time among the Mennonite farmers. By 1860 the distillery had been sold to a distant relative, Abraham Bomberger.

Post-Prohibition, most Pennsylvania distilling operations either moved to Kentucky or just went defunct. Louis Forman came to own the distillery in 1942 and eventually renamed it Michter's, a portmanteau of his sons' names, Michael and Peter. He would release an Original Sour Mash Whiskey, re-created based on an old recipe found in the attic of one of the buildings.

Drinkers yearned for yesteryear even when it was yesteryear.

By 1972, right at the start of the glut, Dick Stoll took over distilling operations, and he would continue adding to the glut, producing some whiskey that was world-class (the distillate for what would become the vaunted A. H. Hirsch), but a lot that was used for gimmicky purposes (see the King Tut decanter).

In 1990 the distillery went bankrupt, and the brand had no choice but to lock the doors and turn over the keys to the bank. Over the next three years, looters would help themselves to much of the memorabilia, bottles, and even full barrels still in the facility.

By 1996, Joseph Magliocco, a lawyer who was also owner of Chatham Imports, a wine importer, was looking to add a whiskey brand to his portfolio. Around then he came to notice that the Michter's trademark had lapsed and not been renewed. He'd actually been a Michter's salesman while in college at Yale.

"It seemed like a shame to let this iconic American whiskey brand disappear," he thought, and so he acquired it for a mere $245 and some paperwork.

By then, Pennsylvania didn't really have distilling operations to speak of. So Magliocco moved the company to Kentucky, which was still three years away from even launching a Bourbon Trail. He sourced some quality bourbon and rye from United Distillers in Louisville, bottled it at Julian Van Winkle III's facility, and began releasing Michter's 10 Year Old Bourbon and Rye, selling for around $38 apiece.

They didn't exactly look like the brand's bottles from the past, and they in no way tasted like it, but it didn't matter. Michter's now had a past, a present, and a great future. Today it's one of the industry's most coveted modern brands.

Two of the hottest "new" releases of 2022 were also of the faux-vintage variety.

The Maryland Heritage Series seemed to come out of nowhere, offering three different bottles with vintage labels. In the summer, Sherbrook Unfiltered Straight Rye Whiskey, Sherwood Pure Rye, and Mount Vernon Straight Rye Whiskey Aged 14 Years, appeared on Seelbachs.com, an online craft spirits retailer owned by Blake Riber. Though they all presented labels nearly identical to those glorious dusties from the 1940s and '50s that recalled the state's once-abundant rye-distilling history, none of these modern releases were of a Maryland rye style.

Instead, the owners of these labels—two Maryland liquor store owners—sourced MGP rye whiskey, something they readily admitted in marketing materials. Aged fourteen years, it was admittedly good stuff, and though it tasted nothing like the vintage bottle of Sherbrook I had once tried a few years back at Copper & Oak in Manhattan, collectors didn't seem to mind. Two hundred three-bottle sets sold out immediately at a whopping $1,199.99 price tag.

Around the same time came Fortuna Bourbon from Pablo Moix, who, earlier in the year, had also launched Rare Character, a whiskey company designed to hearken back to the era of private label bourbon and rye, with single-barrel releases produced exclusively for bars and restaurants.

"I'd always loved the look of the Fortuna labels," says Moix of the brand once produced by Louisville's Glencoe Distillery as early as the 1880s and up until Prohibition. The labels are an almost shimmery silver color with cerulean lettering. It's certainly very unusual compared to other brands, and they certainly pop on the shelves. "As a Latino, I also love that it's a Spanish-enunciated word," says Moix. "*Fortuna*. Meaning 'fortune.' And as someone who collects whiskey and drinks a lot of old whiskey, I love a lot of old Glencoe whiskey."

Post-Prohibition, National Distillers and Bardstown Distillery would bottle Fortuna until the late 1950s. Eventually the facilities and label names were acquired by Heaven Hill, where Moix's friend Andy Shapira was part of the family that has long owned it. Moix acquired the trademark, and Shapira became his business partner in Fortuna. Moix also sourced barrels of whiskey that someone else had distilled, though his source remains undisclosed. Unusual for these brands from yesteryear, however, is that Moix tried to make his Fortuna blend match a vintage flavor profile, tasting it alongside dusty bottles of Fortuna he had acquired.

It seems to have worked. Soon after his first release, an older man reached out to Moix. He told Moix he had a vintage bottle of Fortuna that he cherished, and that he had been slowly sharing with his son over the years. When he tasted Moix's Fortuna, though, he found it so similar in flavor profile, so equally enjoyable, that he now realized he could save the dusty Fortuna and just drink the modern incarnation instead.

To me, that revelation was eye-opening.

Yes, I realized, this was the next logical step!

Like rich guys who keep real works of art in a vault while displaying facsimile paintings around their house, it seemed that a good yesteryear label could offer the exact same sensation to vintage booze collectors simply in the hobby to feel something from the past.

The past could now become the present, and be made scalable.

WHEN I SPOKE to Owen Powell in late October 2022, he was expanding his bar space even more, business was booming so much. At the time he had been living at his fiancée and co-owner Danie Elder's house while using his own house to store his collection. By the end of December, he had added a large vintage bottle shop component to Neat and begun moving his full collection in. In January, the two would marry.

Meanwhile, Bonds opened a larger, six-thousand-square-foot space he unofficially dubbed "Willy Wonka's Vintage Wonderland," now with a full liquor license, able to do 1950s Old Grand-Dad "on tap," vintage bottle pours, and even past-era cocktails.

"I think vintage spirits are God's gift to us," says Bonds. "It's like your grandma's cooking in a bottle. *Trapped.* And so I get to share that with people and share my passion."

These vintage bars of the future—many of which are improbably focused completely on vintage pours—have been able to happen only because consumers have become more and more aware of the category, more and more interested in traveling back to the past, and tasting it too.

"Guests have quit asking me, 'Are those bottles safe to drink?' More frequently, they pull their phones out, display a relative's old booze, and ask what it's worth," says Kristopher Peterson, who continues his spirits archivist role at Mordecai today while also consulting for Billy Sunday. He says guests want to study these old bottles, want to learn the distilleries' histories, want him to regale them with any interesting stories around the bottles.

"People want to feel connected and transported to the past. It's romantic, sentimental, and nostalgic—all qualities people love investing in," Peterson's former colleague Tom Lisy once told me.

Bourbon connoisseurs who have long cared only about the latest and greatest—mostly meaning Pappy, Pappy, and more Pappy, with maybe a side of Blanton's—have also started to see the beauty, and more favorable economics, of drinking vintage. Why spend $1,500 on a bottle of Pappy that is just going to be made again next year when that same $1,500 could buy a bottle or two from back when Franklin D. Roosevelt was in office?

It's not only in Kentucky either.

By 2023, Manhattan finally had a vintage amaro bar, One Fifth, a Greenwich Village Italian joint opened by acclaimed chef Marc Forgione. And across town, in the East Village, longtime bar owner, dusty expert, and human decanter lead tester Joshua Richholt had opened his own dream bar, Down & Out.

Unlike many American collectors, Richholt was raised in Alberta and thus has an infinity for vintage Canadian Club, owning a bottling from every single year dating back to 1911. While most aficionados would never drink that brand today, the vintage versions are great, light and creamy, but hardly thin in mouthfeel. Like Caroline Paulus from Justins' House of Bourbon, Richholt is also a former archaeologist, with a master's from the University of Lethbridge. He traded a low-paying career of discovering thirty-eight-thousand-year-old mammoth tusks in Belgium for a more drinkable form of carbon dating.

The most on-the-nose opening of the pandemic, however, might have been The Doctor's Office in Seattle. The twelve-seat tasting room bar is owned by an actual doctor, Dr. Matthew Powell, a hospital medicine specialist for Virginia Mason Medical Center and MultiCare Auburn Medical Center and a longtime cocktail geek, having tweeted under the name @CocktailMD for years.

A former serviceman as well, Powell had the grave misfortune of opening his bar in late February 2020. Thus, he would spend the bulk of the early pandemic working ninety-hour weeks fighting COVID and saving lives while earning extra income to single-handedly keep his bar afloat.

"It was more stressful than when I was stationed in Afghanistan," he told me.

Indeed, it's hard to imagine that many people—other than those who became seriously ill, or worse—had as hard a pandemic as him, being both a health care professional and a small business owner in the hospitality space in the very city where the first confirmed COVID case in America was reported.

Dr. Matthew Powell had better luck, however, surfing the web one night, when he stumbled upon a Profiles in History auction for a certain "lot #1401."

It was simply described as

"Howard Hughes (90+) vintage liquor bottles."

14

DUSTIES ON THE AUCTION BLOCK

IF SOME VINTAGE spirits enthusiasts, bored at home during the pandemic, decided to go out and start their own quasi-vintage labels, or open their own vintage bars, others simply decided to keep it a hobby and move it strictly to the online realm, bringing the auction market to the forefront for many American collectors for the first time ever.

Alcohol auctions have existed for centuries, of course, though they've rarely been focused on spirits, they mostly weren't held in America, and they were conducted strictly in person.

In Germany, as early as 1806, Kloster Eberbach, a Cistercian monastery, auctioned off new vintages of wine from a group of local estates. The first French wine auctions were held in Burgundy beginning in the mid-1800s. The earliest wine auction in the States was held by Christie's, in Chicago, in 1969. By 1980, the auction house was attempting to hold its first New York City wine auction when local retailers whined to the New York State Liquor Authority, and the event was canceled. By 1981 the first-ever Auction Napa Valley was held—and in the following four decades, it has raised more than $200 million for charity.

By the time auction houses began to deal with spirits, it was often our old friend Cognac, but especially single malt Scotch whisky.

In 1996 the first online wine auction site, WineBid, finally emerged. In 2020 alone, its revenue exceeded $400 million.

Finally, in 1997, there was WhiskyAuction.com out of Fockbek, Germany, launched by buddies Klaus Rosenfeld and Thomas Krüger; the latter had been collecting whisky miniatures since 1974, when he was just thirteen years old. (Even when he reached age twenty-one, he was hesitant to drink whisky, concerned he might like it so much he would deplete his collection.)

"When I started collecting, I hoped so much that whisky would be something special. But I never thought that it would become so valuable," says Krüger.

By the 1980s, Krüger was pursuing full-size bottles of original single malts, U.S. whiskeys from the Prohibition era, and whiskeys distilled in atypical producing countries like his native Germany. As he was building his collection, he realized the in-person auction markets were quite awful for whisky—he had bought miniatures from Christie's in London and Sotheby's in New York and not enjoyed the experience at all. Fellow miniature collector Rosenfeld knew a little bit about the early internet and had a site up after a year and a half of designing it.

Their first auction offered a couple of dozen of Krüger's own miniatures. An Italian guy made the first purchase. Even early on, people from across the globe were using WhiskyAuction.com, finding the site via Yahoo! and Alta Vista searches. Back then, and somewhat still today, Europe's biggest collectors of old whisky were based in Germany, Italy, and Sweden. Few came from Great Britain.

"At that time, nearly nobody in the U.K. collected whisky," says Krüger. "They all drank it."

Their current website still looks like it's from the early 2000s, and that's after a recent revamp—well into 2022 it still looked like a Geo-Cities monstrosity from the 1990s. A bit hard to navigate and use, nevertheless it continues to offer great dusties across the board. Though one vintage auction player told me, "This website just hurts my ass to look at it. It makes me fucking sick."

Despite its aesthetics, in the emerging vintage spirits world, you couldn't simply set up a fly-by-night operation. You needed to have the logistics and manpower to be able to receive individual bottles from across the globe, assess them, make sure they weren't counterfeit, then price them, list them, and distribute them back out across the globe. Early on, there weren't enough experts around to handle these types of things.

"I think some of the auction sites seem to have been started by people who had collections to sell rather than an actual trading platform for buyers and sellers," Isabel Graham-Yooll, a longtime professional in spirits auctions, told me.

You needed a robust website, one that wasn't going to choke when inundated with bidders; it likewise would need to be set up with technical systems that didn't allow people to snipe bids in the final seconds just because they had faster internet at home. (Many sites would eventually institute what are called "anti-sniping" or "soft close" or "dynamic bidding" or "popcorn" technology, extending final bids for a few minutes every time a new bid comes in late.)

The Glasgow-based Scotch Whisky Auctions (scotchwhiskyauctions.com) would be the first U.K.-based online site, started in 2010 by Tam Gardiner, who then had a small retail whisky shop called Tam's Drams. He wanted to start an online auction site with his buddy Bill Mackintosh but assumed it must be illegal. After a couple of calls, they learned that, so long as they had an off-premise license, they were good to go.

Their first auction, on May 1, 2011, offered a little more than one hundred bottles, many from Gardiner's own collection. An Ardbeg 1977 went for a mere £240, and a Port Ellen 1979 was won for just £740. Both are worth at least four to five times that these days. They've held an online auction just about every month since, with, at the time I write this, their 143rd auction having just occurred, one offering around eight thousand lots.

Other early sites included Whisky-Online Auctions (whisky-online auctions.com) coming out of Blackpool, England, Whisky Auctioneer (whiskyauctioneer.com) from Perth, Scotland, and Just Whisky (just -whisky.co.uk) out of Dunfermline, Scotland, all still running strong. With so many online auction sites now residing in the same country where the vintage and rare single malt had been distilled and was being released, it was a lot easier for both buyers and sellers.

In 2015, Whisky.Auction would be launched by perhaps the most prominent name in all of vintage spirits collecting.

* * *

NO MATTER WHO I spoke to for this book, no matter what subject we were discussing, whether miniature bottles, the auction market, vintage single malt, or old rum, everyone would eventually and inevitably mention one guy's name:

Sukhinder.

He was the man who had opened the 1780 bottle of Harewood House rum and acquired the remaining existing flagons of British Royal Navy rum.

He was the owner of the miniature 1919 Springbank and James MacArthur's Malt Mill that sold at auction for big bucks.

He was one of the earliest guys to play the auction markets and likewise one of the earliest to sell online, when he launched Whisky .Auction.

He was the owner of the best single malt collection in the world.

Sukhinder Singh is perhaps the king of vintage wheeling and dealing on either side of the pond, not only having cofounded The Whisky Exchange, but having collected vintage spirits via the auction markets since the 1980s.

His parents had come to the United Kingdom in the mid-1960s and, like many Indians of the era, opened a grocery store. One loyal customer at the time persuaded them to open a liquor component, which they did. The Nest, in Hanwell, West London, was issued a liquor license in 1972, making them the first Indian family in the United Kingdom to receive one. As a young boy, Singh was captivated by their single malts, all stocked on the top shelf, and which he'd have to get a ladder to retrieve for any interested buyers.

He soon shifted from a childhood stamp-collecting obsession toward collecting miniature bottles of single malt. Early on, he won an auction for a collection of eight thousand miniatures. Only five hundred were single malts, and he moved the rest. Within a decade, he had more than five thousand miniatures of single malt.

Singh eventually moved on to full-size bottles, spawned by inadvertently coming across a dusty of 1930s Kirkliston Pure Malt while buying miniatures; from then on, anything he personally liked he would stock up on, more concerned with quality than quantity.

He took an early gamble on the now-vaunted Black Bowmore, distilled in 1964 and first released in 1993 for just around £80. (It was nearly black in color due to extended sherry cask maturation.) Noticing how quickly it was selling out at his parents' store, he went around London, hitting various locations of Oddbins, a liquor retail chain, and cleared out their Black Bowmore stock. Today it goes for easily over $50,000.

"When I found liquid which I really liked, doesn't matter about age, whether it was young or it was old, if I had an opportunity to buy a small parcel, I would buy the parcel," he recalls.

He was early on with The Macallan as well, "blown away" by the 1950s and '60s distilled bottlings he tasted while traveling in Japan. He collected every single release there was. Even today he misses The Macallan from this golden era—as do many collectors.

"They find it too expensive. They find the quality probably not as good as it was," he says.

In 1999, when his parents retired and sold the business, he and his brother Rajbir decided to go into the whisky business full-time, immediately using the money to buy a small warehouse. Within six months they also had a website.

Being online so early in the game gave The Whisky Exchange a huge advantage over other retailers. As with bourbon in the 1980s, Japan was also at the forefront of single malt whisky in the 1990s and early 2000s—many Japanese bartenders and personal collectors would order from Singh, favoring 1970s bottlings of Brora and Ardbeg. Singh, in turn, would buy some of the earliest releases of Yamazaki.

And the whole time, he continued collecting the past:

A 1903 Glenfiddich bottling that the distillery doesn't even have.

A Longmorn 1971 "Scott's Selection."

The famed Macallan 1926 60 Year Old.

More than ten thousand bottles of single malt, almost certainly the best collection in the world, though very few modern releases from the last decade or so, as they hold little interest to him for taste or certainly historically.

In 2021, Singh sold The Whisky Exchange online and its three London-based brick-and-mortar sites, along with Whisky.Auction and all his other events and businesses, to the Pernod Ricard beverage group. He and his brother have remained as managing directors.

He continues collecting, unable to stop himself.

FAKES, REFILLS, COUNTERFEITING, AND TEENAGE FUNNY BUSINESS

We've now reached a section in the book that you may be interested in, but that I don't really wish to write about:

FAKES!

Yes, a sad fact of the human condition is that when anything becomes valued and coveted, counterfeit reproductions of said thing will arise. All the more so if the valued and coveted is rare and little seen.

Until very recently, fakes were not really an issue in the bourbon world. That's quite unlike the wine industry, where a mysterious German man could dupe a Koch brother into paying £105,000 for a supposed Thomas Jefferson–owned 1787 Château Lafitte (now spelled Lafite), or an Indonesian con man could sell millions of dollars of vintage fakes he had made in his apartment. True stories!

In bourbon, there was never anything of a high enough value to merit faking. A few dusty geeks might care about mid-century Stitzel-Weller, but no one else did.

That has all changed in the last decade with Pappy-mania, though most of the fakes on the market are what we would call refills.

REFILLS

By 2015 or so, a curious thing started to occur. If you'll recall, eBay banned liquor sales in 2012. Nevertheless, *empty* bottles of Pappy Van Winkle began to appear on the auction site. They weren't cheap either. Back then, a single, liquid-free bottle of 20 Year Old was going for $200. Mind you, its MSRP at the time, if you could find it, was just $149.99 for a full bottle.

Hmmm . . . why would anyone want these empty bottles?

Well, the answer is fairly obvious. You take an empty Van Winkle bottle, fill it with a more accessible, cheaper, but still wheated bourbon (Maker's Mark, Larceny, Weller if you could swing it), and suddenly you had turned an empty $200 bottle into a full $1,000 bottle.

This is still occurring today, with eBay overflowing with listings for Pappy empties, often at a "Buy It Now" price higher than your average person has ever paid for a full bottle of alcohol.

"It's about opportunity," says Jonah Goodman, who has seen unused tax strips for sale on Facebook and found labels for The Macallan 12 Year Old offered on Alibaba, an Amazon-like China-based e-tailer.

The most noted superhero combating refill culture for the past decade has been Adam Herz. Back in 2016, when I interviewed him for *Esquire*, he had started spending his free weekends cataloging all the empties on eBay. At first he noticed the same three or four users were buying all the empties.

So he began to write down the unique, hand-numbered codes on all visible 23 Year Old and Van Winkle Family Reserve Rye listings. When he matched those numbers of supposed empties to bottles for sales in one Facebook private group, he knew the secondary market had a major refilling problem, which still prevails today.

BREAK YOUR EMPTY BOTTLES!

But an empty bottle, once opened, has had its foil seal broken, you argue. Not a problem for a refiller—Amazon sells the same exact bottle coverings, in any color you wish, for a few bucks. With a hair dryer on high, it takes seconds to reseal a refill.

That's why all serious collectors who care about the integrity and legitimacy of the secondary market have no choice but to destroy their empty bottles, especially if they are putting them out with the recycling.

THE EARLY 2000S
ITALIAN CONNECTION

Of course, single malt Scotch is much more valuable than bourbon, and it has been for decades. Nearing the turn of the century, a flood of rare, extremely old, and never-before-known bottles began to mysteriously appear on the auction market, many selling for bonkers prices. The majority of the bottles were The Macallan, and the distillery itself purchased many of these dusties.

Experts eventually noticed plenty of errors in the labeling, and those who tasted some thought they seemed way too vibrant and "fresh" in flavor. By the summer of 2002, paper and glass experts had identified several bottles as clear fakes. Humorously, the Edrington Group, the new owner of The Macallan, had purchased some in order to inform its creation of what it would call The Macallan Replica Series. Of course, these bottles purporting to offer drinkers a replica of what 1841, 1851, 1861, 1874, and 1876 The Macallan—complete with snazzy, replica labels from the past—would have tasted like were simply offering a replica of a counterfeit. Nonetheless, the Replica Series bottles remain fairly valuable today.

The culprits were never caught, but they are thought to have been part of an organized crime syndicate.

"The finger generally points to Italy; it may be terribly unkind to say that, but the Italians are master forgers," said Charles MacLean, a whisky consultant for Bonhams auction house at the time. "From classical times, with major pieces of artwork, there is a long and heroic history of forgery."

A biased statement, perhaps, but most major collectors and dealers I spoke to still refuse to deal with Italian collectors they don't have a long-standing relationship with.

Today the top single malts have terrific tamper-proof systems—bourbon less so, though Buffalo Trace has begun to insert microchips in the Van Winkles and Antique Collection. Nevertheless, most major collectors I know also refuse to buy Pappy Van Winkle unless they fully know the provenance of it.

ANCIENT BOTTLES

Another case of opportunistic fakes involves bottles claimed to be so old they'd be nearly impossible to research. Many collectors and auction houses have taken to carbon-14, or radiocarbon, dating of the liquid in bottles, a process more often used for fossils. Professor Gordon Cook at the University of Glasgow has become renowned for dating rare spirits and uncovering fakes using a Radiocarbon Accelerator Unit.

For many bottles claimed to be from the nineteenth century, simple carbon-14 testing usually find them full of a modern liquid. Exactly dating a liquid from the distant past can be difficult, but dating anything post-1955 is quite easy. That was the year that open-air testing of nuclear devices would greatly increase across the globe; a radioactive isotope of carbon would forever after be found in all organic matter—like, say, the grain used to produce whiskey.

Famously, there's the viral story of the Hotel Waldhaus am See in St. Moritz, which sold a guest a pour for 9,999 Swiss francs from a bottle of what was purported to be 1878-distilled The Macallan. Later carbon-14 dating would find that the bottle was most likely filled with a blended Scotch distilled between 1970 and 1972.

PERIOD FAKES

We tend to think of counterfeiting and refilling of spirits bottles as a modern problem that affects only the high end of things. But for

the entire history of mass commerce, people have made cheap reproductions of widespread items. So, of course, long ago, unscrupulous
people—often organized crime even then—produced knock-off bottles
of booze, filled with who knows what. Usually just grain spirit and
coloring.

"If you're concerned about your health and safety, the minute you
know that something is fake, you shouldn't be tasting it," says Graham-
Yooll.

No one expected these bottles to be saved for decades until they
were old and collectible; they simply wanted to dupe a buyer, get some
cash, and get out of town before anyone tasted it. The only reason these
contemporary fakes have begun to emerge is because of the unexpected
boom in value of vintage spirits.

BUT CAN A KNOWN-FAKE HAVE VALUE?

"This delves into a sort of philosophical question for me," says Graham-
Yooll. "As a historian, I think they have great value."

For her, these period counterfeit bottles can tell the history of what
brands mattered enough to counterfeit in the past. They can likewise tell
the story of what people were drinking illicitly during Prohibition. They
can reveal weird anomalies, like bottles of "Scotch" that were imported
from Germany and never touched Scotland. These bottles reveal all sorts
of avenues of crime and fraud during past eras.

"Now, for me, that's fascinating," says Graham-Yooll. And yet
Whisky.Auction refuses to list them. Not that it hasn't considered
that explains Graham-Yooll. "We've discussed it on occasion because
we thought, well, this has got huge historic value, if not monetary
value."

Ultimately, it decided, if you start selling some clearly counterfeit bottles, you have gone down a rabbit hole with no ethical end in sight. But Graham-Yooll still collects these past-era counterfeits.

TEENAGE FUNNY BUSINESS

Having said all that, most "fakes" that are presented to auctioneers are actually not nefarious but, rather, the result of a comical error.

Say someone who has a modest, nearly lifelong liquor collection, but is a non- or infrequent drinker, brings in some booze—only for the auction house to find that the dusty Scotch bottle is full of apple juice and the old gin is nothing more than tap water.

What had happened is classic teenage shenanigans: Kids had helped themselves to their parents' liquor many years ago, and no one noticed until it was time to bring these dusty bottles to auction.

"Imagine their surprise when we tell them, you know, forty years later, that they've been keeping a bottle of iced tea in the liquor cabinet this entire time!" says Graham-Yooll.

Back in the United States, Bonhams was a rare, early entrant into the rare whiskey auction game, though strictly in person when it launched its series in 2009. However, for the most part, vintage spirits were kind of given short shrift to the fine art the auction house seemed to care more about, though that's been changing of late. That's good, because the cost of shipping bottles from overseas can be prohibitive.

The rules and regulations for fifty separate state liquor commissions make it very difficult for the United States as a whole to do online liquor auctions in the same way the United Kingdom can. But there are a few advantages for American auction houses.

"We didn't have world wars [on our continent] destroying collections in cellars and basements and whatnot. So a lot of the really old stuff can still be found here versus there [Europe] in some regards," says Joseph Hyman. For the past two decades he's been a whiskey consultant for the auction world, today a specialist of whiskey and rare spirits at Bonhams Skinner, the new house formed by a merger in March 2022. "Also, because we had Prohibition, a lot of people just bunkered and hid stuff they thought that you weren't allowed to have."

That's what has led to quite a few viral stories of new homeowners finding Prohibition-era collections buried in basements, sealed under staircases, or bricked into walls, such as the 2020 story about a couple who found sixty-six bottles of Old Smuggler Gaelic Whisky hidden in the walls and floorboards of their upstate New York home, which had once been owned by notorious bootlegger "Count" Adolph Humpfner.

"Most of the auctions here [in the United States] are through larger auction houses versus over in Europe, where most of them are stand-alone entities," says Hyman, explaining that in most European countries you can run a legal auction out of your tiny apartment.

———◦◦◦———

ONCE YOU GET Joseph Hyman on the phone, he's hard to get off. The man has a deep knowledge of the industry and strong feelings about the business. He even had thoughts on how my book should be written.

"You know, J. P. Morgan was the first dusty hunter," Hyman casually told me toward the end of one call. "The Morgans used to go up and buy collections from people."

Like that of Captain John Ridgely, who for decades owned the Hampton Mansion, north of Baltimore, the largest private residence in the country when it was built. According to typewritten log books, Morgan, then in his sixties, showed up one day in 1902 and bought an entire liquor collection for $7,600. It mostly consisted of Maryland rye from the era.

Like a lot of rich people of the Gilded Age, Morgan drank a lot and entertained a lot and needed a lot of booze to go around. He famously was a member of the Zodiac Club, which gathered together twelve titans of industry (each assigned a Zodiac sign) six times a year for bacchanalian feasts at high-end restaurants like the Metropolitan Club, Delmonico's, or Sherry's. Morgan, known as "Brother Libra," would serve the most and best alcohol when he hosted the dinners: not just the best vintages of Burgundy and Bordeaux but Cognac and Scotch too.

"They drank heavily at these dinners," says Joshua Feldman, a vintage collector and historian who works as a network administrator at the Morgan Library & Museum in Manhattan, where he has researched the man's collecting habits. "There's documentation in the collection about the drinks to be transferred from the seller for the purposes of these dinners."

Like a lot of people in his era, cellaring services were just a part of running a massive household, and Morgan employed Louis Sherry, his restaurateur friend who owned Sherry's. When Morgan died in 1913, Sherry decided to resign rather than work for Morgan's son, J. P. "Jack" Morgan Jr., but he agreed to do one final assessment of the family's wine and spirits cellar. Feldman has seen this handwritten document, which thoroughly lists all the clarets and ports and Madeira and champagne, dutifully noted with their vintages. The spirits were less thoroughly cataloged. Line 792 in the cellar book, just a single line, simply lists "ryes and Scotches," with a count of several hundred bottles of his whiskey.

"Was he a whiskey collector? Was he a dusty hunter?" asks Feldman. "[Previous] cellar books show a lot of really old bottles, like 1860s bourbon, rye, there's demijohns. So is that collecting, or is that just having a well-stocked cellar for guests with very fancy tastes? Part of being well-heeled back then was being able to offer an impressive set of selections for people, I'm guessing."

Feldman uncovered a story of Morgan collecting dusty booze even on the final trip of his life. En route home from Egypt, while in the South of France, staying at a hotel near the port of Marseille Fos, he scored a case of vintage-dated 1887 Chartreuse. Morgan would die in his sleep a few days later while at the Grand Hotel Plaza in Rome.

His son and heir had a lot of immediate concerns to deal with, yet he seemed especially worried about that dusty Chartreuse. He even had his butler write a letter to the concierge of the hotel to make sure that dusty Chartreuse got shipped safely back to New York.

"It's so funny to me," says Feldman. "There's a lot going on for Jack at this time. He's transferring the ownership of his father's bank to himself. He's disseminating his father's art collection, which was the world's largest at the time. And in the midst of all that, he's seemingly most concerned with a single case of old Chartreuse."

It would end up that Jack was actually more concerned with the influence-building that an old spirits collection could aid in. So instead of drinking it, he began to dole out gifts of his father's vintage whiskey to politicians like FDR and Harry S. Truman, other captains of industry, leaders of religion and medicine, the clergy—each with a professional nameplate attached to it:

FROM THE CELLAR OF
PIERPONT MORGAN
1837-1913

—

A SOUVENIR TO HIS FRIENDS
1915

One of the bottles the senior Morgan had purchased from John Ridgely would eventually get into the hands of a Supreme Court justice, James F. Byrnes. He eventually passed that bottle on to an anonymous friend, who was the grandfather of the man who passed the bottle to Joseph Hyman in 2021, ready for it to go to auction.

The bottle was a brown glass flask with Old Ingledew Whiskey, LaGrange, GA., Evans & Ragland embossed on it, the latter a grocer and whiskey bottler in Georgia after the Civil War. A note taped to the back claimed the whiskey had been distilled before that war:

"This Bourbon was probably made prior to 1865 and was in the cellars of Mr. John Pierpont Morgan from whose estate it was acquired upon his death."

"There'll be tons of people that say 'Bullshit,'" thought Hyman of this whole story. So he decided to get it tested.

Various chemical analyses were taken, and, though nothing is foolproof, Hyman assessed that these showed that the whiskey was probably distilled between 1763 and 1803 and that it was likewise made mostly of corn.*

As for Feldman, he's more interested in another Morgan dusty from the past.

A few years earlier, Boston Harbor Auctions had auctioned off items taken from Morgan's yacht, the *Corsair*, including fine china, Tiffany ashtrays and cigar cutters, game tables, and art. One of the items was another one of Morgan's bottles, this of J&G Stewart's of Edinburgh, a premium Scotch brand before Prohibition. It sold for $6,500.

---

* The *Guinness World Records* entrant for oldest whiskey, however, remains Baker's Pure Rye Whiskey, an 1847 Monongahela rye owned by Adam Herz, counterfeit bottle expert on the weekends, but more famously the writer of *American Pie*. He is also an expert on the vintage dating of whiskey. Herz strongly disputes that the Old Ingledew could be that old and claimed that Hyman had interpreted the data incorrectly.

"For me, that bottle has always been my unicorn," says Feldman. "I bet you it is really good. Just guessing."

THE ONLINE AUCTION market would really explode by 2015 or so. Asian customers were starting to get involved—one collector told me he would willingly pay 20 to 30 percent over market price, screwing things up for Western collectors—and Japanese whiskey had also become massive auction fodder by then. Some saw this whiskey as an investment, not something you'd ever drink. Though I hate the cynicism, as of this moment in time, those investors have been proven correct. But, to be clear, there were still plenty of people buying it to drink it.

Kurt Maitland, a whiskey collector and spirits writer from the Bronx, started playing the auction markets by 2014. Like many Americans, he realized once eBay was shut down for booze sales, that looking to Europe was the best ploy.

"I wanted to track down the shit that I was reading about and get a taste," he explains. "Shit" like Karuizawa, a cult Japanese whiskey, famous for its intensely sherried single malts, that had been off the market since 2001. Japanese whiskey expert Dave Broom describes it as tasting "earthy, feral, sooty but also of resin, old churches, and deep forests." Today bottles auction off for tens of thousands of British pounds, but back in 2014, few knew about Karuizawa and Maitland could still win an auction here or there.

"I mean, it wasn't cheap, but it wasn't as expensive as it is now," he explains. He opened everything himself or with a whiskey tasting club he was a part of, the latter often defraying the costs of pricey auction wins.

Maitland also wanted to purchase old Scotch to learn why it was so often considered better than today's incarnations.

"When you think about the actual making of Scotch whisky, what exactly is the same from the fifties?" he asks. "Your grain source is different, probably relatively local back then. Your heating source is different, coming from direct fire. How you deal with barrels is different. There's a reason why guys bitch about, like, new Macallan not tasting like old Macallan. Because it doesn't. It shouldn't!"

"Before online auctions, it was a smaller pond of dusty hunters," says Isabel Graham-Yooll, who took over as auction director of Whisky. Auction in 2016. "Now the values are so high and the ease of selling is so significant that a lot of these bottles turn up at auction. I think, in the same way as the internet has democratized all sorts of things, auctions are one of those things. It means anyone can pick these vintage bottles up."*

Graham-Yooll continues to think there are "extraordinary" bottles still to be hunted down: bottles and collections she is aware of and those she isn't—"known unknowns" and "unknown unknowns," she jokes, knowingly using some Rumsfeldese. She's aware of several people, not necessarily collectors even, with a cache of extreme rarities. Forget the old lady dying in Kentucky; Graham-Yooll is excited about the aging English doctor who didn't drink but was continually gifted expensive Scotch and Cognac for his entire career.

She's most excited about those "unknown unknowns" that continually pop up.

She told me the recent story of an "enthusiastic drinker" who didn't want his wife to know about his habit, so he hid cases of booze in the attic. When he had a stroke, he could no longer climb the rickety stairs to retrieve the bottles, and once he died, his wife never knew of the stash of three-decades-old bottles until she finally sold their house. The new owner was thinking about pouring the dusty booze down the drain but then decided to call the auctioneer on a whim.

---

* I was a bit nervous to talk to her, as Isabel's father was the late Andrew Graham-Yooll, the famed news editor of the *Buenos Aires Herald*, who had to flee to London in 1976 before he could be "disappeared" by the rising military dictatorship he was covering. And here I was quizzing her about the quality of old Scotch blends.

"The vintage bottle's story is about the journey. It begins at the point that it gets to its first home and then follows all the different love affairs that bottle has had over its lifetime," says Graham-Yooll. "Has it just had one lifelong partner until now, or has it been traded around a bit? These stories add interest, if not value, to the bottles."

For what it's worth, even today Maitland thinks you can get great deals on bourbon via European auction markets—they simply don't care about it as much as Americans do. He jokes that a brand-new release of Michter's 20 Year Old will go for $5,000 the second it hits store shelves in the United States; for that same bankroll, you could get perhaps three bottles of Karuizawa or Brora, dead distilleries that haven't produced anything in decades. Or simply land old bottles of, say, Bowmore or Springbank or Bruichladdich.

"There's so many different brands, depending on what somebody likes, because they've been producing whisky for so much longer," says Maitland. "You can still find something cool and vintage, and it won't be cheap, but it won't be the crazy prices we pay for old bourbon."

ONE NON-AUCTION ONLINE site of note is Old Spirits Company, launched in 2015 by a Canadian whose initial expertise was in seventeenth- to nineteenth-century British and French furniture.

Edgar Harden was working at Christie's auction house in New York when he started getting into vintage wine after tasting spectacular vintages like a 1961 Romanée-Conti. While he was clearing a customer's cellar of 1982 Château Mouton Rothschild, a case of dusty 1960's Gordon's Gin was tossed in for free. Harden tried it and was hooked.

Because of his knowledge of the world of antique furniture, he was also aware of the sorts of people with old country estates, potentially full of vintage booze. It was usually a lot of gin, vermouth, and other fortified wines, French liqueurs procured on vacation, "all the classic sorts of British Empire drinks." Harden had no interest in getting into vintage whiskey—plenty of sellers were already into that, and he needed a way to differentiate himself.

Indeed, visit his website today and you'll be blown away by the breadth of vintage categories he offers. He always has around five thousand to six thousand bottles, stocked both in Europe and in a processing center in New Jersey—50 percent of his customers are now Americans. The pandemic shifted the majority of his orders from bar customers to private individuals, who proudly flex their dusty scores on Instagram, an unexpected boon for business.

The last time I spoke to Harden, right before we hung up, he politely wondered if he could flip the script and finally ask me a question. I said sure.

"Do you see an end to this coming?" he wondered, meaning the whole vintage spirits game.

If, before I wrote this book, I thought I was reporting on a trend that was approaching its end days, by now I've come to realize that vintage spirits collecting is here to stay.

There are still so many bottles out there, so many collections yet to be found, so many new bottles being made today that will be vintage themselves in two decades. It doesn't matter how many people join the hobby, there's plenty to go around, plenty of new old things to get excited about, to pursue.

Thomas Krüger, the man who started the online vintage auction scene, knows that better than anyone. He has been collecting whiskey for some forty-five years, through the ups and downs of the industry, the ups and downs of his own life. When he's feeling sad sometimes, he goes and looks at his collection, using key bottles to jog his memories of the good times from the past, making himself happy again.

"That's why people like these old bottles," he says. "They're a time machine. You can still drink something from bygone days. It's not impossible. Spirits are the perfect taste from old times, the ideal way to revisit the past."

BRIAN CHANES, A LONGTIME employee of Profiles in History and a Hollywood memorabilia expert, had been invited by an anonymous person to 7000 Romaine Street to check out what Hughes had left behind in death some four decades earlier.

Among the materials that the owners wanted to unload was film equipment including a 16 mm movie camera and projection lenses. In Hughes's actual former office there was still his personal credenza made of Italian burl wood and a similar chest of drawers. There was a large piece of artwork from TWA, the airline Hughes owned for two decades, showing a map of the world—"Gorgeous," thought Chanes, though that was one item he was unable to pry away from the building. There was also a large stock of liquor bottles, still "in situ" in Hughes's old office, according to Chanes.

Chanes essentially took the bottles as a "toss-in." He'd never sold any celebrity alcohol collections before, didn't even realize they had much value. Maybe as a celebrity memento, sure, but as something to devote your collecting propensities to? Something to one day possibly drink?!

Until we spoke on the phone in early 2023, it had never even occurred to Chanes that there were people out there like Ackerman, like Goodman, like Moix, like Powell, like me, who would actually want these bottles. People who wanted to obtain Howard Hughes's dusty booze so that they might get to see what it tastes like.

"I would have never thought that someone was going to consume this stuff," he told me, joking that, quite frankly, he's not even sure whether his auction house is allowed to sell booze for the purposes of consumption. "I just kind of thought that they would just want it and kind of keep it as a time capsule, so to speak."

But no, vintage alcohol is the one collectible you can consume, the one collectible you can actually make a part of yourself. I speculated that I supposed you could put on Howard Hughes's dirty old white sneakers or play a round with his golf clubs, but with his alcohol, you could actually consume something that perhaps he held in his hand one day.

"The consumption aspect rather than the donning aspect," replied Chanes with growing interest, as I explained this theory of mine and why it makes vintage alcohol the world's best collectible. He began to understand my point of view.

"Most of those things are just going to be in the museum. No one's going to wear Howard Hughes's clothes. It's just going to be looked at," he responded. "But you could actually take a swig of Howard's booze. I get it."

This was particularly interesting to Chanes because he was such a fan of Hughes himself. Having dealt with the possessions of so many famous people over the decades—Einstein, FDR, Marilyn Monroe, John Wayne—and having had to research their lives to assess the importance of their possessions, he grew to love Hughes more than any other celebrity from the past.

"Who else could say, 'I want to be the best golfer in the world,' and then make it to almost professional level when he was still into it?" asks Chanes. "He wanted to be the world's most famous aviator. And he did hit that for a while. Then he wanted to be the most famous filmmaker in Hollywood, which he kind of was that too. Not to mention you can include him being such a playboy, dating all these starlets, Katharine Hepburn, engaged to Ginger Rogers.

"He lived, like, four famous lives. He's, for me, by far the most fascinating person of the twentieth century."

Not everyone felt this way, of course. In 1972, Gore Vidal asked in the *New York Review of Books*, "Is Howard R. Hughes the most boring American?"

Personally, I was somewhere in between. I suppose I had become like Joan Didion, who wrote in "7000 Romaine Los Angeles 38," "I am interested in the folklore of Howard Hughes, in the way people react to him, in the terms they use when they talk about him."

But I had mostly become obsessed with his dusty booze. And I knew I needed to find the man who now owned Howard Hughes's bottles so I could drink one myself.

THE "HOLLYWOOD AUCTION 96," as it was dubbed, offered a catalog featuring more than two thousand lots of industry props, costumes, set decorations, and other memorabilia, including the handwritten first draft of *The Wizard of Oz*, Irving Thalberg's Best Picture Oscar for *Mutiny on the Bounty*, Sean Connery's James Bond suit from *You Only Live Twice*, and Luke Skywalker's lightsaber from *Star Wars*.

There was also Lot #1401, the one acquired to be auctioned off by Brian Chanes, which was simply described as "Howard Hughes (90+) vintage liquor bottles," dated circa 1930s–40s, and said to have come from the personal stash at the Howard Hughes Headquarters located at 7000 Romaine Street in Los Angeles.

Few bidders seemed all that interested, but that's surely only because most dusty hunters did not even know this auction was going on. Unlike Bonhams Skinner or the European outfits, Profiles in History is not the sort of auction site that the top vintage booze collectors in America pay any sort of attention to.

Except for Kevin Langdon Ackerman, that is, who, if you recall, is also a longtime movie memorabilia collector. He would be bidding against Dr. Matthew Powell who had stumbled upon the listing while doing some mindless web surfing one evening, looking for other rare spirits to stock his new bar with.

Uncertain of the quality of the bottles within the lot, uncertain if this was actually the Hughes collection that had been whispered about for so long, Ackerman eventually bowed out around the $2,500 mark. Other anonymous bidders—dusty hunters, early-era Hollywood buffs, Hughes obsessives, who knows?—drove the price higher and higher.

By the end of the auction, Brian Chanes was surprised to see that this vintage booze—this "toss-in"—actually ended up having the second-highest hammer prices among all the Hughes items up for sale, just behind a 28 x 20 x 46 inch wood-slatted "mystery crate" possibly containing a sealed projector.

With his $5,440 winning bid, Powell scored a few cases each of whiskeys like 1938 Hiram Walker Canadian Club, Old Forester Bottled in Bond from 1946, Ballantine's Scotch and Johnnie Walker Red Label from the '40s, and Coon Hollow Whiskey, a pre-Prohibition brand started in Nelson County, Kentucky, in 1870 that was bottling Canadian bourbon by the 1930s.

There was Minerva, an Argentine gin, Fleischmann's and Gilbey's gins, all from the 1940s, a Hiram Walker's Dry Martini ready-to-drink cocktail, some pre-Prohibition wax-sealed Angostura bitters, along with a bunch of other bottles with missing labels and busted closures. Some of the cases and boxes still had invoices attached to them, sent from Vendome Foods and Wines of Distinction in Beverly Hills to Mr. John Meyer.

Powell would do all he could to legally import these bottles to Seattle to sell at The Doctor's Office, as soon as this pesky pandemic wrapped up.

A FEW KEY SCOTCH AND SINGLE MALT DUSTIES

Just as bourbon had its glut years, Scotch had its "Whisky Loch" years—as in a loch, or lake, of surplus—in the mid-1980s when distilleries over-produced and undersold thanks to changing tastes. (And some beloved distilleries completely went out of business.) Vintage bottles from this era and before are much sought-after and often offer an example of how Scotch "used to taste." Likewise, many casks from the era were never bottled until single malt was again in favor, creating a sort of dusty barrel culture that led to many well-matured and now pricey "luxury" releases in the 2000s and still today.

Unlike bourbon, which can often have a certain sameness of taste due to strict production regulations, the Scotch world offers a far wider breadth of flavor profiles. Thus, many collectors pursue what they like to drink and not simply what's "in," whether it's the elegant richness of The Macallan, the earthy, bright notes of Springbank, or the briny, peaty smoke of Islay malts like Laphroaig, Lagavulin, and Ardbeg. Scotch also has a worldwide audience of collectors compared to the more parochial pursuers of bourbon, rum, and tequila.

Finally, Scotch whisky has also been around a lot longer than bourbon, meaning there are simply more distilleries and brands (and ghost distilleries and defunct brands) to pursue over a longer period of time. That makes it a lot harder for me to sum up a few key things to be on the lookout for, as I have done for the other categories.

THE BRAND THAT PROBABLY MERITS AN ENTIRE BOOK

THE MACALLAN

If it seems like The Macallan—always *The* Macallan (eye roll)—went from unknown to the biggest thing in the world in the twenty-first century, coveted by the well-heeled collector, flexed with by the finance bro, that's because it sorta did. A licensed distillery since 1824, its oily, creamy whisky became sought-after for blends like The Famous Grouse, and production grew until The Macallan had twenty-one compact stills by 1975. Then the 1980s and the Whisky Loch came; all of a sudden, The Macallan had a surplus of maturing casks and not enough blended brands that wanted them; thus, it decided to focus on the emerging single malt market, releasing an 18 Year Old aged in sherry casks in 1984.

Two years later, it released its first limited edition 50 Year Old, distilled in 1928. The Macallan 60 Year Old, distilled in 1926, bottled in 1986, might be the granddaddy of all vintage spirits these days, rarely appearing at auction, but going for a minimum of seven figures when it does. By 2000, The Macallan had released its first single cask, distilled in 1981 and dubbed Exceptional 1; a visitors center opening the next year would solidify the brand's status as an icon.

The Macallan famously used direct fire stills until 2002, something that many believe creates a sort of Maillard reaction in the grains, causing a richer, deeper flavor, while making the liquid capable of aging much longer without being overtaken by wood or sherry notes—thus, vintage collectors particularly pursue any Macallan distilled before the early 2000s.

In the twenty-first century The Macallan would lean heavily into being the most luxurious, most collectible whisky around, releasing decades-mature single malt in extraordinarily expensive, increasingly ostentatious crystal Lalique decanters, driving the retail price of some bottles well into six figures and becoming the darling of the world auction scene. In fact, nine of the top twenty hammer price auctioned whiskies of 2022 were from The Macallan.

(And, for the record, there actually is a book, *The Definitive Guide to Buying Vintage Macallan*, a slim, fifteen-page affair produced in 2002 that has become a vintage collectible itself.)

OTHERS OF INTEREST

CADENHEAD'S DUMPY BOTTLES

Scotland's oldest independent bottler (meaning it doesn't make its own whisky) has been around since 1842, specializing in sourcing single-cask whiskies. Its "dumpy" bottles—so dubbed because of their squat brown glass shape—produced from 1977 through 1991, and featuring just about every single Scotch distillery at one time or another, remain coveted among collectors.

PRE-CLOSURE ARDBEG

This Islay distiller had been offering its heavily peated stock for blends as early as the mid-nineteenth century. By the 1960s, a fan base had begun to develop around its single malt, distilled from barley it had malted itself. By 1974, however, it had started sourcing peated grain from nearby Port Ellen, and for some collectors, that marks the end of a certain era of top-notch Ardbeg. By 1981, the Whisky Loch had shuttered Ardbeg. Today a revived Ardbeg, purchased by Glenmorangie and reopened in full in 1997, is still producing pretty good single malt with a devoted fan base, but nowhere near as collected as the pre-Loch stuff. (Of note: many pre-closure Ardbeg casks were eventually bottled and released by the new owners, which became French luxury goods giant Moët Hennessy Louis Vuitton in 2004.)

DIRECT-FIRED SINGLE MALT

Just as with The Macallan, pre-closure Ardbeg, and Karuizawa (see below), many collectors simply prefer the flavor of direct-fired whisky, as in literally using a direct flame, powered by coal or peat, to heat the still. From brand to brand, across the board, the demarcation line will differ—heck, Glenmorangie was using steam-fired stills as early as 1887. Look for Caol Ila before 1974, pre-1986 Glenlivet, pre-2005 Glendronach, and older Springbank, among others. (Pablo Moix long held the post-Loch Springbank 1996 "Green Thistle" bottling as his white whale, until he recently enjoyed one. Though an age-stated 12-year-old, the rumor has long been that some disgruntled employees dumped mostly 30- and 40-something-year-old casks into the batch. Bottles approach $10,000 today.) Glenfarclas is one of the only major single malt distilleries to still completely use direct fire, though other things have obviously changed with the brand, which remains quite good.

THE GHOSTS

While dozens of great distilleries have been shuttered over the years (Banff, Ladyburn, Millburn, Rosebank, and St. Magdalene, to name some), a few continue to capture collectors' curiosity above all others.

PORT ELLEN

For many, this is *the* Islay single malt, and one that has rightly attained cult status and astronomical value. Originally a malt mill when it opened in 1825, ownership changes and economic events led to its getting moth-balled for the first time in 1930, before reopening in 1967, then ultimately being mothballed for good in 1983, then demolished. Innovative for a past era, early owner John Ramsay was also an importer of sherry and Madeira, whose casks he would use to mature his whisky. This lent Port Ellen its sui generis, heavily peated, heavily sherried flavor profile adored by so many drinkers—though, when it was an active distillery, Port Ellen would have mainly been used as a blending component. Port Ellen wouldn't actually be bottled as a single malt until it was released as a 20-year-old by the Rare Malts Selection in 1998 and onward. Diageo's annual Special Releases series would include a Port Ellen expression each year from 2001 until 2017.

BRORA

Originally known as Clynelish, by 1969 its name had changed to Brora, and by 1983 it, too, was mothballed. There are three distinct eras of flavor profiles for the brand: an early "earthy" style, heavily peated malts from 1972 to 1980, and a low-peat, "waxy" profile produced until it was shuttered for good. There are, thus, not only fans of the brand, but fans specifically of each flavor era. In 2017 liquor conglomerate Diageo announced plans for a reopening of both Port Ellen and Brora, releasing a limited edition Brora Triptych set that featured three bottles of old liquid most reflective of each specific era. While not a dusty per se, it retailed for some $42,000 and remains a major unicorn.

KARUIZAWA

A relatively unknown Japanese distillery, it began operations in 1956 but has been mothballed since 2000. Though the smallest distillery in the country, the production sounds like the stuff of a boozy fairy tale: produced strictly using Golden Promise barley, fermented in wood washbacks with water from Mount Asama, a still-active volcano, then distilled in tiny, coal-fired pot stills, before finally being matured in sherry casks stored within ivy-covered warehouses. Used mostly for blending at first, in the 1980s and 1990s single malt began to appear in Japan, though few outside the country were aware of it. Popularity finally soared in 2007 when independent bottler Number One Drinks started releasing single casks of the whisky exported to Europe, some distilled as long ago as 1960.

OTHER JAPANESE WHISKY YOU SHOULD KNOW

Well, you probably already do know Suntory, and yes, all Suntory whisky from the past, even if it isn't remarkably old, well-aged, or even tasty, has value. The first Suntory single malt, the ur-Yamazaki, if you will, was Suntory Pure Malt Whisky, aged twelve years, which was distilled in 1972 and released in 1984 in a fancy wooden box. Outside of Suntory, Ichiro's Malt Card Series is perhaps the most coveted vintage whisky series of all time, and no, you can't afford it, nor will you ever taste it (nor have I, nor will I). The fifty-four bottles, released between 2005 and 2014, represent a full deck of playing cards (with two jokers), each created from barrels from yet another ghost distillery, Hanyu Distillery, which shuttered in 2000. A complete set sold for $1.52 million at Bonhams in 2020.

SLEEPER BLENDS FROM THE PAST

Remember, aside from independent bottlers like Cadenhead's and Gordon & MacPhail, there really wasn't a lot of single malt pre-1980s; no single malt had really made it to non-Scottish markets before 1963, when Glenfiddich started promoting its offerings worldwide. Thus, much of this great single malt, and much of it of a mature age, was going into blended Scotch, and thus, dusty blends from the past are a ton better than one might expect—at the least, wildly different in flavor profile from today's incarnations. Specifically look for dusty bottles with spring-cap closures, which keep an incredible seal.

WHITE HORSE

Probably the most well-known and desired among blended Scotch dusties, old White Horse is famous for including well-aged Lagavulin in the blend. Noted for its rich caramel, butterscotch flavor with a wisp of smoke, the White Horse from as late as the 1980s and 1990s is also quite good, Isabel Graham-Yooll thinks. Higher-end White Horse was sometimes known as Laird O'Logan, Logan's Deluxe, or Logan over the years. There's also Mackie's Ancient Brand Scotch, which is said to contain whisky from Malt Mill, so mythical that the plot of a movie, 2012's *The Angels' Share*, centers around the theft of a cask of it.

FAMOUS BLENDS THAT KINDA SUCK TODAY

Johnnie Walker Black and Chivas Regal, which you might drink these days only when you're at an open bar wedding and the sole other option is a supermarket Chardonnay, are likewise much better from the past. Johnnie Walker Black, for instance, has distillate in the blend from the vaunted Brora. Some old Chivas is composed of very well-matured, direct-fired Strathisla, something no one cared about as a single malt back then.

BLENDS YOU MIGHT NOT HAVE
HEARD OF TODAY

Kristopher Peterson also thinks many of the blends from a pre-1990 era are so tasty because they potentially included paxarette (pax), a blend of vino de color, Oloroso and Pedro Ximénez sherry, and wine must that has since been banned as it was designated a flavor additive. Pax or no, other tasty blends from the past include The Antiquary, Vat 69 (specifically from the 1970s), Whyte & Mackay, Bell's, and King's Ransom, a higher-proof blend at one time purported to be the most expensive Scotch in the world, aimed at the luxury market, and produced from the mostly sherried, solidly peaty Edradour. It was discontinued in 1980.

15

THE WHOLE STORE SCORE

ANYONE WHO HAS ever dusty-hunted, especially those who have come in late to the game, has had the same insane thought:

If only I had a time machine.

They think, I wouldn't use it to go back and kill baby Hitler or to make sure Bo Jackson never injured his hip on that January night in Los Angeles, I'd just return to 1960 or 1980 or even 2005 and buy everything on my liquor store's shelves.

And then a man living in the year 2022, without bending the laws of space or time, kinda figured out how to do that.

Jon Lilley was once a regional account manager for Southern Glaz-er's, the largest wine and spirits distributor in the United States, which he assured me has nothing to do with this story at all, but I print it for journalistic accuracy. For years he'd been a bourbon collector, and in the last four years had shifted his focus from the rare, allocated releases that had become increasingly hard to find to hunting for dusties in the area of Napa Valley where he and his family reside.

Even as someone in the liquor store business, someone who used to enter liquor stores on a daily basis for his previous job, back when he was a salesman for a California distillery, the days of finding vintage

bottles on the shelves had all but dissipated. Instead, Lilley would hunt
for dusties via Craigslist (where he claims to get more than two hundred
alerts per day for keywords he has flagged), yard sales, and estate sales,
including a recent one where he found an entire half-gallon "swing" of
1957 Old Fitzgerald. The deceased's son had unfortunately opened this
$8,000 piece, taken a single sip, and not found the sublime liquid to his
liking. Lilley was more than willing to take it off his hands for a song,
even if he doesn't really drink his collectibles anymore.

"I taste it, I just don't get fucked up," he assured me.

In July 2022, Lilley was doing his standard morning loop of internet
auction sites when he came up with an idea. He googled, "sites like
HiBid," referencing an auctioneer in the past he'd had some luck with.
The first thing that popped up on his search was another auction site
he'd never heard of: Sullivan Auctioneers, an Illinois-based outfit that
mainly deals in farm equipment. Nevertheless, Lilley dustily typed in
"liquor" on its internal search engine—and suddenly was taken to the
estate sale of one Edmund Bickett, "a legend in the southern Illinois
and northwestern Kentucky area," according to the listing.

In actuality, Bickett was just a guy who once owned pretty much
everything in Old Shawneetown, Illinois (population: 114). He had died
in 2017 at age eighty-five.

There were several "rings"—different categories—among his estate:
real estate, which included thirty-nine commercial, residential, and
recreational lots; his vehicles and farm equipment, including at least
fourteen tractors, two backhoes, a Cat Dozer, a telescopic boom lift,
a fertilizer spreader, a Batwing mower, Ditch Witch equipment, a
twenty-eight-foot pontoon boat, a forty-two-foot lowboy trailer, and a
1983 Cadillac DeVille; and household items such as a SentrySafe digital
safe, an infrared space heater, cookware, a "large quantity of scissors,"
and a Busch beer neon sign.

The fourth and final ring was for the entire contents of the Shawnee Package liquor store and its storage basement, which Bickett had unceremoniously shuttered in the late 2000s. He wasn't selling much liquor, and his son claimed Bickett got fed up with people stealing from him.

It was a Friday when Lilley saw all this, and the live online auction was scheduled for Monday.

"This is twenty-five hundred miles away from where I live," Lilley thought. "How the fuck can I find a way to make this happen?"

And at first he thought he couldn't. He couldn't leave his wife, Megan, and ten-month-old son, Julius. He couldn't take off work. Did he even have available the tens of thousands of dollars it might cost to win the auction?

He slept on it, and then he did something really stupid:

He woke up first thing on Saturday morning and Facebook messaged a few dusty-hunting friends, sending them a link to the listing, Kevin Langdon Ackerman among them.

Upon hearing this, Lilley's wife prodded him: What are you doing? We can find a way to make it work. In fact, she would help fund it. She trusted her husband's business acumen and had seen it pay off before.

In fact, Lilley himself had recently seen a friend buy the entire wine cellar from the Machus Red Fox restaurant in Bloomfield Township, Michigan, better known as the last place Jimmy Hoffa was seen alive. A score that man had quickly turned into a cool $35,000 profit.

So Lilley quickly unsent the Facebook messages, something I didn't even know you could do. His fellow dusty hunters were now none the wiser; nor was, as far as Lilley knew, any other major vintage spirits collector in America.

"There's a lot of jealousy in this game," says Lilley.

Suffice to say, on Monday morning Lilley won the auction. It wasn't completely a cakewalk. In fact, he had never been as stressed-out as he was during the hour as he jockeyed for the top position. Only one other person even seemed to be seriously bidding on it all, though, and that person didn't seem to be willing to go as high as Lilley, who still went 35 percent higher than he had planned to. All told, however, Lilley would estimate he spent around $5 per bottle.

Now logistics came into play. He would have only until Thursday, three days from then, and just six days after he'd even discovered the auction, to get all the bottles out of Shawnee Package and back home to Napa Valley. Over the weekend, Lilley had put a strategy in place. No, he still couldn't go to Old Shawneetown himself, but his brother, Matt, was willing to fly from Las Vegas to Phoenix and then on to the closest major city, St. Louis, and pick up a twenty-two-foot Penske box truck to drive another 149 miles to Illinois. And Lilley's brother-in-law, also named Matt, was willing to take a red-eye from San Francisco to Charlotte, then drive a rental car to the package store for added loading help.

At least for a dusty hunter's purpose, 2009 would have been the perfect time to shutter a liquor store. Despite Shawnee Package being just across the Ohio River from Kentucky, it had sat quietly in this penurious, one-horse, zero-gas-station town in the final days before dusty hunters had completely picked over the country. Even back then, Kentucky locals crossed the river mostly to buy lotto tickets, not booze, there.

"How did no one ever see their collection?" Lilley would eventually wonder. But, the fact was, it had closed right before anyone was hunting that kind of stuff.

So cracking open the boarded-up wooden door and entering the humble, A-frame store, a simple board still reading "SHAWNEE PACKAGE" over the door, granted the two Matts access to that time machine every dusty hunter has always dreamed of. This was Howard Carter and Lord Carnarvon opening King Tut's tomb—if they cared more about bourbon made by National Distillers than about fucking scepters and pairs of golden sandals.

"It looked like Bickett had basically turned off the lights one day and boarded it up," says Lilley.

There were still help-yourself sliding-door beer coolers stocked with six-packs of Budweiser and Miller Light, malt liquor forties, and Jäger-meister minis, recalling a past era when they were still a popular party bomb. Near the front door, an ATM, presumably empty of cash. Advil and Motrin single-serving pill packs behind the register. BIC lighters at checkout. All the fixtures and furniture and liquor advertisements from the era. It was a bit dirty, and it was incredibly hot and humid, being the end of July in southeastern Illinois, though probably not as bad as the Egyptian desert in 1922.

And, of course, there was shelf after shelf after shelf of still perfectly stocked bottles from the past, most still neatly organized, lined up single file like soldiers, unbothered over the years.

"Everything was pristine; the tax stamps were perfect," says Lilley, who FaceTimed with his brother as they assessed the collection. "This just doesn't happen."

There was a whole case of Old Heaven Hill Bottled in Bond from 1987. A never-opened case of Old Grand-Dad Bonded from 1998. Sealed Old Forester Bottled in Bond. Six Old Fitzgerald Primes from 1985. Eleven cases of 1984 W.L. Weller Special Reserve 375 mLs. Ninety-six bottles of Old Forester 86-proof 200 mLs—something Lilley could easily flip at $75 apiece.

"It's crazy shit. There's just crazy shit in there," says Lilley. "And it's still one of those things where I'm like, 'How did this happen? How did this even happen? How did I stumble upon this?'"

It wasn't all winners, of course. Lilley was now the owner of tons of crap from the 1980s, blended Scotches, bottom-shelf vodkas and gin,

1990s Everclear (vintage Everclear!), mixto tequila, and, of course, a case of 1986 DeKuyper Peachtree Schnapps, from the heyday of the Sex on the Beach.

By the time it was loaded up, the twenty-two-by-twelve-foot interior of the Penske was completely full of one single layer of cases of alcohol.

That's 264 square feet of dusty booze!

Lilley's brother-in-law, who has long had the cockeyed dream of becoming a long-haul trucker, gladly drove the Penske back to Napa Valley, in just forty-two hours. It cost $1,200 in fuel to move what Lilley estimates is some $250,000 in booze, which would reside for the time being in a ten-by-twenty-four-foot storage locker he was now paying an additional few hundred bucks a month to rent.

By September 2022, Lilley had made his money back, despite the $1,300 in shipping costs. At that point he had sold only 5 percent of his haul. He figured it would take another six months to a year to move the rest of it. He was already lamenting some of what he had sold, especially those Weller bottles from the 1980s, something he thought he would surely never see again.

It had just made him even hungrier to top himself.

"Every day, every fucking day, I look for another one of these scores," he told me the last time I spoke to him.

AS WITH A portion of Lilley's haul, eventually all vintage collectors acquire some, well, crap.

But even crap can teach us something useful about the past.

Like what people were flocking to during the bourbon glut. Sure, some of those spirits, like vodka, remain significant today. Others, namely peach schnapps, recall an era better left forgotten.

An era of childish cocktails, both in name and contents, like the Sex on the Beach and Fuzzy Navel, which was the number one most popular cocktail in America at the end of the 1980s (the Long Island Iced Tea was number two).

There was the Orgasm, a truly vile combo of amaretto, Kahlúa, and Baileys Irish Cream. The Silk Panties, made with vodka and peach schnapps, and named "Drink of the Year" by *Bartender* magazine in 1986, gave way to the Slippery Nipple, aka the Buttery Nipple (Baileys and sambuca or butterscotch schnapps), the Slow Comfortable Screw (sloe gin, Southern Comfort, vodka, and orange juice), the Redheaded Slut (peach schnapps, Jägermeister, and cranberry juice), and even the Blowjob Shot, made by slowly layering Baileys, Kahlúa, and amaretto and then topping it with whipped cream. It was to be drunk by putting your hands behind your back and moving your mouth agape toward the shot glass sitting on the bar . . . or in a man's waistband.

Peach schnapps is in most of these drinks, and so the innovator in the category, DeKuyper Peachtree Schnapps, would end up moving twelve million units in its first year on shelves, 1985, making it the fastest-selling new alcohol product since Prohibition. By 1987, it was the ninth-best-selling overall liquor in the country, selling for a mere five bucks a bottle.

So yeah, a lot of it is still left in the world gathering dust. And a lot of it inherently ends up in the hands of vintage collectors.

A few years back, Mordecai's spirits archivist Kristopher Peterson and Stephanie Andrews, then beverage director of Billy Sunday in Chicago, met up on his patio for an impromptu tasting of disrespected dusties. The bartenders mixed up vintage Sex on the Beaches using that same 1980s Peachtree Schnapps along with some "neon yellow" citrus vodka from the 1990s.

"They were definitely not the most complex cocktails we've ever whipped up, but it was a ton of fun," Peterson recalls.

He owns a bunch of 1980s tax strip Midori—once so popular it had its own neon billboard in Times Square, looming over 45th and Broadway for much of the decade—which he has played around with in vintage Midori Sours. He's even taken the disrespected drinks back to Mordecai's menu, in October 2021 selling vintage Rusty Nails using 1970s Hudson's Bay Blended Scotch, 1980s Drambuie (so well-made back then that you could still taste the Scotch base), 1980s Aper Al Carciofi, and 1970s Strega. Paired with a foie gras torchon, he was able to charge $38.

If it's easy to look back and laugh at what people used to drink, to see the 1970s and 1980s as a "lesser" era of quality drinking, it was still part of America's drinks history. And that inherently makes it important for any serious drinker or spirits collector. People weren't drinking Rusty Nails and Midori Sours and Fuzzy Navels as a gimmick—they were drinking them because they thought they tasted good!

Thus, tasting vintage versions of these cheesy cocktails from the past allows us modern snobs to perhaps understand what people from the past saw in blended Scotches, flavored vodkas, and brightly colored fruit liqueurs. Perhaps that's why the prices on vintage versions of them are steadily increasing—old Peachtree will set you back a bit these days!

Tasting them can also allow us to be thankful for the era. Because if Americans didn't once have a taste for all these now-derided drinks, then there wouldn't have been a glut bourbon era, and there wouldn't have been all sorts of great "real" liquors gathering dust on shelves, for us to find one day, and realize what all these silly people from the past were once passing by on store shelves, so that they could grab another bottle of Kahlúa.

WHAT'S NEXT?

By the 2020s, this vintage madness was getting so crazy that I even encountered people who were pursuing vintage water.

Yes, you heard me, vintage water.

Running out of reasonably priced dusty bourbon, Cognac, and European liqueurs, the collector's mentality moved on to something stranger and surely less-tasty, yet way more economical.

I first noticed this in 2019 when a man posted an auction in a vintage whiskey private Facebook group that I—and about eight thousand others—was a member of:

"Auction for 1 bottle. Mr Wellers [*sic*] Pure limestone water 4/5 quart Straight from Kentucky."

The comments on the post came quick, the most incisive one simply asking: "Water?"

But then a funny thing started to occur: Bids started coming in as well. First $60. Then $80. By the end of the auction, the bottle of 1967 vintage, yes, water had sold for $120 to a Kentucky man, Larry Baldwin.

"I don't ever really plan on drinking them, [they're] just for show," Baldwin told me. By then he had about a dozen bottles of vintage water. "They're definitely more rare to find than dusty bourbon bottles of the same age!"

Of course, that Mr. Weller's may have been straight from a Kentucky tap, but it was no ordinary water. By now you realize that "Weller" on the label tells even the most green bourbon enthusiast that this product has the bouquet of Pappy wafting from it—and, indeed, it was bottled by the Stitzel-Weller Distillery. Baldwin speculates these bottles were gimmicks even back then, just something silly to promote the brand—and the fact that he has acquired a 1960s Old Fitzgerald

Prime Limestone Water *gallon*—in a swing, no less!—makes me think he might be right.

Julian "Pappy" Van Winkle Sr. was a salesman par excellence in the post-Prohibition days of bourbon, so it's perhaps no surprise he'd have the chutzpah to try and sell water too (mind you, commercially widespread bottled water doesn't really appear until the late 1970s, early 1980s). It was even less of a surprise that this Pappy Van Water would become highly desirable on the online secondary market, which was reaching a fever pitch of insanity by the end of the 2010s, in the final few months before the dystopian March 2020.

To a certain extent, it even felt like an indictment of bourbon culture, a "self-own" as the kids say. And the fact that vintage water was now selling well confirmed many people's notions that the liquid in the bottle had begun to not really matter at all. Whether it was a bottle of 2019 Pappy Van Winkle 15 Year Old or, say, some 1985 Weller Water, which, by 2019, was fetching $150.

Vintage water or vintage whiskey, the dusty bottle had become an asset. Something to display on one's shelf, something to post on Instagram, something to never ever open—until it becomes worth more than you paid for it, and you sell it to some other schnook who repeats the cycle.

Seriously, what was much different between this and the non-bourbon drinkers gobbling up Elvis and King Tut decanters in the 1970s?

Like Dutch Golden Age tulips or late 1990s Beanie Babies, the vintage spirits industry is at a critical point.

So if not vintage water, what's left? What's next in dusty hunting? What is there still to collect? Is there anything? I have some thoughts. . . .

CALVADOS AND ARMAGNAC

Let's start with the two French brandies that have long been red-headed stepchildren to Cognac, even today. Which makes little sense, because, in many ways, Calvados (apple and/or pear brandy from the Normandy area) and Armagnac (grape brandy from the historical region of Gascony) actually offer more of what sophisticated drinkers crave: quality ingredients, old-fashioned production methods, and minimal corporate interference. The fact that modern Armagnac releases are beginning to finally make waves with bourbon bros leads me to believe vintage enthusiasm will soon follow. Of course, with vintage Calvados and Armagnac, there are no "big" names from the past like, say, Hennessy with Cognac, so purchases will often be a bit of a dice roll. Luckily, these two categories are still way undervalued, and there's many, many decades of old stuff to find. You'd also have to think dusty bottles from Laird's, the apple brandy maker that is literally the oldest licensed distillery in the United States (1780), would eventually gain traction, though few ever seem to appear on the secondary market.

CANADIAN AND
IRISH WHISKEY

If American bourbon and rye, Scotch, both single malt and blended, and any Japanese whiskey demand prices through the roof, there are still two major whiskey-producing regions that are often ignored by vintage collectors. True, there are not a lot of vintage options from our neighbors to the north, but old Canadian Club is quite good—lower-proof and delicate, but with a full, creamy mouthfeel. Irish whiskey suffers from a similar problem, as you're mostly going to find only dusty Jameson or Bushmills. (Remember, by the 1980s the only

Irish distilleries left were Bushmills and the New Midleton Distillery, which produced Jameson, among other labels.) Both are fine, but the defunct distilleries from the Emerald Isle offer way more exciting scores. Key Irish dusties might include whiskey from Coleraine (which once produced a 34 Year Old single malt), Comber, Locke's, Midleton bottlings distilled prior to July 1975 at its old distillery, and stuff from the old Tullamore distillery (1950s bottles of Irish Mist can be a great, cheap get), among others.

GENEVER

It's a little surprising this Dutch liquor isn't already more popular among vintage enthusiasts. A juniper-flavored malt distillate that is sometimes barrel-aged (look for "oude" genever), in many ways it combines the best of both gin and whiskey. Bols is surely the most famous brand from the past—and today—but the category has existed for such a long time that there's a lot of esoteric bottlings out there, though mostly in Europe. Of note, since 1952, Dutch airline KLM has issued, strictly to business class travelers, miniature Delft Blue ceramic decanters, shaped like tiny houses, and filled with genever. These have become highly collectible, though, like American bourbon decanters, less so for the contents than the vessels.

KÜMMEL, OUZO, AND OTHER OFTEN-IGNORED REGIONAL LIBATIONS

Liqueurs that have never really made inroads in America, whether as neat sippers or a modern cocktail ingredient, also show great potential to be "rediscovered" by vintage enthusiasts. Look for kümmel, a German caraway- and cumin-based liqueur; aquavit, the caraway shooter favored in Nordic countries; and the anise-flavored aperitifs of Europe such as pastis (France), ouzo (Greece), sambuca (Italian), and raki (Turkey). For the moment they are uncool and undervalued, though many are quite tasty if you truly explore them.

MINT LIQUEUR

As mentioned in "Key (and Necessary) Vintage Cocktail Ingredients" (see page 166), no one buys dusty mint liqueur, but Edgar Harden of Old Spirits Company actually thinks the ignored category is one worth pursuing. "I really rate a lot of the mint liqueurs, peppermint, crème de menthe," he says.

1970S AND '80S FAVORITES

From a purely speculative standpoint, it would seem that pursuing the unfashionable alcohols of the 1970s and 1980s might actually also be worth a shot. Surely they'll be back in style again one day? And then you'll be the person with loads of dusty schnapps and amaretto and Galliano, and why not grab some vintage Goldschläger too? Gold is only going up in value.

16

ASK THE DUST

YOU SCRATCH YOUR arm and skin cells are sloughed into the air. Comb your hair and follicles disperse. Throughout the day, your body volatilizes the deodorants, soaps, and other fragrances that you applied in the morning.

Eat a sandwich for lunch and crumbs fall to the floor. Throw your clothes in the hamper at the end of the day and fibers are tossed about. Kitty cleans herself and dander escapes. Pollen and pesticides fly through the open kitchen window. Tiny bugs take tiny shits and then die a tiny death. Microscopic mites are born, feeding on all of this.

Like a snowball rolling down the hill, this mass floats through your home, absorbing more and more iotas as it becomes larger and larger. It picks up the flame-retardant decabromodiphenyl ether found in furniture foam, the phthalates from plastics, the polychlorinated biphenyls once used in electrical cables and wood floors, lead paint chips, and insecticides from aerosol spray cans—many of this stuff banned years ago but still existing all around us every day.

All still there in the dust.

We, too, become dust, slowly at first, then quickly, and when it comes down to it, dust is nothing more than the past itself.

We track it into buildings on the soles of our shoes. When we touch things and move through rooms, we agitate the settled dust already long there, resuspending it in the air—perhaps to be seen by the naked eye only if the morning sun is shining into the room—where it picks up further dirt, particles, hairs, mites, crumbs, and contaminants.

Eventually the dust floats down again toward a surface, any surface, where it embeds itself in carpets, thinly coats dressers and cabinets, and hugs the necks of bottles of booze.

I needed to see the dust, touch the dust, and drink from the dust-covered bottles once owned by Howard Hughes.

I flew to Seattle in late February 2023.

On a frigid Thursday around midday, I checked into the Hotel Sorrento—"Welcoming guests since 1909," and advertising seventy-six different "vintage" rooms and suites. I'm not sure most guests could have told you exactly what that meant—my corner room was nice, but fairly typical and certainly modern—but today everyone thinks that vintage anything is cool, the past is cool.

"Vintage" has become a marketing buzzword no different from "small batch" or "handmade." So call it vintage if you need to. You can probably charge more for that.

I walked from the hotel—located, perhaps, fittingly, in an area surrounded by hospitals—and down the steep slope of Boren Avenue before cutting over to Bellevue and toward the hip Capitol Hill neighborhood.

On East Olive Way I passed a kitschy hula bar and a few tacky cannabis dispensaries, a taco shop, and a Belgian beer bar, before I realized I'd somehow missed The Doctor's Office. Tracking back on the sidewalk, I finally found a withdrawn wooden door, surrounded by an intentionally rusted facade, "THE DOCTOR'S OFFICE" etched into it, neatly, as if on a MedicAlert bracelet, along with the bar's logo, that slithering snake so typically wrapped around the Rod of Asclepius—though, this time, instead of a staff, the base of a coupe glass.

And there was Matthew Powell, the good doctor, unlocking the bar on this Thursday afternoon. His hair had grown long since the pandemic started and was now up in a tight bun. He wore Air Jordan 5s, a modern reissue of a shoe that originally hit the market in 1990, when I was in fifth grade.

Powell escorted me into The Doctor's Office, the first customer of the day. It was like entering another realm. I walked through a small, pitch-black antechamber, still unable to see the bar, before turning the corner and finally emerging into the intimate space. It recalled the alleyway bars of Tokyo's Shinjuku Golden Gai district, though really no other U.S. locales. That was why Powell had opened the bar in the first place.

"If this kind of bar had already existed in Seattle, I wouldn't have needed to," he told me.

There were five barstools, one banquette, one tiny table. No windows, the bulk of the room's light coming from the thin illuminations behind the impressive wall of bottles, many unrecognizable to the average bar patron.

I took my seat at a place setting with a hot hand towel, a spritz bottle of hand sanitizer, and a welcome half glass of champagne. I clicked my iPhone on a QR code in order to access the thirty-two-page Google Docs menu.

The Doctor's Office offers great cocktails like a Vesper and a flaming Spanish Coffee, crafted by local industry vet Keith Waldbauer, but in the year and a half since it's been reopened post-vaccine, it's been honored as having one of the best spirits lists in the entire world. It was hard to argue with the plaudits.

I spied some 1990s Karuizawa bottled in a gold ship decanter, some Black Tot Royal Navy pre-1970s and Japanese market Caroni, Bénédictine from the 1940s and Amer Picon from the '60s, and 1960s Sauza, a 100 percent agave tequila from well before Robert Denton's days.

I was already a very knowledgeable spirits drinker and consumer back in 2020 when this project started; writing and researching this book had made me even more skilled at reading a vintage spirits menu, at delving into the past, at knowing what mattered and when it mattered, which I was realizing was now a bit of detriment to my happiness (and bank account).

Now, unfortunately, now that I knew better what everything was, what it represented, how it differed from a lot of the junk on the market today, I knew how much I wanted to taste all these spirits from the past.

And yes, I saw how much they were going to cost me.

When you have the collector's mentality, however, you have to find out. There's no other choice.

You have to find out why a defunct distillery like Karuizawa is so coveted.

You have to find out if the Royal Navy's rum blend was actually as good as everyone once thought.

You have to find out, to paraphrase Pablo Moix, if it's true that once you try vintage tequila, you'll think, "This is the first time I've had tequila."

I can confirm, indeed, that the 1960s Sauza Tequila Plata was mind-blowing; it was rustic, vegetal, a little nutty even, and still a major steal at just $30 a glass. It was like nothing I had ever tasted before. Certainly unlike any tequila on the market today. When I got back to my hotel room later in the evening, I would go online to see if I could acquire a bottle myself.

But there was also the key reason I'd flown all the way to the Emerald City: an entire section of the menu labeled "VINTAGE: HOWARD HUGHES' COLLECTION."

"These bottles were owned by Howard Hughes himself and we are fortunate enough to have obtained the contents of his liquor cellar," read the section's introduction. "Take a step back in time and enjoy some spirits from the 1930s and 1940s—literally the exact bottles he would have reached for!"

The cheapest, at $125 an ounce, was a 1940s Fleischmann's Gin; the priciest, at $300 a pour, was some 1920s Coon Hollow.

The Hughes collection had quickly proven popular among Powell's customers, selling at a surprisingly decent clip despite the high prices. So many drinkers were loving the chance to try something not only rare but historical. With The Doctor's Office in a part of a town with a lot of start-ups, many of the tech bros and founders who came into the bar surely wanted to feel the power of another great entrepreneur by sipping on his spirits.

I suppose so did I.

I considered whether I should try his Canadian Club from 1938. That was the year Hughes completed his record-breaking flight around the entire world, the one where he relaxed with a whiskey and soda as his limousine drove him back into Manhattan. Or perhaps that limo highball had used the Ballantine's blended Scotch whisky that was also on the menu, $200 a glass.

Another one of Hughes's famed aviation stunts was in 1946—though he wasn't sipping anything after crashing his XF-11 reconnaissance plane into three houses in Beverly Hills and nearly killing himself. It's probably the most exciting scene in the Scorsese movie.

And now I could have a pour of 1946 Old Forester Bottled in Bond bourbon for just $250.

I watched Waldbauer carefully pour from the dusty fifth, the tax stamp broken, the label dirty and frayed, its top left corner torn, and thus the "O" in the brand name missing. Despite being a mere four years of age, the liquid appeared a dark amber in my tasting glass.

The nose was rich and aromatic, burnt caramel, vanilla, leather. The taste was even better, toffee and marshmallows, cinnamon and holiday spices, a little apple and bananas, and some oak, of course, though hardly too woody. It was utterly delicious.

Was this 1946 bourbon that much better than, say, a modern pour of Old Forester I could get on the same menu for just seven bucks a glass?

From a pure taste standpoint, probably not. The 1946 certainly tasted a lot better than modern Old Forester, a brand I'm familiar with, a brand I'm a big fan of. But was that worth nearly forty times its cost?

The fact is, you don't just drink with your mouth but with your nose and your eyes. That dusty bottle of Old Forester, sitting in front of me on the bar as I drank it, *did* matter. Drinking is not just a physical process, but a mental one as well.

Drinking this 1946 Old Forester, I couldn't help but think of a World War II–era Kentucky. By the spring of 1941, when this bourbon was distilled, the Kentucky distilleries had been back in business for less than a decade since Prohibition had ended, and now here they were, facing turmoil yet again.

By December of that year, when the United States officially entered the war, Brown-Forman was the first Kentucky distillery to distill high-proof industrial alcohol for use in the war effort, producing munitions, antiseptics, and rubber. How many boys working at the Brown-Forman plant were sent to Europe, perhaps never to return home?

And yet these barrels of Old Forester continued aging safely in a bonded warehouse in Louisville, through the bombing of Pearl Harbor and Battle of Midway, through D-Day and Iwo Jima, through the days when "Little Boy" and "Fat Man" were dropped on Hiroshima and Nagasaki, until the fall of 1946, when the barrels were finally pulled and dumped. The war had already been over for a year by then, and perhaps some of the same workers who had once helped distill the whiskey, who had put the colorless liquid into the barrels, had returned home in time to finish the job, though surely the worse for wear.

These barrels of Old Forester had faced turmoil and survived, as the brand had always faced turmoil and survived ever since it first hit the market in 1870. These barrels were combined and bottled and put into cases and sent out across America, where they were distributed to liquor stores like Vendome on North Beverly Drive.

One of these cases was purchased by Johnny Meyer. Some fifths he must have opened, drunk, shared with friends and associates, maybe even Howard Hughes, who was surely still recovering from the broken ribs, crushed collarbone, and third-degree burns he'd suffered from his recent plane crash. Might he have used the Old Forester as a pain tonic, or by then had he already moved on to the opioids he'd gobble up until the day he died?

Of course, Hughes may have never actually touched this bottle in front of me. May have never even been aware Meyer had spent his money on them. May have never once noticed it sitting in 7000 Romaine.

But I could still dream. I could still romanticize how this bottle finally found its way to The Doctor's Office, and then my glass.

That's what truly matters with vintage spirits.

As Isabel Graham-Yooll once said to me, referencing pre-phyllox-era Cognac, "What you're tasting, it's not just whether it tastes good. It's whether you can feel that magic. Do you believe that you're being transported in time by tasting it?"

I did feel the magic. I did feel transported. Maybe I was a sucker for paying $250 for a pinkie finger-worth of it, but it made me happy in a way the modern stuff never did anymore. In a way no other collectibles did either.

And why else do you drink but to feel happy?

It reminded me of an anecdote Salvatore Calabrese had once told me.

One time at Dukes, in the late 1980s, a famous rock star was sitting at his bar, quietly drinking martinis while Calabrese served a less-famous customer from bottles of vintage spirits he had lined up for him.

It wasn't unusual for rock stars to be in Dukes, and Calabrese frequently served people like Carlos Santana, Jon Bon Jovi, even Paul McCartney and Mick Jagger. They were mostly left-alone by the well-heeled crowd and mostly kept to themselves, drinking simple cocktails, rarely curious about the liquid history available to them.

But for whatever reason, those dusty bottles of Cognac on the bar got this one particular rock star's attention. He was curious, he eyed them, he studied them until he could handle his compulsions no longer. The rock star eventually reached over, put his pointer finger on the neck of an old Cognac bottle, and wiped away a line of thick dust like a plow going through the freshly fallen snow.

Calabrese stopped what he was doing and glared at the rock star.

"Now you owe me twenty pounds," he stated matter-of-factly, holding out his palm.

The rock star was confused; he had done nothing, he had taken nothing, he had consumed nothing.

Oh, but he had.

Calabrese looked at the rock star, showed him the now-scarred bottle, and explained to him the true secret of life:

"THE DUST HAS VALUE."

ACKNOWLEDGMENTS

JUST LIKE STUMBLING upon a bottle of Stitzel-Weller Very Xtra Old Fitzgerald at a liquor store in 2023, a lot of being a writer is just dumb luck and good fortune.

A stranger named Kevin Langdon Ackerman DMed me on Instagram in September 2020, telling me that he'd just discovered Cecil B. DeMille's booze collection and that I should write about it.

So I did.

Thanks, Kevin!

(I am also extremely grateful for his insight into the Hughes collection and the dusty booze hobby in general.)

Then another stranger named Doug Grad read my story in the *New York Times* and asked if I'd meet with him.

So I did.

He was a literary agent who just so happened to live down the block from me in Park Slope. I met him at my favorite local beer bar, the Double Windsor, at an outside table, of course (there was no indoor drinking in New York just yet), and I drank a Zombie Dust while he told me he thought my article could be a book.

I wasn't sure about that at all, but I told him I'd scribble out a proposal and he could knock himself out.

He sold it, and now here I am, writing the acknowledgments to that very book.

Thanks, Doug!

Life is weird.

People always assume that I'm an expert on alcohol because I own a lot of it, drink a lot of it, and write a lot about it. I always tell them, oh no, I may be in the 99th percentile, but the people in the 99.99 percentile would make me look like a dummy who doesn't know anything. This book is about that 99.99 percentile, and they taught me so much. (Perhaps I'm up to the 99.01 percentile now.)

For the key dusties to collect sections that follow many chapters, I received invaluable advice on what bottles, brands, and distilleries to include from people like Owen Powell, Jonah Goodman, Seth Weinberg, Martin Cate, Ernesto Hernandez, Kristopher Peterson, Kurt Maitland, Joe Hyman, Isabel Graham-Yooll, Edgar Harden, and numerous others. If there are any glaring errors in those sections, blame me, not them, or at least blame the passage of time, which radically alters what matters in this esoteric world of vintage spirits collecting. Goodman and Ackerman also aided me in fact-checking.

I would also like to thank the many publications and editors I write for in my "day job," who have helped me and given me a platform over the years for exploring many of the ideas expanded on in this book:

Alexandra Jacobs at the *New York Times*, my big softball crew at *Esquire* (none of whom work there anymore), Talia Baiocchi and Chloe Frechette at *PUNCH*, and Adam Teeter, Tim McKirdy, Joanna Sciarrino, and many others at *VinePair*.

Thanks to Jamison Stoltz at Abrams Press, who truly seemed to get the concept and pushed me in directions I hadn't thought of.

I dedicate this to the memory of Randy Baker, my favorite high school English teacher.

And thanks always to my family: Betsy, Ellie, Wilder, and Hops, who allow me to keep thousands of bottles of booze in our living room, so long as I dust them occasionally.

VINTAGE RESOURCES

TOP BARS FOR FINDING VINTAGE SPIRITS

WEST COAST

Smuggler's Cove
650 Gough St., San Francisco, CA 94102
smugglerscovesf.com

Tommy's Mexican Restaurant
5929 Geary Blvd., San Francisco, CA 94121
tommysmexican.com

canon: whiskey and bitters emporium
928 12th Ave., Seattle, WA 98122
canonseattle.com

The Doctor's Office
1631 E. Olive Way, Seattle, WA 98102
tdosea.com

Rumba
1112 Pike St., Seattle, WA 98101
rumbaonpike.com

MIDWEST

Billy Sunday
3143 W. Logan Blvd., Chicago, IL 60647
1115 N. Brevard St., Charlotte, NC 28206
billy-sunday.com

Delilah's
2771 N. Lincoln Ave., Chicago, IL 60614
delilahschicago.com

Milk Room
12 S. Michigan Ave., Chicago, IL 60603
chicagoathletichotel.com/restaurants/milk-room

Mordecai
3632 N. Clark St., Chicago, IL 60613
mordecaichicago.com

The Office
955 W. Fulton Market, Chicago, IL 60607
theaviary.com/the-office

THE SOUTH

Bardstown Bourbon Company
1500 Parkway Dr., Bardstown, KY 40004
bardstownbourbon.com

Neat Bourbon Bar & Bottle Shop
1139 Bardstown Rd., Louisville, KY 40204
neatbottlebar.com

The Silver Dollar
1761 Frankfort Ave., Louisville, KY 40206
whiskeybythedrink.com

The Crunkleton
320 W. Franklin St., Chapel Hill, NC 27516
1957 E. 7th St., Charlotte, NC 28204
thecrunkleton.com

Reserve 101
1201 Caroline St. Ste. 100, Houston, TX 77002
reserve101.com

EAST COAST

Down & Out
503 E. 6th St., New York, NY 10009
downandoutnyc.com

One Fifth
1 5th Ave., New York, NY 10003
onefifthnyc.com

Jack Rose Dining Saloon
2007 18th St. NW, Washington, DC 20009
jackrosediningsaloon.com

TOP VINTAGE RETAIL

Revival Vintage Bottle Shop
5 E. 8th St., Covington, KY 41011
revivalky.com

Justins' House of Bourbon
601 W. Main St., Lexington, KY 40508
101 W. Market St., Louisville, KY 40202
thehouseofbourbon.com

INDEX

Abbott's Bitters, 168–69
ABC. *See* alcoholic beverage control
Los Abuelos, 153
Ackerman, Kevin Langdon, xi–xii, xvii, 51–55, 57–58, 60, 61–65, 107, 109
agave, 147, 149
age, 78–79
airline bottles (nips), 193–94
Alchemy Consulting, 117
alcoholic beverage collector law, 94–95
alcoholic beverage control (ABC), 91, 94
alpine liquors, 124
amari, 97–98, 101, 121
American Costcos, 181
Amer Picon, 122
AMS bottling, 184
AMS Special Old Reserve, 90
ancient bottles, 232
aniseed liqueurs, 124
"Antique Spirituous Liquor," 91
Ardbeg, 37, 249–50
Armagnac, 27, 197–98, 200, 265
auctions, 223–25, 239–41, 242–43, 245–46, 263
Aviation cocktail, 169, 170

Bacardí Massó, Facundo, 128
Bachman, Alex, 97–99, 101–2
Baldwin, Larry, 263–64
Baltimore, Maryland, 32–34, 36
Bardstown Bourbon Company (BBC), 92

Bénédictine, 115, 123
Bergeron, 130–31
Berghoff, 210
Berman Liquor Co., 187
Bermejo, Julio, 141–42, 145–46, 150
Berry, Jeff "Beachbum," 131–32
Bickett, Edmund, 256–57
bitters, vintage, 168–69
Blanton's, 17–18, 22, 45, 85
Bonds, Brad, 37, 110, 214, 215, 220
bootlegging, 61–62
Bottle Blue Book, 72
Bottle & Bond, 92
Bottled-in-Bond Act (1897), 73, 151
bottling year, 70–71
Boudreau, Jamie, 46–49, 160–61
bourbon, xiii–xiv, 8–9, 14, 15–18, 19, 37, 110–11, 184–85, 186–89. See also specific bourbons
Bourbon Blue Book, 72
Bourbon Exchange, 52
Bourbon Secondary Market (BSM), 68, 79–80
brandy, 119
brandy based cordials, 169
Brora, 251
Brown-Forman, 15–16, 84–85
BSM. See Bourbon Secondary Market

Cadenhead, 249
Calabrese, Salvatore, 25–29, 30–31, 108–9, 159–60, 275–76
Callaway, Dan, 92
Calvados, 265

Camarena, Don Felipe, 147–48
Campari, 120–21, 190
Canadian whisky, 192, 265–66
canon restaurant, 46–48
caramel taste, 139
Caribbean rum, 129
Caroni rum, 137–38
Castro, Fidel, 136
Cate, Martin, 127–29, 130
Champagne, 27
Chanes, Brian, 243
Chapel Hill, North Carolina, 88–89
charred oak, 110
Chartreuse, 116–17, 120, 237
Chartreuse Eau-de-Vie, 119
"Cheesy Gold Foil," Wild Turkey, 36
Chicago, 44–46, 101, 102
Chinaco, 143–44, 151–52
Chivas Regal, 253
cocktails, 159–64, 261–62. See also
    specific cocktails
Cocquyt, Olivier (Don Henny),
    112–13
Cognac, 26, 27, 29–30, 111, 276
column still, 136
conglomeration, 76
control states, 31
cordials, fruit, 170
Corti Brothers, 92
Costcos, American, 181
counterfeiting, 229
COVID-19 pandemic, 211–13
crème de violette, 169
Croizet Bonaparte Cognac Fine
    Champagne (1914), 27
Crunkleton, Gary, 87–90
Cuba, 129, 186–87
Cuban bourbon, 186–89
Cuban rum, pre-Castro, 136–37

dating old bottles, 69–71
decanters, 10–14
deciphering old bottles, 69–71
De Goñi sherry, 57
DeKuyper Orange Curacao, 130–31
DeKuyper Peachtree Schnapps, 260,
    261
Del Maguey, 156
demijohns, 137
DeMille, Cecil B., 52, 55–56, 58

Denton, Robert, 142–44, 147, 149,
    151–52
Didion, Joan, 201
direct-fired whisky, 250
Direct Martini, 25–26
distilled spirit plants (DSP), xiv, 71
Distillerie P. Garnier, 170–71
distillery equipment, 77–78
The Doctor's Office, 271–72
Don Henny (alias). See Cocquyt,
    Olivier (Don Henny)
Donoghue, Dan, 72
Dowling, Mary, 184–85
Drinks Planet (website), 40–41
DSP. See distilled spirits plant
Duke, Doris, 178
"dusty hunter," 32–34. See also specific
    hunters
Dusty Hunters (TV show), 108

Eberbach, Kloster, 223
Elijah Craig 18 Year Old, 67
empty bottles, 230
entry proof, 77
equipment, distillery, 77–78
Ezra Brooks 15 Year Rare Old Sippin'
    Whiskey, 38

Facebook groups, 67
Faith, Nicholas, 144
fakes, 232–34
Famous Grouse, 61
FDA. See Food and Drug
    Administration
Feldman, Joshua, 35, 238
Fern Creek Bourbon, 216
fernet, 98, 123
FOAF. See "friend of a friend"
Food and Drug Administration
    (FDA), 11
Ford, Gerald, 69
Fortaleza, 153
Fortuna Bourbon, 218
four chamber bottles, 170–71
Four Roses, 17, 23, 84
Foursquare Distillery, 138
freelance dusty hunting, 98–99
"friend of a friend" (FOAF),
    53–54
fruit cordials, 170

Gardiner, Tam, 225–26
genever, 266
gin, 25, 29, 164–65, 166–67
Glenfarclas, 250
Goldfarb, Stanley, 203–5
Goodman, Jonah, xiii, 179–83
Gordon's Gin, 241–42
Graham-Yooll, Isabel, 225, 233–34, 240
grains, 76
Grand Marnier, 169
grapes, 29–30
Guyana, 138–39

Harden, Edgar, 241–42
Harewood rum, 133–34
Harvey Wallbanger (cocktail), 7
Hawaii, 139–40
Heaven Hill, 259
Heaven Hill Distillery, 21, 68, 85
Hennessy, 112–13
Hennessy 8, 113
Hepburn, Katharine, 61, 178, 244
Herradura, 145–46, 155–56
Hollywood Auction '96, 245–46
Horse Shoe Straight Bourbon Whiskey, 185, 187–89
Hughes, Howard, 60, 61–65, 109, 178–79, 272
    aviation and, 273–74
    7000 Romaine Street and, 201–3, 205–6, 243–45
Humpfner, Adolph, 235
Hyman, Joseph, 235–36

imperial measuring units, 69
Instagram, 39
Irish whisky, 265–66
Italy, 231–32
I.W. Harper, 16–17

Jack Daniel's, 84–85
Jack Daniel's collectors loophole, 93–95
Jack Rose Dining Saloon, 43
Jack Rose event, 35
Jägermeister, 124–25
Jamaican rum, pre-column-still, 136
Japan, 14, 15–22, 23
Japanese whisky, 252

Jasinski, Mike, 31–36
J&G Stewart's, 238
El Jimador Añejo, 150
Jim Beam, 9–10, 83–84
Jim Beam decanter, 14
Jimmy Russell, 18
Johnnie Walker Black, 253
Jose Cuervo, 153
Joshua Feldman, 4
Julian Van Winkle III, 20–21
Justins' House of Bourbon, 92–93

Kane, Charles Foster, 64
Karuizawa, 239, 251–52
Ken's Choice, 23
Kentucky, 3–4, 91–92
Kentucky Alcoholic Beverage Control, 93
Kina Lillet, 122
Klimek, Oliver, 75
Krüger, Thomas, 224, 242–43
kümmel, 266–67
Kunett, Rudolph, 5–6

labels, misleading, 184
Landon, Matthew, 79
large-format bottles, 194–95
laws, 87–89, 91–92, 94–95
lead poisoning, 11–12
Lee, Elmer T., 45
Leilani Hawaiiam rum, 139–40
Leonis, Jean-Baptiste "J. B.," 56
Lilley, Jon, 255–60
Lipman, Michael "Lippy," 144–45
liqueurs, 120, 124, 267
"liquid history," 27–28
Livigni, Steve, 95–96, 102–3
Lombardo, Guillermo Gonzalez Diaz, 143
Longman & Eagle, 45–46
Loredo Pass, 21

The Macallan, 228, 231, 248–49
Mad Men (TV show), 7
Magliocco, Joseph, 217
Maine Course, 185–86
Mai Tai, 131, 135
Maitland, Kurt, 239–40
Maker's Mark, 86
Manhattan, 161

maraschino, 170
Martin, Gilbert, 6
Martini, 25–26, 161
Martin Mills 24 Years, 18
Maryland Heritage Series, 218
Massee, William, 116
Matsuyama, Ken, 23
maturation, bottle, 75
McCormick Elvis decanter, 13
McGee, Paul, 163–64
medicinal whisky, 4, 47, 184
Mellon family, 182–83
Merges, Matthias, 101
Metric Conversion Act (1975), 69
metric measuring units, 69
Mexican bourbon, 184–85
Mexico, 141
mezcal, 154
Michael Mokotov (alias), 41
Michter's King Tut decanter, 13
Middle East, 183
Midori, 262
The Milk Room, 163
Mill Creek Distilling Co., 186–87
Miller, Mike, 44–45
miniature booze bottles, 190, 224,
    227
Minnick, Kevin, 185–86, 188
mint liqueur, 267
Mitcher's, 216, 217
mixtos, 156
Moix, Pablo, xiii, 95–96, 102–3, 145,
    213, 218–19
Mona, 127–28
monks, 116, 118
Monongahela rye, 3
Moore, Tim, 89–90
Morgan, John Pierpont, J. P., 235–37
Moscow Mule, 6

nabbing, 59
Neat, 213–14
Negroni, 161
New York Times, 57–58
nips. See airline bottles
Noe, Booker, 22–23
Noe, Fred, 9–10, 22–23
NOM. See Norma Oficial Mexicana
NOM 1079, 152–53
Norma Oficial Mexicana (NOM), 151

oak, charred, 110
The Office speakeasy, 46
OGD. See Old Grand-Dad
Old Crow, 56
Old Crow Chessmen, 92
Old Fitzgerald, xvi, 256
Old Forester, 43, 274
Old Grand-Dad (OGD), 83–84
Old Grow Chessman decanter, 12
Old Ingledew Whiskey, 238
Old Lightning (speakeasy), 102–3
Old Overholt, xii, 181–82
Old Rip Van Winkle 15 Year Old, 43
ouzo, 266–67

Pappy Van Winkle, 37, 38, 208, 220
Parsons, Brad Thomas, 121
paxarette (pax), 253–54
period fakes, 232–33
Pernod, 124
Peters, Josh, 36–37
PEZ dispensers, 38–39
phylloxera, 29–30
Pietrek, Matt, 134
piñas (agave hearts), 147
pints, 68
Porfirio, 154–55
Port Ellen, 250–51
Powell, Matthew, 221, 245–46, 271
Powell, Owen, 67–68, 71, 79, 188–89,
    213–14
Pre-fire Heaven Hill, 85
pricing guides, 72–73
private labels, 18, 207
Prohibition, xvi, 3–5, 47, 61–62, 129
proof, 70, 77
Pusser's Rum, 137

Rathskeller Rye, 209–10
razzles, 72
r/bourbon Reddit thread, 80
Rebel Yell, 37
Reddit, r/bourbon thread, 80
Red Hook Rye, 36, 103–4, 209–10
refills, 229–30
Remsberg, Stephen, 127–28, 130
Revival Vintage Bottle Shop,
    214–15
Richholt, Joshua, 221
Rineer, Dan, 189–91